T0294111

Ted Egan AO is an Australian leg[end] bush musicians. He played to hun[dreds of thousands] *Ted Egan Outback Show* in Alice Springs over 30 years; he was the presenter of the acclaimed TV series *This Land Australia*, and later *The Great Outdoors.* He is an inaugural Life Member of the Australian Stockman's Hall of Fame and has Lifetime Achievement Awards from the Golden Guitar Awards, the Country Music Association of Australia and the Australian Folk Federation. He served as the Administrator of the Northern Territory 2003–2007.

* * *

'I had heard of Ted Egan long before I met him. Old Buddy the stockman told me about him. Johnny Raaen the stuntman told me about him too. The legend of the man who could hold a room spellbound with just his voice and a VB carton. Sounded a bit far-fetched to me. Then I met him, in big places, small places, out under the stars listening to him sing, snapping out a rhythm on that green box and I was indeed spellbound. Ted Egan is a national treasure.'

Russell Crowe, actor

'Every time I hear stories of Ted's incredible life, I simply cannot believe them! People aren't real Australians until they have read Ted's book.'

Dick Smith AC, entrepreneur

'Ted Egan is an Australian living legend. As a true Australian, as a Government servant, as a Northern Territory Administrator and as a singer he ticks all the boxes.'

Baillieu ('Bails') Myer AC, co-founder of the Myer Foundation

'Sit down with raconteur Ted Egan and you'll be entertained and enlightened by myriad aspects of his, and our, history. The indefatigable composer of "Gurindji Blues" and "The Drover's Boy" makes for engaging and inspiring company.'

Margret RoadKnight, singer

'Ted Egan is wonderful narrator and a splendid raconteur whose words take the reader or listener right to the time, the place and the people. His love for Australia, especially for the Territory and its characters, shines through everything he says, sings or writes.'

Sheila and Peter Forrest, historians

TED EGAN

OUTBACK SONGMAN

my life

ALLEN&UNWIN
SYDNEY·MELBOURNE·AUCKLAND·LONDON

First published in 2019

Allen & Unwin
83 Alexander Street
Crows Nest NSW 2065
Australia
Phone: (61 2) 8425 0100
Email: info@allenandunwin.com
Web: www.allenandunwin.com

 A catalogue record for this
book is available from the
National Library of Australia

ISBN 978 1 76052 987 1

Page 279: 'Shelter'. Words and music by Eric Bogle © Copyright Happy As Larry
Music Publishing Pty Ltd. Print Rights administered in Australia and New Zealand
by Hal Leonard Australia Pty Ltd ABN 13 085 333 713 www.halleonard.com.au
Used by permission. All rights reserved. Unauthorised reproduction is Illegal.

Back cover image (right): Jeff Carter, Ted Egan singing with a beer-carton
instrument, Kiama Folk Festival, New South Wales, c. 1995. National Library
of Australia. PIC/11536/9.
Set in 12.5/18.5 pt Adobe Garamond Pro by Midland Typesetters, Australia
Printed and bound in Australia by Griffin Press, part of Ovato

10 9 8 7 6 5 4 3 2 1

To the members of the AFF society. Ad familiam felicem.

Contents

1

THE COLDEST DAY

My mum always said, 'Teddy, you were born on the coldest day for 30 years.' When I eventually looked up the news-papers of that day, 6 July 1932, it was described as a 'normal Melbourne winter's day'—early-morning frosts and fogs, rain later. Things haven't changed!

I guess life seemed somewhat bitter to Grace, my ma, having her fourth baby—first boy—in the middle of winter, during the worst financial depression Australia and the world had known. I was born at home, 4 Higinbotham Street, Coburg; Nurse Regan was the midwife. I weighed in at a fairly hefty 12 pounds (five and a half kilograms).

For my first five years, my dad—I always called him Pop—was out of permanent work, due to the Depression. He rode his bike into the city every day, seeking jobs at the Labour Office, but was often 'on the dole'. Our house was mortgaged to the State Savings Bank of Victoria, where Pop had managed to do a deal: he'd pay off a mere sixpence each week, just to 'keep in touch'.

When I came into the world, I had three sisters: Patricia (Pat), aged nine, whose birthday was St Patrick's Day; Margaret (Peg), who was seven; and Shirley (Sal), who was almost two. Mum was Grace Brennan, born at Banyena, in western Victoria, on 8 March 1901, the daughter of Peter Brennan, an Irish-born farmer who'd married Martha Williams, a 'native' of Australia, as white people born in this country were then classified. My dad, Joe Egan, was born at Timboon, in western Victoria, on 26 January 1898. Throughout his life he thought his parents were John Egan—born in Tipperary, Ireland—and Ellen Hogan, another 'native'; years later we learned otherwise.

Our neat little suburban house was built of weatherboard, with a galvanised-iron roof. It had two bedrooms, a lounge room and a dining room—which was, in fact, a spare bedroom for the many relatives who visited regularly. There was a bathroom, but we didn't have reticulated hot water; when it was bath night we would carry buckets of hot water from the washhouse, where Mum had a wood-fired copper. We had a good-sized kitchen, with first a wood stove, and later a gas one. We didn't even have an ice chest until 1941. There was a dresser for storing food-stuffs, and a Coolgardie safe with wet hessian walls, where butter and meat were kept cool.

For all of my childhood I slept on the back porch, adjacent to the washhouse. In the backyard was a lavatory, fortunately sewered. We had many country relatives whose houses still had the old dunny can, and we city-ites used to dread going to 'the lav' when we visited them. (When did we start to use words like 'toilet' and 'the loo'?) In the spacious backyard we had a clothes line, a cricket pitch, a big plum tree and, from time to time, chooks and vegetable beds.

My first memory is of starting school at St Paul's in 1936, aged three. I don't know why Grace sent me to school so early, but it was a handicap for my entire school life. I was always the youngest in my class, which turned me into an absolute smart-arse, convinced I could get away with murder. I never had problems with lessons or passing exams, but I gave some fine teachers hell and didn't grasp the fundamentals of anything, in real terms.

We lived a narrow, xenophobic lifestyle. As Irish Catholics, we felt very free to ridicule anybody who was not just like us. If we weren't having a party (which was not a lavish affair but singing and dancing in the lounge room), there was constant political consideration of 'what the English did to the Irish'. Or there were card games. Two Irish priests, Fathers Lynch and Duggan, were regular visitors for a game called Forty-Fives, and the table shook as players trumped one another's cards.

Our family delights in recalling a night when, at 11.30 p.m., Father Lynch recalled that he hadn't finished saying his office for the day, the Latin panegyric all priests had to recite aloud. He retired briefly from the game, knelt in the corner of the room and rattled off the remainder of his office. He then returned to the table, saying, 'Right, now, who led that bloody ace?'

The Sisters of Mercy who taught us at school wore long black habits with thick leather belts and long rosary beads that rattled ominously at their waists. Starched white coifs framed their faces and gave them awe-inspiring countenances. Very occasionally a wisp of hair was erotically exposed, but the most striking thing was that they had no ears!

There were two long-term lay teachers, Miss White in Grade Five and 'Cocky' Reardon, who taught Grade Three. Cocky's nickname derived from her high-pitched voice, but she was a great favourite and an excellent teacher, much loved for her mannerisms, her beautiful copperplate handwriting and her unforgettable teaching methods.

I have only a few specific memories before 1939, when war broke out. I do remember vividly, though, how few cars there were. The residents of Higinbotham Street were all working-class people, and only two or three families had cars. That left the street clear for horse-drawn vehicles.

The milkie came with his four-wheel cart in the early hours and filled the billycan we left on the front verandah. His horse moved slowly from house to house. The bread man had a different turnout altogether. His was a light, two-wheeled jinker, with a breadbox at the back of a precariously high seat. He came midmorning, travelling at a brisk trot, coming to absolute stops, whereupon he would run to about six houses at a time, carrying a basket, calling 'Baker!' as he delivered the lovely hot, crusty, high-tin loaves and accepted his cash payments.

Mr Howlett delivered wood in the winter and ice in the summer to those lucky enough to have ice chests. He was a kind man who always chipped us kids a piece of ice, which we wrapped in our hankies to make it last longer. Mr Howlett's wagon was pulled by two Shetland ponies, and we loved to pat those sturdy little animals. Mr Howlett's beautiful daughter Glenys was stricken with infantile paralysis in the awful polio epidemic of the late 1930s. Her classmates wheeled her to school in a long flat pram.

The dustman—lesser Sydneysiders called him the garbo—came twice a week with a dray pulled by a big Clydesdale draught horse. As the driver emptied the rubbish tins onto his dray, the huge horse would stand to attention, never moving an inch, but we always tried to be around, hoping to get some horse manure for the garden. We were fascinated whenever the horse disdainfully lifted its tail and had a chaffy, steaming shit.

Occasionally there would be a fish man, or a fruit man, but fruit, vegetables and meat were available at the nearby shops in O'Hea Street. Fish and chips—vital to Catholics, who were not allowed to eat meat on Fridays—were purchased at the shop near the railway line that ran from Coburg to the city, five miles (eight kilometres) away. There was also a very efficient Number 19 tram service to the city.

The postman came twice a day! It is sobering to reflect that, in those times, a letter posted in Geelong in the late afternoon would be delivered in suburban Melbourne by 10 a.m. the next day.

Given the absence of cars, games in the street were great fun, especially in summer. Boys and girls played together, with parents sitting on their front verandahs or patches of lawn, supervising.

There would be cricket, footy, hide-and-seek, release, hoppo bumpo, branders, Simon says. We kids would perch in the trees, conducting spelling bees. Oh, the fun of it.

I sometimes go back to Higinbotham Street, but there are no trees there now. You just can't imagine how all those games were played on such a grand scale. It's the cars! They have displaced the trees and stopped the games. I feel so sorry for kids these days. Even with all their smartphones, video games and electronic toys, they are constantly bored. Never once was I bored as a child. Never once.

2

SO MUCH HAPPENED IN '39

It was a long time before I knew anything about the 'facts of life', so I was absolutely amazed when, on New Year's Day in 1939, my brother came into the world, weighing a massive seven kilograms (fifteen pounds). My sisters and I had been sent off to Ballarat, on the train, to spend the day with our old uncle J.P. Williams. When we returned, Grace was sitting up in bed. We had a new brother. Easy as that.

'What's his name?' I asked.

'Francis Geoffrey. He'll be called Geoffrey.'

We never knew why she chose those names!

So the year 1939 got off to a good start, but that soon changed. Black Friday, 13 January 1939, saw bushfires raging all over Victoria, New South Wales and South Australia. Seventy-one

Victorians were burned to death that day. The nation was in a state of shock.

And then Germany invaded Poland in September. Nobody was surprised, really. Even though there were stark reminders of the horrors of World War I, in the shape of the thousands of wounded old diggers still in our midst, nobody demurred when the new prime minister, Robert Menzies, took us into the war on the side of Mother England. Get it over and done with, most said. Good for the economy, others reckoned.

Grace just shook her head and said, 'They'll never learn, will they?'

Most young men and some women rushed to enlist. What amazed me was the speed with which sleepy Australia mobilised. Who made those uniforms so quickly? The badges? The boots? The hats? The guns? The bullets? The aeroplanes, even? The paradox with war is that the armourers always seem to have it planned in advance.

The starkest reminders of World War I were the sad old veterans who manned the lifts in all the big city stores and offices in Melbourne. They sat on their stools, with one or no legs, their crutches beside them. *What are you thinking now*, I wondered when I saw them. *You wasted that leg, didn't you? It's on again.*

Even though we were 12,000 miles (19,000 kilometres) away from the action, Melbourne was buzzing with excitement from the outset. The wharves at Port Melbourne rang out with 'Waltzing Matilda' and 'The Maori's Farewell' as the wild colonial boys again sailed off to war.

My sisters Pat and Peg were both teenagers, and got jobs at the Royal Arcade Hotel in the city. Pat was a bar attendant in the ladies' bar, and Peg was a secretary/typist. In their different ways, they participated in the hectic social life that swirled around all the servicemen and women. They both took up smoking, which was novel for women but de rigueur for young men. Peg loved dancing, while Pat was not so keen, but together they attended socials and dance parties, commanding the attention of many young swains, as they were both good-looking and very smart dressers.

The cigarette companies had us all by the throat. The people promoting smoking on the wireless and in posters were, ironically, the world's leading singers. They assured us that the 'smooth-ness' of the cigarettes was the reason they sang so beautifully. Smoking was permitted in cinemas; I found it fascinating that every time Spencer Tracy lit a cigarette for Katharine Hepburn, the audience would all light up and puff and cough in unison. Later, soldiers became the models in cigarette advertising, telling us to pack Craven A fags in their ACF (Australian Comforts Fund) parcels.

I began to compile quite comprehensive 'war books' based on the daily wireless reports and the movements of our many cousins who joined the armed services. That knowledge was given a boost when, late in 1941, I began, at age nine, to sell evening newspapers. My stand was on the corner of Bell Street and Sydney Road, Coburg, in front of Brown's Pub, right at the Coburg tram terminus—always a busy spot, but teeming with people now that the war was in full swing.

I would cross from the pub to attend each departing and arriving tram. I became expert at swinging from one tram to another, on the wrong side, risking a kick in the bum from the conductor each time. I threaded through the crowds of men in the public bar—no women allowed—and witnessed the barbarity of the six o'clock swill, when blokes drank as many beers as they could before the pubs closed, peremptorily, at 6 p.m. and then staggered onto the street, leaving the bar staff to hose down the premises.

Most of my school holidays were spent at Dennington, near Warrnambool, in western Victoria, where Mum's brother, Bob Brennan, his wife, Rita, and their large family had a small farm. It is fascinating to recall, today, that my mother would take me to Spencer Street Railway Station in the city, purchase my ticket, open a carriage door and ask: 'Anybody here going to Warrnambool?'

Invariably someone was.

'Look after this boy, please,' Mum said as she bundled me into the carriage.

What fun! I would be asked: 'Can you play cards? Do you like singing? How about some fruit cake?' And, after a six-hour trip on the train, there would be my beloved Uncle Bob and a few of his kids—my cousins—in their little car, ready to take me to the farm.

Uncle Bob made me feel ever so important, as he plied me with various questions. I realised later in life that he was a latter-day Socrates, for he'd had such an eventful life himself, yet cleverly brought out the best in those he met. Prior to World

War I, he had travelled all over Australia and New Zealand as a shearer. He joined the AIF in World War I and spent three horrible years on the Western Front. He was wounded in 1918 and evacuated, but his ship back to Australia was torpedoed; he lost all his possessions and spent three days on a raft. Fortunately, he made it home, met and married Rita Toogood and took up a soldier-settler farm block.

Mary MacKillop wasn't Australia's first saint—Auntie Rita was! She had ten children with Bob, but she was always smiling, relaxed, in control, exuding love and compassion. She spoiled me rotten. My every wish was anticipated. But her own children were never neglected in the process. I got on so well with them all.

The Dennington Brennans milked Jersey cows and grew potatoes and onions on the rich volcanic soil in the Tower Hill country between Warrnambool and Port Fairy. There were lots of other relatives in the region, including Uncle Bill Brennan at Warrnambool, whose wife, Auntie Bess, had a cake shop! I visited all the rellies.

Back in Melbourne, there were two other very important relations. Uncle Martin, Mum's handsome brother, had enlisted in the Light Horse and served at Gallipoli and in the Middle East, where—for a short time—he was a prisoner-of-war of the Turks. He escaped and rejoined his regiment. Sadly, though, he returned to Australia a shattered man—'shell-shocked' was the term applied to the many chaps like him. Uncle Martin spent much of the rest of his life at the Bundoora Military Hospital, where any unexpected noise sent him into a frenzy.

Mum would pounce on people who laughed at him when this happened. 'That's the reward my brother gets for fighting for you and his country,' she would snap.

Auntie Nora—Nornie, as we called her—was always prominent in our lives. We knew her as one of the 'three maiden aunts' who had a fascinating terrace house in Neill Street, Carlton. We visited them regularly, as they were all so fond of my dad, Joe—and, indeed, of all of us. When we visited the aunts at Carlton, the adults played cards and we kids would explore their two-storey house, with all its exciting features: cupboards, verandahs, inside toilets! Then we'd all have supper and sing.

Nornie had given our family a piano, and Pat and Peg taught themselves to play. Shirley had piano lessons with the nuns, but could never emulate Pat and Peg, who could hear a song on the wireless, go straight to the piano and play and sing it. If Mum approved, she would say: 'Put it in the repertoire, girls.' They had typed lists of hundreds of songs that they and we knew. I can still sing most of the hits of the 1940s.

Whenever Nornie visited us at Coburg, usually on a Sunday for lunch and dinner, she and Pop would talk about the football—we all barracked for Richmond—as they cut up the fruit salad that we had on Sunday evenings. They got on beautifully together. Nornie was undoubtedly Joe's favourite sister.

And yet she wasn't. In 1972, eighteen years after Nornie's death, Joe established that Nora was in fact his mother.

In the state of Victoria, you can establish your date of birth by two means. There is an 'entry of birth', which simply gives a name, date and place of birth. Then there is a birth certificate, which lists parentage and many other details. Joe had never travelled outside Australia, so he never had a passport. But at age 74 he applied for the age pension and was required to produce a birth certificate.

The shock was profound. He immediately developed the shakes and became distressed. We, his children, were thrilled to bits. Our wonderful Auntie Nora was our grandmother! We laughed as we reminisced about the happy times we'd spent together. All Mum said was: 'Best-kept secret in the Western District.' She had known all along!

But it was the end of Pop. He died a couple of years later; the doctors diagnosed it as Parkinson's, but there was much more to it than that. I know the intense level to which my father would have reviewed every event in his life and the lives of his various family members. Having met them, I also know the extent to which Joe was loved by the people he thought were his brothers and sisters, all of whom would have been sworn to secrecy— with the dire Catholic warning that to break their oaths would send them spiralling into the Eternal Flames of Hell.

I have, over many years now, tried to consider the circumstances of my father's conception and birth. Probably a one-off roll in the hay for seventeen-year-old Nora, with the young chap named on the birth certificate. Then the agonising awareness of her pregnancy, by a girl who probably had little knowledge of the facts of life. Discovery by her strict Irish Catholic parents. The recriminations.

'Off to confession you go, my girl! Abortion is out of the question. You will stay on the farm, out of sight, and when this baby is born it will be presented to the world as your mother's "change of life" baby. You and your brothers and sisters will swear never to reveal the secret. Nora, you will never have anything to do with any man, ever again.'

How dare they?

My own mother was an admirable woman in so many respects. She and Pop could have achieved so much if given today's opportunities. Joe had only four years of schooling, but he could have been a professor of political science, so profound was his knowledge of world affairs and history. He was a superb wordsmith, a fine poet whose works are treasured to this day. Grace was admirably cool in a crisis. One day she said to me: 'I'd have made a great surgeon, Teddy.'

Mum was especially fond of her nine brothers, but I only ever knew eight of them. Jack Brennan enlisted in the 9th Light Horse at the outbreak of World War I. He had the standard studio portrait photograph taken, in his 'feathers, leggings and spurs', and away he went, to Egypt, then Gallipoli. All Light Horsemen went to Gallipoli as infantry troops, but their horses were left in Egypt. A big, strapping fellow, Jack became a stretcher-bearer and was in many 'willing goes', as he described them in his letters. Sadly, on 10 October 1915, Jack died from wounds he received as he saved another man's life. He was buried at sea, off the island of Lemnos.

As a consequence of the experiences of three of her brothers, my mother was fiercely anti-war. World War I also had a profound effect on Mum's elder sister, Mary. When Jack died, Mary left her job in remote Western Australia and, in 1916, sailed to England to 'do her bit'. She worked in munitions factories in London, and then joined the Land Army. As a farm girl, Mary was able to make a real contribution, driving teams of horses, milking cows, shearing sheep and tending other stock.

Mary returned to Australia in 1920 as a very *worldly* woman— she rolled her own cigarettes, drank beer appreciatively and was a wonderful conversationalist. She married a widower named Pat Carroll, which gave her two stepchildren. She and Pat then had their own daughter, Joan.

Mary was always a great favourite with us. She knew all the details of the family tree and could talk with authority about Australia (and the world) going well back into the eighteenth century; as a young girl, she had always relentlessly asked questions of her grandparents, Robert Victor Williams and Honorah Corcoran, my maternal great-grandparents.

Robert and Honorah had met in Geelong in the early 1850s. Robert was a Cornish sailor who had jumped ship and worked for the Henty brothers at Portland, an early white settlement in Victoria. Honorah was one of Caroline Chisholm's girls, known as 'God's Police'. She was a member of an impoverished family from County Cork, Ireland, and was sent to Australia as a servant girl, aged seventeen, to help fulfil Mrs Chisholm's aim of civilising the many wild white men at large in Australia—free settlers and emancipated convicts.

Honorah and Robert married and settled in western Victoria. One of their daughters was my grandmother, Martha Williams, who married Peter Brennan and produced twelve children, including Grace, my mother.

3

TIMOSHENKO AND
THE YANKS

I remember vividly the day Darwin was bombed, 19 February 1942. It has always been held that the nation was not told the facts, but on 20 February I was selling *The Herald* at Brown's Hotel, and there was the news in bold headlines. What we were not told was the extent of the damage. Darwin was devastated, with ships blown to pieces in the harbour, the airport and fuel tanks annihilated, 250 service personnel and citizens killed. To this day, most people are unaware that Darwin suffered over 60 more bombing raids, up to late 1943.

Many expected Japan to invade Australia at that time, but the Japanese demonstrated that they could easily isolate Australia by cutting off fuel supplies through their occupancy of the Dutch East Indies. They expected to acquire Australia eventually. They almost did.

After the bombing of Pearl Harbor and the arrival of General Douglas MacArthur, who set up the Allied Headquarters in Brisbane, thousands of American troops arrived in Melbourne. What an impact they made! They seemed so attractive and rich, with their toothy smiles, their stylish uniforms, their pervasive accents, their charming (in most cases) manners. The Aussie girls flipped.

The Yanks were great for paperboys. Often I would sell a tuppenny *Herald* and be given two shillings and told, 'Keep the change, son.' But they were not so popular with Australian soldiers, especially those who had fought valiantly in the Middle East and were now brought back, at Prime Minister Curtin's insistence, for the defence of Australia and New Guinea.

A parody of 'The Marines' Hymn' was often enthusiastically sung:

From the streets of Melbourne City
To St Kilda by the sea
All the Aussie girls are showing us
Just how stupid they can be
In the good old days before the war
All the Aussie girls were gay
But now they've gone completely mad
On the twerps from the USA.

Overall, it was agreed that the Yanks were 'overpaid, over-sexed and over here'. Nonetheless, I am grateful for the entry of the United States into World War II. Had they not been around, there is little doubt that Japan would have subjugated every nation bordering the Pacific Ocean. At that time, Hitler looked assured of victory in Europe. While World War I should never have begun, World War II was necessary, as we had aggressive madmen seeking to take over the world. They came so close!

My sisters Pat and Peg, smart young women and skilled stenographers, were by that time employed in the Code Section at Victoria Barracks. Pat and Peg are now dead, but neither ever revealed any of the details of their very secret wartime work. Many of their workmates were Americans, so they often invited American servicemen to visit us in our modest Coburg home. By 1942 we had, in our backyard, a small bungalow for guests and often there were eight or ten young servicemen, Americans and Australians—for many of our cousins were in the services— bunked down overnight. We seemed to have a party every night, with Pat and Peg on the piano, Pop playing his accordion and all of us delivering our party-piece songs.

Our parents were teetotallers, but the boys would have various drinks hidden in our front hedge. There would be dancing, singing and supper, served in that tiny lounge room. The Norris and Sheehan families would also join us. Poppa Sheehan would tell the same (very funny) jokes, time after time. Gert Norris always sang 'Banks of the Wabash', and we invariably sang 'Two Little Boys', which Grace had heard as a child. Everybody considered it to be an Egan family song, for nobody else seemed to know of it.

I subsequently taught that song to Rolf Harris, and he took it to world fame as Song of the Year for 1969, displacing the Beatles at the top of the UK charts. Rolf always acknowledged where he had learned the song and I scored a trip to London for his appearance on *This Is Your Life*. We eventually established that the song had been written by two Americans named Madden and Morse.

In Europe the Battle of Britain was raging, the Germans had Stalingrad under siege for months and millions of Russians were killed. I kept abreast of the war via my newspaper sales. I would deliver the headlines to all and sundry, and I meticulously wrote details into my 'war books' each night. Often on the wireless we heard mention of the great Russian general Semyon Timoshenko. Whenever he heard the name, my young brother Francis Geoffrey would give a salute and shout, 'Timoshenko!' We began to call him Timoshenko. He loved it, and it was gradually shortened to Tim. He has been Tim Egan ever since, and is a fine man indeed. My *aff* brother.

In letters to one another, Mum and her family members always signed off: 'Your *aff* [for affectionate] brother/sister . . .' That has become a family habit, and we nowadays have an AFF Society, which meets each year. The letters AFF also stand for the Latin words *Ad familiam felicem*—Towards a Happy Family—so we have doubly good reason to celebrate. Lucky us.

4

PUBERTY

In 1943, I transferred to St Joseph's Christian Brothers College, in North Melbourne. That meant a tram trip from Coburg each day. We descended from the tram at the old Haymarket, on the corner of Flemington Road and Elizabeth Street. There were quite a few horse wagons operating around the Haymarket in those days, so the prevailing smell was certainly di-*stink*-tive. The Yanks were using the brand-new Royal Melbourne Hospital on the next block as their headquarters and they were all over Melbourne. That provoked plenty of discussion on the trams.

I was still in short pants and was treated accordingly at 'North', as the college was called. It was like a tribal initiation. You could have boys six feet tall but still in short pants and little squirts knee-high to a grasshopper wearing long 'uns. Going into long pants was recognition by the boy, or by his parents, that he was approaching puberty. For most of us it also marked the point where we started to wear underpants. The only kids in short trousers who wore underpants were the rich, or the 'sissies'— mummies' boys—and I was certainly neither. I was still a kid, still a soprano in the school choir and not taken too seriously by anyone other than myself.

Fortunately, I was aware that my parents were determined to give my sister Sal and me the chance to attend secondary school, so I took things very seriously for a change. Sal went to the nearby St Aloysius College for girls. Most children from working-class families would attend primary school only and then go into factories, apprenticeships or other 'menial' jobs. Pop had permanent work with a shipping company, but his wage was minimal. His and Mum's lives were dominated by the sacrifices they made to provide opportunities for their children.

As teachers, the Christian Brothers were very different from the nuns. For a start, it was all very masculine. The brothers were into physical punishment, which ranged from the strap (on our hands) to the cane (on our bums) to random clouts over our ears. Most parents approved. We were constantly told at home to have 'respect for the cloth': while brothers and nuns might be fallible human beings, they wore habits to indicate that they had been chosen by God to teach His children.

One teacher, Brother J.A. Edwards, stands out in my memory. We nicknamed him 'Slick'. He was rotund, with black hair plastered with Brilliantine and parted in the middle. He looked like George Raft gone to seed. A clever cartoonist in our class,

John Murray, did daily sketches of *Slick in Gangster World*, complete with spats and a machine gun. Slick taught me for two consecutive years and spent half of each day giving 'the cuts'—with a leather strap he always had in the pocket of his cassock. It became a joke among us to see how exhausted he was at the end of each day.

Not that the physical stuff ever affected me. I was determined that I would never show the slightest indication of pain; most of the boys had similar attitudes. I always thought that a smart brother would seek to bring out the best in me, but I never met one who tried. Pity. Mum often said of me: 'You can lead Teddy Egan, but you'll never force him.' And yet, strangely, many years later I met Slick and we had a very pleasant conversation. He recalled my class as 'one of his better groups'.

I was something of a phoney at school. Possessed of slightly above average intelligence and always the youngest in my class, I was a dreadful show-off, but I inherited from my parents the need to be aware of myself and develop clever habits that might perhaps disguise my shortcomings.

Educated by the Sisters of Mercy and then the Christian Brothers, I knew that there was a 'Catholic' view of life. My parents, bless them, were classical Irish Catholics. It was the era of 'state aid' arguments and every day of my school life I was told: 'Archbishop Mannix is determined to get justice in education: he will take Australia to the point where Catholic education is funded by the state, on the basis that we provide a better system than state schools.'

A 'better system', in the eyes of the nuns and the brothers, was one where they taught their pupils how to look good. Putting it bluntly, we were expected to achieve better results in public education exams than state-school kids. As a consequence, our teachers were ingenious at instructing us in how to pass the exams at top level. I sometimes suspected they had infiltrated the examination system, for often they'd announce: 'You'll be getting this question on the exam paper. Despite what you think on this issue, here is the answer that will get you highest marks.' Sure enough, the question would appear on the public exam paper.

So my exam results were always very impressive. Usually, during secondary school, I came in the top ten students in the state, especially in subjects that I enjoyed, such as Latin and English Expression. In my Intermediate year, 1946, I was equal first in Victoria in the subject Commercial Principles and Practice, and first in Economics. What a joke! Today, I can't even manage a simple bank account, let alone credit cards; I never have any idea where I filed those papers last month. And there is so much of life where I don't grasp the fundamentals. Give me the job and I'll finish the tools.

Gradually, puberty arrived, I started wearing long pants and my life changed dramatically. My parents had never given me the 'facts of life', so all I knew was that I had a dick that I was not allowed to play with, and that girls—apart from my sisters, who were great fun—were creatures to be avoided. Baby making? That somehow occurred when you got married. I knew the word *fuck* was connected somehow, but I had no idea, really, how to go about it.

The pubic hair started to grow, my tits began to look like girls' tits—not that I had ever seen or touched any—and I started to have erotic, shame-filled dreams. Totally compliant, I embraced

Lana Turner as she kissed me and then did strange things with my exploding penis, but was mortified when I awoke with my pyjamas sticky and my conscience burning.

A good Catholic boy had to go to confession to unburden all the guilt. I couldn't go to our own church, St Paul's, because all the priests knew me as an altar boy and might recognise my voice. So I would visit Uncle Bob and his family—they had moved from Dennington to Brunswick, the next suburb to Coburg—and go to confession at St Margaret Mary's.

Confession! I have such mixed feelings about it. On the one hand, it gives people the chance to 'wipe the slate' and obliterate various misdemeanours. On the other hand, it thereby endorses in the sinner the right to repeat the offence and be cleared yet again. Articulation of the sin becomes more polished. A new start. I am sure many violent men are truly sorry when they confess their sins, but the next time they belt the missus they feel they are doing it for the first time. 'I was guilty of a violent act *once*, Father . . .' And on it goes. *Ego te absolvo.*

The attitudes of the various priests also intrigued me. Some were kind and helpful, others voyeuristic, wanting to know chapter and verse, particularly when the penitent started describing 'impure thoughts and actions'.

In recent years, the paedophilia of various clergymen has been exposed and discussed, and I feel sure that many abused children would have revealed their vulnerability to devious priests in the confessional. At the same time they were told that their various sins were now forgiven: 'Perhaps we should have a private chat, my dear? Come and see me at the presbytery.'

A beautiful girl (NB, I'll call her) caught the same tram as me each day, and invariably brought on in me a huge erection. Schoolkids were required to stand in the crowded trams, and we were often pressed body to body as we got closer to the city. NB used to get on the tram at The Grove, Coburg, and would gravitate to the middle section, where all the boys and a few girls were jammed. There were invariably a few North boys copying my homework into their own books, so they were busy. But I had only one thought on my mind: *How close will she be?* She had superb legs, and I could discern that she had quite well-formed breasts. And she always had that 'aren't I gorgeous?' look on her serene face. Immediately, I would be in pole-vaulting mode. But how to conceal the bulge in my pants? What if I impaled another person—especially her?

One day NB and I were almost locked in a connubial embrace, our thighs rubbing for most of the journey. We never exchanged a word, but I was mortified by my lack of breath, and by that surging monster, my dick. At her stop in Brunswick, she gave a little sigh. 'There'll be a bit more room for you now,' she said and she swung off the tram.

In summertime, I often saw NB at the Brunswick Baths in her red Speedos, her tanned body gleaming, gorgeous breasts, nipples prominent. She was a great swimmer, which I wasn't, so I never had any opportunity to do anything other than adore her from afar.

I hope NB has had a good life! She'd have made her partner very happy.

5

OFF TO QUEENSLAND

As the war came to an end, I started to develop itchy feet. Mum was aware, while never envious, of her sister Mary's travels, both within Australia and overseas. She and Mary agreed that the young people of the post-Depression era should be encouraged to get good jobs and to travel. They always spoke with pride of their brothers, especially the older ones who had gone shearing in New Zealand, chasing gold at Kalgoorlie, farming all around Australia and then served in the war.

Mary's daughter Joan was a brilliant student who went to Europe, then came back to Australia and became a school principal. Bob's daughter Judith went to France, worked as a waitress for four years and became very fluent in colloquial French.

On her return to Australia, Jude established a lifelong connection with Alliance Française as an interpreter.

I was particularly impressed by my Western Australian cousins, the Brennans, the five sons of Uncle Michael and Aunt Isobel. Two of those sons—Frank and Bill—came to Melbourne in late 1945. They had brought their father back to his birthplace of Victoria for a family reunion, but they bragged about the Golden West and their wonderful upbringing. I was spellbound.

During the war, Frank had been in the Army in the Middle East, and then had transferred to the RAAF. He was one of the handsomest men I have ever met. As a teenager I modelled myself totally on him—lifting an eyebrow here, pursing my lips there, smiling disarmingly on a regular basis. Bill, his younger brother, had joined the Merchant Navy at sixteen. By the end of the war Bill had been around the world eight times, torpedoed twice and badly burned at the Allied landing in Italy. Both Frank and Bill had plenty of money and dressed superbly. They were both now in the Seamen's Union, ready to work on the coastal ships. Everybody idolised them.

They both had tattoos, small but impressive. Frank had done his own, so I had two tattoos done on my forearms at age thirteen. I told the tattoo artist that I was eighteen, and he smiled knowingly. The procedure caused a bit of pain, but not as much as the belting that Mum gave me! It was my last 'trip to the washhouse' with her, but she was at her best.

I was determined that I was going to do something exciting. For the present, I'd had enough of school, so I left CBC North at the end of 1946 and got a job at the Moreland Timber Company as a clerk. It was fairly boring, as I handled the simple work easily.

In 1947, my parents decided to pass our house over to Pat and Peg, who had recently married. They both started to have families and they shared our old Coburg home at the outset. Mum and Pop had taken the big decision to work for the Christian Brothers at Victoria Parade, East Melbourne—Grace as cook and Joe as caretaker/cleaner. Shirley took on the job as Grace's assistant. Tim would attend school. I would live with them in a small cottage at the school.

The college principal, Brother Crennan, evinced an interest in me. Although I had passed the Intermediate examination with flying colours at North the previous year—coming third overall in Victoria—and was now at work, Brother Crennan outlined the many opportunities that would come my way if I went back to school at Parade for terms two and three and was able to pass the Leaving Certificate examination. That would give me access to dozens of different areas of employment. He felt that I would be able to make up the leeway, despite already having missed term one.

So back to school I went, and I have never regretted it. It did give me that valuable 'piece of paper'. I passed all the subjects easily enough—without distinction, however. But I had a great year of sport. I was still young enough for the under-15 football team, and in fact also played for the First 18. I was the Under-16 Victorian Handball Champion (Irish handball, not the nonsense they have in the Olympics), and I played a few meaningful games of cricket.

At the end of 1947 I had the choice of many jobs, so I became a 'bank johnny' at the State Savings Bank in Collins Street, in the city. That was a breeze, and I enjoyed the stimulating company of some of my fellow staff members for six months.

I was still living at Victoria Parade with my parents. There was an elocution teacher, Miss Kitty O'Shea, who enjoyed Mum and Pop's company. Over a cup of tea one day, as we discussed my desire to 'do something exciting in life', she suggested that I take a job with a dear friend of hers in Queensland, a 'kindly' man (she said) named Andy Maguire, who had a racehorse stud, Kialla, on the Darling Downs. I said I would love the experience.

Maguire was already famous, because Kialla's stallion, Emborough, was the sire of the incredible Bernborough, who had recently won fifteen races straight, including the Doomben Ten Thousand, carrying 10 stone 5 pounds (65.8 kilograms). I followed all sports avidly, so I knew all about Bernie, as the horse was affectionately known.

I resigned from the bank. Miss O'Shea assured me that everything was in place in Queensland; all I need do was pay my train fare. At her suggestion, I sent Mr Maguire a telegram advising my date of arrival.

The train journey to Queensland was interesting, but at the little Watts Siding, near Greenmount, I was confronted by a surly Andy Maguire—a formidable bloke who had made his money as a professional boxer—who wanted to know what in the hell was going on! I told him of Miss O'Shea's advice that all was in place, but he said he knew nothing of me. What experience did

I have? Nil. With very bad grace he decided that he would 'give me a chance'.

Fortunately, I was in good hands at his stud. I was assigned to a man named Bert Taverner, a very competent English migrant who ran the farm. I had all my meals with the Taverners and shared the men's quarters with the stud groom, Joe Jennings, and the cowboy/butcher, Ted van Dreick.

It was amazing how much I absorbed in the next six months. I learned to drive a truck and tractor, to build yards, to erect fences. I became a good horserider, learned how to slaughter and butcher sheep and when the yearling foals were being prepared for sale, I assisted in their grooming and handling.

Sometimes I had the job of feeding Emborough, a magnificent but very aggressive chestnut stallion. He would allow me into his stall, watch me place his feed of chaff, oats and hay in its container and then rush me. It's one of my lesser claims to fame that Bernborough's father bit me on the arse several times.

I had another very messy task. When the mares were brought in to be served by Emborough, their yearling foals had to be separated from them. I had to hold each foal, for it was to rejoin its mother immediately after she was served, to calm her down. With all the squealing and biting and sheer savagery of Emborough, as Andy Maguire rammed the stallion's huge dick into the mare, the foals went berserk. Without exception, I would get covered in horse shit—plus cop the odd bite and kick. The sport of kings indeed!

I worked so hard for Maguire, but was appalled when, at the end of the yearling sales, he said: 'There's not much to do here over the summer. Finish up next Friday.' The first and only time I've been sacked.

So I took my cheque and my 'port'—which I now knew was the Queensland word for suitcase—and headed for Toowoomba. I spent a glorious week there, eating at Greek cafes and going to the pictures. I then signed on to be the cowboy/butcher at Myall Park Station, at Glenmorgan, near Surat—'out west', the employment agent told me.

Queenslanders are funny about their geography. As a total body of people, they deplore 'southerners', whom they call 'Mexicans', as they're from 'south of the border'. Yet among themselves they are just as selective. 'Out west' is really 'OUT WEST', and the real westerners despise those from 'inner-western' places such as Toowoomba. And try heading north. Yes, Bundaberg is north of Brisbane, Townsville is in North Queensland, and in Cairns you have arrived in Far North Queensland, but only just. In Cooktown you may list your address as FNQ and you are definitely contemptuous of 'those bastards down south in Brisbane'. What would they know about running Queensland?

So Surat was only *just* out west. But I couldn't have arrived at a better time. Myall Park carried 60,000 sheep and the shearing was on, ten shearers. There was a wonderful horse breaker, Lindsay Cant, who was breaking in a hundred horses for the very busy Gordon Brothers, who owned Myall. (They were also world-famous as rose growers!) I got involved in all of the action, as well as performing my routine tasks.

I had to milk eight dairy cows twice a day, chop firewood for all the houses, and slaughter and butcher ten sheep a week for the station and the shearers. I rode with Bede Campbell and Ray Berg to the furthest parts of the run, mustering the sheep for shearing; I helped to keep the pens full for the shearers. At night I sat in awe among the shearers and came to understand the 'ethos' of shearing, the source of much of Australia's folklore. The shearers paid for everything, so all their actions and talk inferred that they were kings. Not quite, for the shearing contractor was in charge of finances, and the classers and pressers had skills of their own that had to be recognised. But the rouseabouts were definitely the shearers' punching bags. I came to realise that shearing is about the hardest day's work imaginable.

The food served at the homestead (for we workers) and by the shearers' cooks in their mess was of superb quality, three solid meals a day, plus two smokos. It was an exciting six months for me, at seventeen years of age, and then I felt it was time for the next chapter of my life—another adventure, somewhere new. First, though, I would go back to Melbourne, for the old maxim had again been confirmed: absence had made the heart grow fonder. I needed to see the family again.

I had Christmas in Melbourne and met up with an old schoolmate, Ron Smith, who had only that year finished at CBC North, although he was eighteen months older than me. Smithy said he was thinking of going to Brazil, to be a cowboy.

'What a good idea,' I said. 'I'll come with you.'

6

BRAZIL NUTS

'Here's the deal,' said Smithy. 'We'll go to Mildura first and pick grapes, get a cheque together and then we'll go to Darwin. Plenty of jobs in Darwin, big money. Six months there and off to Brazil.'

To this day I'm not sure whether Ron had any idea how one travelled from Darwin to Brazil, but it sounded exciting. Fortunately, my parents agreed. They knew and liked Ron very much.

Six weeks at Red Cliffs, near Mildura, was a fascinating experience. I was aware that grapes were grown along the Murray River, but had no idea of the extent of the dried-fruit industry. Most of the grapes we harvested became currants, raisins and sultanas, and the picking was done by hand. Because of my experience with horses, I was given the job of collecting and carting the buckets of grapes, driving a light wagon pulled by a good old horse. Smithy offered to help me one day, but when he put the collar on the horse upside down I asked him if he was sure he wanted to be a cowboy in Brazil. He assured me I was in good hands.

The buckets of grapes were emptied onto wire racks to dry. Most of the pickers were DPs—Displaced Persons—from Europe, and I immediately loved being among people of such diverse backgrounds. We had Latvians, Lithuanians—they were called 'Balts'—and Poles. The lingua franca seemed, incongruously, to be German, but there were certainly no Germans. None of the 'New Australians' had much English, but my schoolboy French was helpful. Many had been in concentration camps, and seemed to think that 'Attention please' was the way to start each sentence. 'Attention please! Good morning' became our standard greeting.

One day a lovely Polish chap named Jan had stopped picking his grapes when I drove up to collect his buckets. He seemed petrified. 'Attention please, Ted. Snoke!' He pointed to the top of a post.

There was a lovely frill-necked lizard. I clapped hands, the lizard took off and we had a good laugh together. Jan was a fine man. I'll bet he did well in Australia. He was a better French speaker than me, but we could sing 'La Marseillaise' together and he taught me *Après la Guerre*. He also instilled in me an appreciation of fine wine.

We earned good money at Red Cliffs, so Ron and I went to Adelaide by coach and then booked our passage on *The Ghan*, the old steam train that would take us to Alice Springs.

What a journey! Four days it took. While that seemed like a lifetime, I was told it was a quick trip, considering the railway line went through treacherous country. The few bridges and culverts were dodgy. There was no ballast; given even the smallest shower of rain in the desert, the train would be stuck.

We played cards, the passengers drank enormous quantities of beer, we sang and took turns sleeping, anywhere we could find space. The crew on *The Ghan* were wonderful, always able to find ice and sandwiches, and they shared the fun with us. Especially the beer!

We spent just a few hours in the tiny town of Alice Springs, and then we caught a Bond's bus to Darwin. The scenery around Alice was stunning, with the huge ghost gums and stark red mountains set against the bluest sky I had ever seen.

The 'coach' was simply a converted semi-trailer, open sides with a canvas top. The 25 passengers sat on benches behind our driver, Jack Day, who drank longneck bottles of beer as he drove. As did we. At each town we had to wait patiently as Jack had his 'Christmas drink', often with the local policeman! It was April.

I had only just started to drink beer and could handle it fairly well. From day one I had realised that food was essential with alcohol, and I've never moved from that attitude. On the coach there was a huge 'hot box'—a funny name for a container that we filled with ice and beer that cost us six shillings a bottle!

We stopped overnight at Banka Banka, Daly Waters and Mataranka Homestead; we were well fed and there was a party each night. I was starting to like the Northern Territory . . .

I have never been averse to singing—in fact, to this day the issue is not starting me, it's stopping me. Jack Day constantly encouraged me: 'Come on, young Egan, sing us a song!' I used to sing all the great American country songs, among them '(Ghost) Riders in the Sky', 'Cool Water' and 'Mule Train'.

Yippee-ai-ay! What a life!

As a result of the prodigious drinking and revelry, Smithy and I had run out of cash when we hit Darwin. We both had money in the bank, but we arrived on Easter Thursday evening, which meant it was four days until the banks opened again. We had two shillings—two bob—and a tin of sardines between us.

7

THE FLYING CHINAMAN

Darwin was an ugly, scarred town in those days, nothing like the lush tropical city it has become. There were straggly coconut trees here and there, a few turpentine mango trees, some big calophyllums around the town centre, and quite a few frangipani trees. The rich frangipani scent made a big impression on our southern nostrils.

It's funny how your senses are heightened at first acquaintance. Nowadays there are thousands of beautiful frangipani trees in Darwin, but I don't notice the smell. I had a similar experience outside Gage Roads at Fremantle Harbour, one time, coming by ship from the United Kingdom. I had been away from Australia for the first time in my life, and I was immediately conscious of the lovely scent of eucalyptus. Never again.

Because it was Easter and we were broke, Smithy and I camped at Darwin Oval, near Government House. We ate our sardines the first night and then survived on six penn'orth of bread and butter for each of the four days of Easter, purchased at the Rendezvous Cafe in the main street. The weather was kind, and there were not many mosquitoes; we used the shower in the change room and there was a primitive dunny, which we later found out was called a 'flaming fury'.

The town was very quiet, so we walked around and took in the sights. We were appalled. All the damage from the air raids was still evident. The devastated post office—where many staff members had died—the Bank of New South Wales, Gordon's Don Hotel, flats, houses, all blown to pieces and left unrepaired. The nearby Darwin Harbour, over which we looked from the grandstand, was dotted with shipwrecks, looming at stark angles, to remind us how concentrated and how comprehensive the bombing raids had been.

Most of the shops in both Smith Street and Cavenagh Street were run by Chinese people. We saw a few old Chinese women wearing the traditional silk pyjamas and conical hats, but most men of all races were very neatly attired in white clothing: long pants, long-sleeve shirts, the occasional necktie, black or white shoes.

On the Tuesday morning, Ron and I went to the Commonwealth Bank, took out £20 each and had a slap-up feed at the Rendezvous. George Fortiades, the owner of the cafe, suggested we go to see Alan Jones at the Department of Works and Housing to look for a job. The first question Alan asked was: 'Do you chaps play cricket?'

Did we play cricket? Ron Smith had been a great athlete at school, especially at cricket. I was a useful leg-spin bowler and fairly effective as a slogging batsman. So we were signed up as clerks and given lodgings at the No. 3 Hostel, which was locally known as Belsen Camp.

It was called Belsen after the notorious European concentration camp, because it had been built for nurses during the war and surrounded by a high barbed-wire fence. The fence was now gone, leaving 50 attractive little fibro huts, shared in each case by two employees of the department established to rebuild Darwin.

Ron and I shared a hut and with three meals a day being served at the mess, we immediately got to know all the residents. We also quickly met many other townsfolk. Because the old Town Hall had been severely damaged in the raids, much of Darwin's social life revolved around the Belsen Recreation Hut. We were only a short distance from town, near the Catholic Church, where St Mary's Cathedral was subsequently built.

I worked with, and became a lifelong friend of, one of the great Northern Territory characters. He was a fifth-generation Australian, a tall, handsome man whose Chinese name was Chin Xu Hoong, although he was known to the Darwin locals as Ronald Gordon Chin, or 'Hoonga, the Flying Chinaman'. People spoke in awe of him—and his football ability. He had played in four premierships for a team called Buffaloes.

Ron Smith and I both played cricket during the Dry Season— April to September—and Works won the premiership that year. But what we were really gearing up for was Aussie Rules football, which was played in the Wet Season—October to March.

Football in the summer? Well, it was too wet to play cricket in the summer, but the principal reason was that, before 1953, there was no lawn grass in Darwin. It was held that planting lawn was a waste of time, as ants and various grubs would eat it. Grass grew to a prolific height in the Wet, but it was rank 'spear grass,' which was useless; it was burned as soon as possible each Dry Season.

So the Darwin Oval, where footy was played, was basically a gravel pit, its surface a bit softer when wet. Hence gravel rash—the most prevalent hazard for players—was minimised. To this day, Aussie Rules is played in Darwin in the summer, although the players now enjoy superb grass ovals.

The Flying Chinaman helped us start a new Aussie Rules team for the local competition, called Works, better known as Tigers. The three principal initiators—Frank Whiteman, Bertie Garrett and I—were Richmond supporters from the southern VFL competition, so our natural choice of club colours was yellow and black! In later years the new team came to be called Nightcliff, but they're still the Tigers.

Early on, in 1950, my cousins Frank and Bill Brennan came to Darwin on MV *Dulverton*, one of the ships of the old State Shipping Service of Western Australia. By an amazing coincidence, our cousin Leo 'Sandy' Brennan—son of Bob and a famous RAN diver—arrived simultaneously in Darwin on HMAS *Australia*. The *Dulverton* was to spend a week in Darwin, so I took a week off work and joined my cousins as we all bunked on *Dulverton*. Frank said to me: 'It'll give us time to teach you to drink, Ted.'

What a time we had. We did drink a lot of beer, but always with food (kindly supplied by the State Shipping Service), and the sessions were dominated by conviviality. We talked family issues, sport, politics, whatever. I sang them a few songs and most nights we would swim from the *Dulverton* to the nearby wreck of the *Neptuna*, only 50 yards from the wharf. We sat on the *Neptuna*'s upturned hull, pulling on longneck bottles of beer, taking it in turns to swim for more coldies as we continued my drinking lessons. No concerns about crocodiles. Or the huge groper that lived inside the *Neptuna*!

It was agreed that in November 1950—six months hence—Frank would stow me away on the *Dulverton* and take me to the Golden West, to meet my relations in Perth. Already Ron and I had stopped thinking of Brazil.

8

DARWIN FOOTY

The 1950 Darwin footy season began, and Works were totally outclassed by the three established Darwin teams, Waratahs, Wanderers and Buffaloes. The standard was excellent, especially the Buffaloes, who were mainly of mixed Aboriginal descent, led by a magnificent player named Steve Abala.

Waratahs were an 'all-white' team, mainly bank johnnies, public servants and policemen. Wanderers fielded a few whites, mainly mixed-descent 'coloured' players and a few 'full-blood' Aboriginal players. Our new team, called Works and Jerks, was mainly young white blokes like us, a couple of Chinese—the Flying Chinaman and the Irish Chinaman, Wellington Patrick Chin—plus quite a few naval ratings from HMAS *Melville*, the Darwin RAN outpost, based in the old stone buildings that, pre-war, had been the town's court house and police station.

My first game was at fullback for Works, and my Wanderers full-forward opponent walked towards me at the start of the game, offering to shake hands. He was the blackest person I had ever seen. I knew his name but assumed his English would be limited. I said, 'Ted Egan,' very clearly for this chap as we shook hands, and was taken aback when he responded: 'Nice to meet you, Ted. Bob Wilson. Welcome to Darwin.'

He proceeded to give me a football lesson. He kicked six goals and Works copped their first hiding. Bob and I later became good friends; he eventually changed his name to Robert Tudawali, as he became a famous film actor, first starring in the classic 1955 film *Jedda*, followed by many other roles.

The year rolled on, and in November, as planned, I joined Frank on the *Dulverton*, sailing for Fremantle. All the other crew members were alerted to the presence of a stowaway, and I shared the bunks of various crew members as they worked their eight-hour shifts. The officers were totally unaware of my presence; in any case, Frank was revered among both crew and officers—and by me—so there was never any need for surveillance. I simply kept a low profile, slipping ashore at each port—Wyndham, Derby, Broome, Onslow, Port Hedland—to have a look at these fascinating frontier towns.

In Perth I stayed with Frank and his wife, Dot, at Palmyra, met again my Uncle Michael and Aunt Isobel at Shenton Park, and spent a couple of weeks playing tennis with Bill and drinking with Frank and Bill at the P&O pub in Fremantle. When my money was spent I took a job at Wagin, south of Perth, as a 'wheat lumper'.

I stayed at the Federal Hotel in Wagin and worked in the railway sheds nearby, carrying 180-pound (82-kilogram) bags of wheat onto stacks in the sheds, then onto trains. We also went to nearby Katanning on odd days to do the same work there. The season had been very good and it was a big task to handle the thousands of bags that had been harvested. I had never done the work before, but quickly became quite skilful. Using a steel hook, you had to get your knees right as you picked up the very heavy bag. Then swing it onto your shoulder and run up the stack, to unload it exactly in place.

After two months of that, ever so fit, I returned to Fremantle, where my cousin Bill had agreed to stow me away to Melbourne on the MV *Duntroon*. It was a rough trip across the Great Australian Bight, but I survived okay and it was good to see my family again.

I needed an injection of funds, so I went digging potatoes at Nar Nar Goon and Koo Wee Rup. I had learned to dig spuds on Uncle Bob's farm and was fortunate that it was a record crop. We alternated between digging with the fork and 'picking up' after the new harvesting machines. I earned a massive £35 a week—the basic wage was £7—working seven days each week, digging, sewing the bags and loading them five bags high onto trucks. I was with a team of Yugoslavs—and boy, were we good! I returned home with £250 and gave half to Mum.

I wasn't too sure what would happen next, but I was aware of homesickness for the first time, as I missed the free and easy lifestyle of Darwin. My decision to go back north was finalised after a visit to Melbourne by the Flying Chinaman. He and I had a delightful week together in Melbourne; my parents had never met a Chinese person before and Hoonga charmed their socks off.

Hoonga returned to Darwin, but I elected to go first to Brisbane, where another Belsen Boy—Ron Bridgett, aka Bridgo—was on holiday. I still had a good bank balance and did I need it! Bridgo and I went to the races at Doomben and we drank at the Grand Central in the city most days, where he told barmaids that he was a station owner and I was his head stockman. The girls were duly unimpressed.

We went by train to Townsville, and then by another train to Mount Isa. By that time Bridgo had dissipated all of our money, playing cards on the train. We hitched a ride on the tray of a truck to Tennant Creek, spent a freezing night on a bench in Paterson Street and then heaved a sigh of relief when the Bond's coach rolled in the next morning. On board was another Belsenite, Charlie O'Dwyer; we each borrowed £5 from him and travelled back to dear old Darwin.

Bridgo resumed his job at Works and Jerks and was allocated a hut at Belsen. I had resigned prior to going to Western Australia, but I moved in with him as a non-paying guest and took a job as a builder's labourer with John Stubbs and Co., a building company enjoying a 'cost plus' contract to build houses and flats for the Department of Works.

Fortunately, I was in good physical condition. I was assigned to the gang building the new three-storey sisters' quarters for the Darwin Hospital. Every day we did a huge concrete pour, using shovels and wheelbarrows. Many years later I was proud of that association, for the sisters' quarters survived Cyclone Tracy unscathed. It was demolished later.

I had three months with Stubbs and then got a job as Housing Clerk with the Northern Territory Administration in Cavenagh Street. That position also entitled me to live legally back at Belsen. I accumulated a considerable knowledge of pre-war Darwin. During the war, all private property had been 'acquired' by the Commonwealth. Post-war, the old families were seeking either the return of their old accommodation, or compensation for the loss of their original houses. There was a huge list of people desperate for accommodation, and I got to know many of the families and their backgrounds.

The 1951 footy season got underway, and this year Works had a better team, winning a few games.

Around this time I came under the influence of Aloysius Puantulura, a remarkable Tiwi man who lived only a hundred metres from Belsen. Aloysius and his wife, Mena, worked at the Catholic presbytery, looking after the bishop and various priests and brothers. I was a staunch Catholic—a daily communicant at the time—and Aloysius was likewise. He and Mena were the first Tiwi couple to be married in the Catholic church on Bathurst Island by the famous Father (later Bishop) Gsell—who today is revered in Tiwi circles as 'Patagitjali'. The Tiwi run names together like that, so at first they called me 'Tidiganni'—a few years later Aloysius gave me my 'real' name, Murrumungajimirri. It will be on my tombstone.

In 1952, I was instructed (not asked) by Bishop O'Loughlin to be a founder (with Father Aubrey Collins) of the St Mary's Football Club in Darwin. His Lordship was keen to see the undoubted skills of Tiwi footballers given a chance to flourish; equally importantly, he saw an opportunity for them to broaden their general social experience in Darwin. Two large contingents of Tiwi men were employed, full-time, at the Army and RAAF bases in Darwin. Their contacts with the Armed Services had been very productive during the Pacific War of 1941–45. The men wore service uniforms at all times.

That meant three months in Darwin for 60 men at a time. Their families, in most cases, stayed on the islands. They all received the princely wage of £2 per week, half of which was sent to their families back home. In those days Aboriginal people were forbidden by law to drink alcohol, so the Tiwi blokes, all still proficient hunters and gatherers in the manner of their ancestors over countless centuries, were just so fit. Hard-gutted physiques. And they seemed to be so much bigger than today's Tiwi men; we always had four or five 'six-footers' in Saints' teams.

Aloysius was ever so perceptive. He came to me early in the piece, after we nominated Saints to join the local Australian Rules competition, and said, 'Good that you started the football team, Tidiganni, but our boys don't think in English. They think in our language. The team is mostly Tiwi, so I'd better teach you my language, then you can talk to them during the match. And remember, Ted, the opposition won't know what you're talking about.'

Good tactic! We started my regular lessons, two or three nights a week, so I could 'bookim down' the Tiwi language. Or some of it! I was never as good as people thought I was, but it was fun. Ironically, today I can read and write Tiwi fairly well, although I don't get enough opportunities to speak it anymore.

I certainly learned the footy fundamentals very well. *'Ingarrdi pakataringa ningani: Pipwa! Pipwala!'* equals 'The rain's pissing down—mark the bloody ball on your chest.' *'Yirukwa'* means 'Straight down the hi-diddle-diddle.' *'Kwa, mani'* translates roughly as 'Pass the ball to me and we're certain to win.'

St Mary's Football Club has been a remarkable success. I was their first captain in 1952–53, and took the club to our first premiership in 1954–55. The Tiwi players became a wonderful component of the St Mary's legend from day one, but I must also mention a place called Garden Point, run by the Catholic Church at Pirlangimpi, in Tiwi country on Melville Island.

Garden Point was established to enable the Catholic missionaries to care for the children of mixed race, invariably born to Aboriginal mothers and 'other race' fathers, in various regions of the Northern Territory, during a regrettable period of exploitative miscegenation. The birth entries invariably gave the mother's name and listed the father as 'unknown'.

Principally because of embarrassment, the policy in the Northern Territory from about 1912 to the early 1950s was for these 'yellerfellers' to be removed to institutions—out of sight, out of official mind. Comparable policies had been established in the various states of Australia many years earlier. The aim was to segregate the 'part Aboriginal' children from 'tribal' influences, so they could become 'like whites', but that was largely rational-isation. Today they are known as the Stolen Generations.

The policy only applied to children of mixed race, never First Australians of full descent. In many cases, the embarrassed non-Aboriginal father arranged the removal of his children. In the crudest of terms, it was articulated that 'fucking them white' was the best means of resolving 'the Aboriginal problem'.

But I think it is fair to say that, however cruel and unjust the policy was, at Garden Point the nuns, priests and brothers did an admirable job of looking after the separated children, who were often as young as three years of age. The true test of their work was demonstrated when the old laws concerning the removal of children were repealed. I only know a few cases where adults reared on Garden Point as children are critical of their upbringing; to this day, most are loyal to the church and many of them elected, eventually, to continue to live and work on Melville Island rather than be accommodated and employed in Darwin. Naturally, all are censorious of a government policy that separated them from their families in the first place, but in my appraisal a new 'tribe' was created, for among them an affinity and identity with Garden Point and one another continue.

I enjoyed wonderful times on the Tiwi Islands in the early 1950s. The Garden Pointers intermingled with the native-born Tiwi, learned traditional skills and language from them and were happily accepted by the locals. Indeed, many of the children had Tiwi mothers and Japanese fathers, from the pearling days prior to 1940. Pirlangimpi today is a town in its own right, accorded 'land rights' by the traditional Tiwi; it is a very proud community.

So from the 1950s to the 1990s, most St Mary's footballers came from two groups: the 'full-blood' Tiwi, called *tunuwui*, and the Garden Point 'mixed-race' men, called *monari*. We have won 34 premierships in 60 years, and have produced champion players such as Billy Roe, David Kantilla, Basil Campbell, Austin Wonaeamirri, Ronnie Burns, Scott Chisholm, Benny Vigona and the Rioli family—Maurice, Sebastian, Emmanuel, Willie and Cyril from the first generation, and their sons and grandsons Cyril Junior, Dean, Daniel and Willie Junior in recent years. Michael Long, a product of Garden Point, starred for Essendon in two of their premiership teams, and today enjoys immense status in Darwin. Interestingly, the local consensus is that Mick ranked third in talent among the six Long brothers, who together played 1000 games for Saints. Their dad, Jack Long, played 250 games, before and with his talented sons.

I often think of those St Mary's players of earlier years who never got the opportunities to go interstate. In my judgement, there are a great many unrecognised champions in that category.

Since 2007, there has been a separate team in the Darwin AFL competition. Tiwi Bombers have now taken most of the *tunuwui* from St Mary's; that development was understandable, given the depth of talent on the two islands. Most of the *monari* Garden Point families still play for St Mary's, though, and the social relationship between the two clubs remains strong.

I think my connection with St Mary's Football Club was the major turning point in my life. We started a team that wins more than its share of premierships, but more importantly the club is based on sound family principles. In the licensed clubhouse, adorned with photos and many premiership banners, occasionally unruly young people are admonished by an old Aboriginal woman: 'Excuse me, we don't behave like that around here.'

I constantly think of the Stolen Generations; I worked for twenty years for the government agency responsible for observing and enforcing the policy. I was never actually involved in the separation of a child from its mother, but I could have been. As a consequence, I could not sign the 'Sorry Books' quickly enough when they were introduced, for I am now determined that we must never again contemplate discriminatory laws based on race.

With Kevin Rudd's Apology in 2008, there should have been a generous payout to all genuine claimants. The long-term trauma of being separated from their families purely on the basis of race has been disastrous for most of them, despite the fact that many acknowledge that they were well treated. Most were permanently damaged.

9

OFF TO THE LOO

The much-maligned Sir Paul Hasluck, Minister for Territories during the 1950s and early 1960s, used to come to Darwin regularly; he always went to the football. In 1952, he heard me give a half-time pep talk one day, incorporating some Tiwi phrases; Saints went on to an impressive win. He said to me after the game: 'Come and talk to me at the government offices next Monday.' That's how I started my career with the Native Affairs Branch, as it was called in those days.

I began as a cadet patrol officer. Fortunately, the legendary Bill Harney was still a patrol officer at that time. Bill was enigmatic. He was the acknowledged father of two mixed-race children from 'full-blood' mothers. While such associations carried a mandatory six months' imprisonment for the white man involved, Bill was never charged with 'cohabiting'. On the contrary, because he enjoyed such prestigious status among First Australians, he was appointed a patrol officer by the government. So profound was his knowledge that anthropologists sought to conduct research under Bill's guidance. He became a prolific writer, and was appointed the first resident ranger when Uluru was declared a National Park. He was the best raconteur I ever met.

Bill Harney suggested to Frank Moy, the Director of Native Affairs, that I should be given the opportunity to mix with 'full-blood' Aboriginals in bush situations. So I had carte blanche and I grabbed it. Much of my time was spent at Bathurst Island, where I progressed with my language lessons, coached kids at football and basketball, and organised the movements of footballers to and from Darwin for St Mary's. I travelled, whenever possible, on the various boats serving the coastal Aboriginal communities, visiting all the Methodist Missions in Arnhem Land and Umbakumba on Groote Eylandt, where I met the celebrated trepanger Fred Gray.

Trepang, or bêche-de-mer, are 'sea cucumbers' that live in tropical waters. Harvested, smoked and dried, they are considered a delicacy by Asians. Fred Gray worked trepang for many years with groups of Arnhem Land Aboriginals and in 1938 he was asked by the government to be in charge of a 'settlement' at Umbakumba, to establish and maintain contact between Aboriginals and the new Qantas flying-boat base established there.

Fred and his wife, Marjorie, ran the best community I ever encountered, although they served the most aggressive Aboriginals in Australia.

When in Darwin, I attended police court cases involving Aboriginals. I shudder nowadays to think of the many prohibitions placed on First Australians in those times. At the same time, I always felt that my role was to be on their side—to apply to their benefit any skills that I had and to seek at all times to be benign, rather than punitive. I tried to follow the directive Paul Hasluck had given me: 'Always try to work yourself out of the job.'

All Aboriginal people were subject to the supposedly protective Aboriginals Ordinance, unchanged since 1918. They were not allowed to be in town areas 'between sunset and sunrise'; they were not allowed to drink alcohol; they could not vote, and were not officially recognised as human beings in the census; their personal freedom could be removed at the whim of the Director of Native Affairs; and they had to seek the Director's permission to marry. If they wanted to be 'exempted' they had to participate in the demeaning issue of a certificate, which came to be called the 'dog tag'. I used to issue permits for Aboriginals to attend the pictures at the Star Theatre each Wednesday night, which was Cowboy Night.

I achieved minor national recognition in 1953 when I defended a chap named Bob Secretary, who was charged with 'being in the town of Darwin at 7 p.m. without a permit'. Bob was a member of the local Larakia tribe and was, in fact, walking across town to work for the Army, where he was on night shift, when he was 'arrested and brought before the court'. I protested to Magistrate 'Fatty' Nichols: 'This man, Your Worship, was on his way to work! And if that is not enough, he is a Larakia and the Larakia are the owners of this town.' Fatty Nichols gave me a derisive glance—as if to say, 'You'll learn, son'—and convicted Bob: '£5 or fourteen days hard labour'. Fortunately, I never did learn.

I began courting a beautiful local girl named Rae Pierssené. Rae was born in Darwin, and her family was related to the Gadens, well-known buffalo shooters. Rae's mum, Eunice, had travelled to Darwin from Sydney in 1920, as a companion for her cousin, Mrs Ada Gaden, who lived with her husband and family at Kapalga, on the East Alligator River in Arnhem Land. Rae's father, Bert Pierssené, was a crack shot who returned to Australia after World War I and took employment with the Gadens. Rae was the second of their eventual six children.

Bert and Eun Pierssené had moved into Darwin before World War II; Eun and the children were evacuated to Sydney just before the first bombing raid in 1942. Bert remained in Darwin and was working at the Darwin post office on the day it was bombed, 19 February 1942; most of the staff were killed. Bert had built a new home in Darwin in 1939, but they lost that house in a subsequent bombing raid. The family returned to Darwin in 1946. When I met Rae, they were renting a small house only 200 metres from Belsen.

The Pierssené family treated me very kindly. Bert was the strongest man in the Territory, with film-star good looks. Eun had a wonderful overview of NT life. Rae worked in the Territory Administration, in the records section. She was immensely popular at work and among all the old 'pre-war' Darwinites. Through Rae, I got to know and be accepted by many old-timers, and to delight in the history lessons I was given by her parents, by the Gaden family and by the many unique characters always camped around the Gaden household at Salonika, Darwin. My mother's advice to be a good listener was never more useful.

Rae visited my parents in Sydney; they totally approved of her and gave me their blessing to become engaged to her. Rae and I got on very well—we were the same age, and we both played 'basketball' at the Darwin Stadium. Women actually played netball, but it was called 'women's basketball'. The women's games were much better patronised than the men's; the standard of the Darwin women of those days was very high.

Rae and I were married at St Mary's Church in October 1953. The celebrant was Father Frank Flynn, an extraordinary man who was an ophthalmologist, author and missionary. We had a wonderful reception at the nearby Catholic Palais de Danse—a flash name for a converted Sidney Williams hut—and a honeymoon at Coolangatta on the Gold Coast. To get to Coolangatta, we travelled by bus from Brisbane and passed through a little village named Surfers Paradise, which consisted of just a few shacks and a pub. At the time it was inconsequential; the surf break there was held to be inferior to that at the Greenmount and Kirra beaches at Coolangatta.

Back to Darwin at the start of 1954, Rae and I did 'caretaker tenancies' at a few homes and then were allocated a derelict government flat in a block called Seaspray Flats, on the corner of Peel Street and The Esplanade—very prestigious real estate these days but riddled with white ants and very unattractive in 1954.

Yet 1954 was a memorable year in other respects. I was captain of both St Mary's basketball and football teams, and each won the premiership. I was selected to play for the Northern Territory in its first interstate sporting team, which participated in the Australian Basketball Championships in Brisbane. But the greatest thrill was the birth of Gregory Joseph Egan on 1 October 1954, a beautiful boy who would grow into a lovely child and a great man.

In 1955, I was still with Native Affairs, working mainly around Darwin, but often doing annual inspections of Arnhem Land mission stations. On a couple of occasions I travelled with patrol officer Ted Evans on his cattle station inspections to Wave Hill and Victoria River Downs. I learned so much from 'Ted Heaven'—as Aboriginals called him—and he was important in my life thereafter.

In 1956, I graduated to patrol officer after successfully completing the course at the Australian School of Pacific Administration in Sydney. That was an incredible experience, as five NT patrol officers came together with twenty from Papua and New Guinea. I formed lifelong friendships with a few of the PNG lads and marvelled at the contribution they were making to a unique component of world history: Stone Age to world stage.

Back in Darwin in May 1957, I was one of the party that started the Maningrida outpost on the Liverpool River in Central Arnhem Land. Four whites (Dave and Ingrid Drysdale, Trevor Milikins and I) travelled for four days on MV *Temora*, with twenty Aboriginals from that region, who had been living, aimlessly, on the outskirts of Darwin. We took with us supplies for three months; Dave, Ingrid and Trevor were to stay on at the new station; my job as a patrol officer was to spend six months in the region, assisting in establishing the new station, but particularly to walk the region extensively, to announce the government's policies and to ascertain the numbers of quite traditional First Australians who would come under its influence.

I was ordered not to encourage people to come to reside at Maningrida; I passed that instruction on very definitely. Most were invited to have a short visit and then return to the traditional lives they still led at that time.

It was exciting. Many Aboriginals were still naked, and all were living off their land in traditional fashion. Some of the commodities that had lured them to Darwin would be available at Maningrida—basic Western foods such as flour, tea and sugar, plus tobacco and clothing. Visitors to Darwin had in many cases become familiar with alcohol, and in many cases addicted to it, but that was not to be available. The aim was to encourage these skilled hunters and gatherers to trade various items, such as crocodile skins, mats, baskets and bark paintings, for the desired 'white-man' commodities; they were expected to stay in their regions. One of our specific aims was to establish a medical centre as quickly as possible.

Dave and Ingrid were very experienced, as they had worked on mission stations in Western Australia. Dave was an enterprising farmer, baker and mechanic; he immediately started work with a gang of Aboriginals who built an airstrip for the flying doctor in six months. Ingrid was a saintly woman, and began treating the many unfortunate people in the region who were suffering from leprosy. Over the ensuing years, Ingrid and another superb woman, Eileen

'Tuffy' Jones, worked in collaboration with the inimitable Dr John Hargrave to eliminate leprosy in that region. The Maningrida Hospital to this day is named after Ingrid Drysdale.

In order to encourage men and their families to stay in their homelands, I organised teams of commercial crocodile hunters. They were very skilful already, as they occasionally ate crocodile meat, but they needed salt, plus assistance with the preservation and marketing of the skins. It was a very rewarding pastime for them, which the men really enjoyed. As they were paid at the standard rate of eight shillings per inch—measured across the belly width of the crocodile skin—they immediately began to make impressive money. I had a ton of fun learning the various skills myself and the men were patient teachers. I developed wonderful friendships with three men in particular: Harry Mulumbuk, Jack Nabulaya and Frank (Left Hand) Malgaura. It was a laugh a minute being with them.

I returned to Darwin in time for the birth of Margaret Mary Egan on 15 October 1957. A beautiful healthy baby, Marg has always been a loving daughter, her principal attribute being compassion. In later life she has been such a reassurance to so many friends in need.

In November 1957 I was posted to Borroloola, in what is called the Gulf (of Carpentaria) Country. Rae had resigned from her old job at NTA. She, Greg, Margaret and I travelled with a very dodgy pilot in a De Havilland Dragon, an old biplane. Sid, the pilot, had no idea how to get to The Loo—as Borroloola is called. Even though I had never been there, I instructed Sid to fly south-east until we spotted the very obvious Roper River; I would direct him from there to the Macarthur River and Borroloola. We arrived eventually, and settled in for our first experience of real outback living. There was no electricity, so we used kerosene for the fridge and lighting (Tilley pump lamps). There were snakes galore. Rae should have been given a medal for bravery.

We lived in the historic old Borroloola Police Station. I was the 'government man' required to be all things to all people on all government matters, but principally I was responsible for the care and supervision of around 300 tribal Aboriginals. Not that that was ever a worry; Borroloola Aboriginals had had dealings with white people, on an understood and reasonably amicable basis, for a century. In the Dry Season, the majority of the young Aboriginal workers, men and women, went westward to the huge Barkly Tableland cattle stations, where their services were greatly valued. Pensioners and some children would remain at The Loo.

We arrived as the station workers were coming back home from the stations. During the Wet, the Aboriginals all lived on the other side of the Macarthur River. They had simple but satisfactory bush dwellings. They had ample money, as a result of the season's work, and it was time for traditional rituals, particularly the initiation of young boys and girls. Rae and I were always invited to these ceremonies, and we really enjoyed the company of these very hospitable First Australians, particularly the people who worked with us around our house and office.

As well as Aboriginals at The Loo, we met up with an interesting bunch of old white blokes, who had been classified by the eminent BBC filmmaker David Attenborough as 'the Hermits of Borroloola' when he made his *Quest Under Capricorn* TV series.

These blokes, about ten of them altogether, used to conduct debates every Sunday morning under the mango trees near Albert Morcom's camp and I always attended. This was erudite stuff. 'Is There a Future in Buddhism?' was the subject one week; 'Should Henry James Be Taken Seriously?' was another I recall. The best debate I remember was a great battle between the supporters of two eminent poets—'Gray v. Browning'. The Gray team won easily, led by an unforgettable bloke named Roger Jose.

I'll never forget Roger's recital of Gray's 'Elegy Written in a Country Churchyard'. Most of the other Hermits had sobriquets—the Mad Fiddler, the Reluctant Saddler, the Whispering Baritone, the White Stallion, that sort of thing—but Roger Jose was just 'Roger' to all and sundry, including his two Aboriginal wives. (I discovered many years later that Roger's real name was James Arthur Edison Hudson.) I heard an ignorant visitor describe him as 'a death adder' one day, so I found myself defending the old chap in my first-ever song:

> Roger Jose lived terrible close
> To a place called Borroloola
> Folks called Roger the Old Death Adder
> But don't let that fact fool ya . . .
>
> 'Roger Was No Death Adder' (1958)

The Hermits had acquired their level of scholarship via the famous Borroloola Library. Around 1900, a policeman, bemoaning the fact that he had been posted to such a remote region, contacted various philanthropists, including the Carnegie Institute in America. There is debate about the source of the eventual gift, but nonetheless Borroloola ended up with a library of around a thousand leather-bound classics. Wisely, it was decreed that the library would be housed in the police cells.

I arrived 50 years later. Most of the Hermits, over the years, had done various stretches in the slammer for crimes such as cattle duffing, trepanging without a licence, supplying alcohol to Aboriginals, or having sexual congress with Aboriginal women. This had given them time to become familiar with tomes such as Homer's *Odyssey*, Virgil's *Aeneid* and *The Rubaiyat of Omar Khayyam*. Roger Jose was a scholar, verily and forsooth. As I put it in my song:

> Roger liked astrology, history, anthropology
> Poetry, politics and theology
> Geography, philosophy, he'd read of all of these
> And liked to sit and argue underneath the shady trees.

We had a wonderful bush Christmas at The Loo. Hector Anderson and I killed and 'overlanded' a bullock; the women cooked up dampers and brownies. There was tinned fruit and custard for the kids. Spear throwing, pillow fights, treacle bun races, footraces, fire-lighting competitions—all were highlights of a simple but delightful occasion. At the end of the day, after all the Aboriginals had gone back across the river, I said to Roger: 'I've got a few cool bottles of beer, old man. Would you like a drink?'

He replied: 'Ted, beer is strictly for bank johnnies. You wouldn't have a cold metho, would you?'

10

THE INUGWAMBA

My next posting was to Groote Eylandt, in the Gulf of Carpentaria—the 'great island' named by Dutch explorer Abel Tasman. There had been some serious assaults of the Anglican missionaries by Aboriginal men over the issue of polygyny. The Anindilyakwa people are difficult for Westerners—indeed anyone—to understand. In most Aboriginal tribes, there's about 10 per cent of the population with whom members of the same tribe have no dealings or contact. The academics call it 'avoidance'. At Groote, it is about 80 per cent that each individual member can't talk to, can't look at. That's *tricky* avoidance.

As I left Borroloola, Roger Jose, typically—in his best Socratic fashion—said: 'Ted, when you're at Groote, see what you can find out regarding the *inugwamba*.'

'What's an *inugwamba*?' I queried.

'That's what I want you to find out!'

Of course he knew, for he had worked trepang with Groote Eylandters for many years.

I eventually learned that although Anglican missionaries had come to Groote Eylandt in 1921, it was several years before they actually laid eyes on a Groote Eylandt woman. Groote Eylandt women were required to carry, at all times, a large sheet of bark that folded into a V. If they were anywhere where contact with prohibited people was possible, they were required to hide behind this bark sheet, called an *inugwamba*, until the danger had passed.

Groote Eylandt men were, and are to this day, fiercely aggressive. The result of their traditional marriage system was that brother killed brother, and thereby accumulated multiple wives. After 1921, the missionaries, who had taken over the island with the backing of ignorant politicians, announced that henceforth there would be a system of 'one man, one wife'. That suited a lot of younger men, who otherwise had to wait their turn for a promised bride. Thus, many monogamous marriages were arranged and condoned by the missionaries. It all seemed to be accepted.

But after a few years, the same men began to assert their right to a second or third wife; behind the scenes, traditional unions were being organised, with the missionaries in total ignorance about what was happening. When the men started to take 'single' girls from the dormitories in which the missionaries had placed them, quite a few assaults took place. I was sent to Groote for three months in 1958 to attempt to sort things out.

Softly, softly was my approach. I asked a party of men of authority—including a few who had knifed missionaries—to take me into the Gulf for a month, with canoes, to hunt crocodiles, dugong and turtles. An additional complaint I had from Groote Eylandt men was that, under the system imposed by the missionaries, they were unable to get anything other than menial, lowly paid jobs, even though they had a commendable work ethic. They often said to me, 'We are soldiers, not pussy cats'.

I financed the trip, paying for basic foodstuffs such as flour, tea and sugar, salt for crocodile skins, plus tobacco, which they called *tambakwo*. They were all heavily into smoking, in long Macassan pipes called *larua*. I had a .303 Lee Enfield rifle and plenty of bullets. They supplied three canoes, one of them the biggest dugout canoe I had ever seen. They had spears and harpoons, and I knew, after my Maningrida experiences, that I would see expert hunters in action.

It was unforgettable. We lived off the land and the sea for a month—yams, fish, oysters, crayfish. We talked deep into each night. I gained their respect and I certainly respected them. We returned to Angurugu Mission with five huge live green turtles, immobile on their backs in the canoes. We had bags of salted dugong meat and twenty very valuable crocodile skins. There was a huge celebration and each man received around £20—a year's wages—from the sale of the skins.

I subsequently took a gang of workers to camp at the Wallaby Creek crossing, on the road to Umbakumba, which was Fred Gray's outpost on the north of the large island. We built a substantial bridge over the creek; previously, in the Wet Season, the road had been impassable there. The bridge survived twenty years of traffic.

Over many nights thereafter, I held meetings with any Aboriginal men and women who wanted to discuss the issue of marriage promises. I had with me the Register of Wards that had been compiled a few years earlier, when we had, to the best of our ability, established in Darwin a Population Register of all Northern Territory Aboriginals of full descent.

We went through the names of every person listed for Groote Eylandt, and I cross-referenced them and double-checked them to establish every known 'marriage promise' that had been agreed to by the various families but never disclosed to the missionaries.

The missionaries were cynical, disbelieving, but the Council of Aboriginal Elders—appointed by the mission—was adamant that I had prepared my material accurately and that they expected the established promises to be honoured. The missionaries protested that God's law was 'one man, one wife', yet they were not impressed by my suggestion that they might, in some cases, be able to cancel some promises by covering, or bettering, the bride price, which was a component of the promise system. I was aware of the intrusive but successful tactics employed at Bathurst Island many years before by Bishop Gsell, 'the Bishop with 150 Wives': Gsell had 'paid out' the bride price with bags of flour, cloth and tobacco, and encouraged young Christian couples to marry in the Catholic church, provided there was agreement that the choice of spouses accorded to the rules of the old kinship system.

The Anglicans, who were delivering biblical quotes on an almost daily basis, were unimpressed when I referred them to Matthew 20:1–16, the parable of the man who employed workers in his vineyard, for the 'payouts' would in most cases have been quite trivial and easy to match. 'Strike a deal with the longest-established, amenable "promise parties" and set that as the payout figure,' I suggested. No way, they responded. The motto of the Church Missionary Society was: 'The best of all is that God is with us'.

But an agreement eventuated: both parties agreed to sit down and debate issues, rather than come to blows.

At that precise time, in 1958, BHP arrived, with a licence from the government to mine manganese on Groote Eylandt. Immediately the missionaries were no longer in economic control, although they remained (as fairly good friends) in a religious sense. Plenty of jobs, with high wages, were available at BHP for any Groote Eylandters who wanted them. Life went on. Sort of.

11

THE DESERT RAT

Back to Darwin, post The Loo and Groote, reunited with Rae and the kids in a nice house in town for a couple of months. Then I was told that I was to be appointed Superintendent of Yuendumu Aboriginal Reserve, 182 miles (293 kilometres) north-west of Alice Springs. We Top Enders called our counterparts in Central Australia 'Desert Rats'—rats in the ranks! Now I was about to become one.

I left Rae and the kids in Darwin for the first month and flew to Alice Springs. I was driven out to Yuendumu by Bill McCoy, the district officer, who looked askance at this 26-year-old pipsqueak, the youngest superintendent ever appointed in Native Affairs. Puffing impressively on his pipe, Bill told me how different I was going to find things. 'These desert blackfellas only respect people with grey hair,' he intoned as he drove me through some beautiful mountainous country around Alice, and into the very dismal landscape at Yuendumu.

He spent two joyless days with me, urging that I would need to be 'hard, but fair'. Then he left me to it, thank goodness. I knew I was facing perhaps the biggest challenge of my life. I was in charge of a reserve of 1000 square miles, with around 800 Aboriginals who were still in many respects Stone Age people. The scarification on the bodies of all adults was very impressive. Cicatrices were common on chests and shoulders. Huge gashes on thighs were caused by 'sorry cuts' and spear wounds. Most men were proud to have considerable scarring on their backs, as a result of *karintjukara*, the highly disciplined stone-knife fights organised to settle differences.

Most adults had pierced noses; occasionally I saw *mara-bindi*—various bones through their nostrils.

It was May, wintertime, and I quickly judged that these were perhaps the toughest people on Earth. Although they wore Western clothing by day, most of them totally discarded it to sleep, on the bare ground, in temperatures that fell to minus 5 degrees Celsius. No blankets. Body, tiny fire, body, tiny fire—rows of them, naked, frost on the ground. And yet in summer they were confronted with temperatures as high as 45 degrees. What metabolisms!

Although there was a reliable workforce around the place, there were always indications of the comprehensive traditional life these First Australians still led. Most adults had ochre and feathers on their faces and bodies, to indicate serious ceremonial activity. I was on an immense learning curve, trying to understand how best I could assist them. They were Warlpiri people—Yapa, they called themselves, as distinct from Gadiya, whitefellas. From the 1930s they were forced to assemble at various government-run 'settlements' such as Yuendumu, because they were considered to be a threat to the local white pastoralists, who had been given leases that indicated 'ownership' of the land. In 1928, these same Warlpiri had been *dispersed*—this was the common euphemism—at nearby Coniston, where the police acknowledged that they had killed 31 men, women and children. The real figure was certainly higher—perhaps 80. So I was working with people who had suffered incredible brutality, on land they had considered theirs for countless centuries.

Bill McCoy warned me not to 'take on an identity'. He said: 'They'll try to take you over. They'll give you a skin name and then you'll be subject to their influence.' (He was referring to the eight identity groups—called 'skin names' in English—whereby kinship relationships were established and maintained.)

Fortunately, sanity prevailed. On my first day alone, a married couple came to me. 'I am Tim Jabangadi,' said the tall, handsome man. 'This is one of my wives, Uni, and she's Nambijinba. I am going to look after you. Do you have a wife?'

'Yes, she'll be here in a few weeks.'

'Good,' he continued. 'So your wife will be Nambijinba and Uni will look after her. I'll call you Jabangadi, and you will be treated as my brother. I'll look after you while you're here.'

No ifs or buts. 'Ted Jabangadi' I am to this day among Warlpiri people. What luck!

Tim Jabangadi, as I discovered, was extremely powerful in ceremonial terms, but he was also very savvy in Western experience. He had worked for the Army all through the war and was an extremely good mechanic. Uni was a striking young woman, exactly the same age as Rae and me. Ominously, Uni was able to work out her date of birth by reference to the Coniston Massacre of 1928; she was born four years later.

Rae arrived, and she and Uni began a beautiful friendship. Tim brought to me two young men, Sandy Jabananga and Johnny Jungarai, both driver/mechanics whom he had trained. Those two fine young fellows were at our beck and call seven days a week, 24 hours a day, for our entire stay at Yuendumu. I am still in close contact with the various families who treated me so well.

I was also lucky with the white staff. In most comparable places, there were too many white workers; I preferred to insist that Aboriginals would be in charge wherever possible. But I had two white blokes—Don Busbridge and Max Trenowden—who were invaluable at many tasks, plus Arthur Hutchins, a wonderful old-fashioned stonemason. All three were magnificent teachers. Each had a great wife, who joined Rae and Pat Fleming, the Baptist missionary, in working effectively with the local women.

Rae and I were able to achieve much at Yuendumu during that five-year posting, with great assistance from the locals—including white families on the adjacent properties, who taught me so much about cattle. We established market gardens and won prizes for our vegetables at the Alice Springs Show. We built stockyards and fences, which eventually enabled us to run 2000 cattle effectively. At our peak, we slaughtered five bullocks a week. We quarried beautiful sandstone and built some impressive stone houses. We started outstations, to make more effective use of the large Aboriginal reserve. At the same time, we encouraged kids to get a good schooling, and provided a commendable health service, in cooperation with the Aerial Medical Branch of the Department of Health. I taught the Yuendumu men to play Aussie Rules football, and in my dotage, many years later, I am pleased that their grandsons are fine exponents of the game.

As superintendent, I had the enthusiastic support of a man named Harry Giese. He never invited staff to call him Harry. He was Mr Giese, the Director of Aboriginal Welfare, and nowadays—he is dead—he is vilified because he supported the policy of assimilation for First Australian people. He is accused by his detractors of deliberately trying to smash the traditional culture. Absolute nonsense. He certainly had some faults, but he was nothing like the monster people talk about. As one example: he started the various eisteddfods in the Northern Territory, to encourage traditional tribal dancing in particular. I was grateful that he found the funds for our cattle station and various other expensive activities that we embarked on.

Not that life at Yuendumu was ever easy. Maintaining health standards was a perennial challenge. The adults were certainly tough, but their children were vulnerable, particularly between six months and eighteen months of age. I developed what can only be called a paranoia about 'blackfella dogs'. People would protest to me that these mangy, disease-ridden mongrels were 'used for hunting'. I argued that they were the cause of most of the sicknesses that prevailed.

Of the babies born at Yuendumu in 1958, the year I arrived there, not one survived. During 1959, twelve months later, over 40 babies died from gastroenteritis, despite the presence of a medical clinic, the availability of penicillin and access to Alice Springs Hospital. I blamed that tragedy largely on the fact that mothers sat on the ground with their babies, among scavenging dogs, allowing the dogs to eat from the same billycans used to feed children who were being weaned onto various foodstuffs.

Dogs remain an issue to this day among people who still follow similar habits. I tried to come to terms with the problem. I had the key to the ration store, where people assembled once a week to receive staple items—flour, tea, sugar, jam. Each week, before the issue of rations, I insisted that I be given the right to go, with a white offsider, plus Sandy and Johnny, to the various camps to shoot at least twenty dogs. When that was done, the rations were issued. The Aboriginals copped it, but they were not pleased. I have to acknowledge that there were still hundreds of dogs. I encourage all Aboriginal people to forsake their dogs; I regularly bore people on this subject.

Rae and I now had three lovely kids, thanks to the arrival in 1959 of Mark Francis, who had a precarious start to life at Alice Springs Hospital, when Rae's life was saved by the skills of Dr George Tippett, the man who also established an orderly, efficient medical service for all Centralians, regardless of their race or background.

* * *

After five challenging years at Yuendumu, I was, in an administrative shuffle, promoted to Superintendent of Bagot Reserve, on the outskirts of Darwin. There were a few permanent Aboriginal residents at Bagot, but it was mainly a staging camp for transients in various categories. Rae and I lived in a magnificent house, on site, our kids were able to attend school in town, and Rae got to be back among her own family again. Apart from those appreciated advantages, I hated the job. There was simply no challenge to achieve anything positive. I sat at a desk all day, numb.

I had always been critical of many teachers appointed to Aboriginal bush schools. Many of them engaged in nothing other than 'bushwalks', teeth cleaning and some boring singing lessons. Where are the matriculants, I always asked—and still do. To this day, I see TV coverage of Aboriginal schools, and so often the children are just doing 'colouring in'!

I was carrying on in that vein to my good mate Jim Gallacher in Darwin one day, shortly after we arrived back in town. Jim challenged me: he was the Director of Aboriginal Education. 'You're always sounding off, Ted,' he said. 'Why don't you do something about it? You obviously hate your new job at Bagot. Why don't you let me put you through teachers' college?' Jim had, to his great credit, initiated a program of teacher training for mature students.

To his surprise, I responded immediately: 'You're on.'

12

SWEET AND SOUR BUSTARD

In deciding to accept the offer of a scholarship to become a teacher, I was influenced by a man named Colin Tatz. Colin is a lifelong friend now, after 60 years of rewarding connection with him and his wonderful wife, Sandy. In 1958, they migrated to Australia from South Africa, where Colin was a strident critic of the National Party government and its apartheid policies. At the invitation of Sir Paul Hasluck, Colin was, in 1959, working on his PhD thesis; his topic was Aboriginal Administration in the Northern Territory.

After a shaky start at Yuendumu, Col and I developed a huge rapport and he encouraged me to commence an external Bachelor of Arts degree. It became a good discipline. By the time I got back to Darwin at the end of 1962, I had passed two of the required ten units, so Jim Gallacher was supportive of me continuing the BA studies, as well as undertaking my teachers' course.

I had to accept a considerable reduction in salary, but was nonetheless enthusiastic as we departed for Brisbane and Kelvin Grove Teachers College. I knew I would be able to get some sort of additional income, and early in the piece I applied for and was awarded a contract cleaning public telephone boxes at night-time in the suburbs around Red Hill, where Rae and I rented a nice home.

Our three kids went to school and we established a friendship with the Portley family. Margaret Portley was one of the nurses who had assisted Dr George Tippett at my son Mark's birth, and so had participated in saving Rae's life. She was now back in Brisbane. Her brother Coll was my Art lecturer at Kelvin Grove. Coll introduced me to my everlasting appreciation of the game of Rugby Union, especially the social aspects! Ned Portley, their father, was quite famous; a bookmaker, he was also a former mayor of Warwick. It was Ned Portley who originally brought Duke Kahanamoku to Australia, to introduce surfboard riding.

The lovely part about my stint in Brisbane was that I knew exactly what teaching skills I needed to acquire. I knew that I would be returning to the Northern Territory to participate in teaching Aboriginal kids in remote regions, invariably (I hoped) in a 'one-teacher' situation. Fortunately, there was a demonstration one-teacher school at Ascot, in Brisbane. That was my target.

Another advantage was that I was now 30 years of age, whereas most of the students at Kelvin Grove were nineteen or twenty, straight out of high school. As I was as physically fit and as good as any of them at various sports, I was able to establish a healthy 'elder' relationship with most of them.

I had been told that the principal of Kelvin Grove, Dr Greenhalgh, was a great Aussie Rules fan. The college had a very good Rugby Union team, but I went to Dr G. early on and suggested I start a Rules team. He was ecstatic; it was probably my cleverest move, in that he consequently saw the sense in allowing me to do the bulk of my practical teacher training at Ascot. And the footy team was a great success.

It was an absorbing two years. I completed two more units, Political Science 1 and 2, at The University of Queensland. I passed my Dip. Ed. with a high distinction for Class Teaching and was awarded a 'Double Blue' for sports—Aussie Rules, basketball and volleyball. I also spent three nights a week cleaning phone boxes; I was physically the fittest I had ever been in my life. As a cleaner, I employed as my offsider a young trainee teacher named Frank Brennan—not a relative—and Frank and I had stimulating discussions as we drove from one phone box to the next. He had been the Irish handball champion at Gregory Terrace, so every Saturday morning we played that great game, the fiercest of opponents. We were both very good players, of about equal ability. Frank subsequently, on my advice, transferred to the Northern Territory, where he had an esteemed career as a teacher, principal and inspector of schools.

The highlight of our time in Brisbane was the birth of Jacqueline Ann Egan, a lively, lovely girl. Jacki has always been proud of her Queensland origins—especially around State of

Origin time—and I have always marvelled at her capacity for work. She is also a ton of fun. When she was five, she appointed herself as my secretary; I have never been so well organised. 'Just ring the bell and I'll be there,' was Jacki's catchcry.

At the end of 1964, we returned to the Territory. Rae flew back to Darwin with baby Jacki. I drove my old Peugeot 403, with Greg, Margaret and Mark, plus my dad. Joe had never been to the Territory previously, and he gazed in wonder as the 'big country' unfolded. We camped in our swags each night. The kids were very easy to get along with, as they were used to long-distance travel. I was thrilled to spend such rewarding time with my dad. I had always been aware of his knowledge; now, during those ten-hour days of driving, we had the time to share it. That's why, to this day, I elect to drive rather than fly if there's an option. Time to think.

* * *

My 1965 posting was to the isolated but historic Newcastle Waters, slap-bang in the middle of the Territory. Cattle country. Newcastle Waters' cattle station was around 3500 square miles (9000 square kilometres) in area, and reasonably good country. The dreaded Murranji Track lay to the north-west, and the Barkly Tableland to the east, with Newcastle Creek running through the property. Fifteen miles away to the south was the little town of Elliot, established during World War II. Newcastle Waters was once a junction for the various stock routes, as drovers walked their cattle back and forth across Australia. It was the homeland of the Jingili First Australians.

The small school there catered for the Aboriginal kids whose parents worked at the huge cattle station. I was the teacher for 22 children, including my own three. Three nights a week I also ran evening classes for Aboriginal parents, most of whom were illiterate.

The parents were most anxious to learn about the 'new money'; the change to decimal currency was set to occur in February 1966. That gave me the opportunity to teach some simple but useful mathematics—all based on decimals—using, for adults and kids alike, the wonderful Cuisenaire rods I had come to value as inimitable mathematical aids.

The kids were just so keen to learn, and we achieved much. I was assisted by the fact that, at the same time, Rae and I had enrolled Greg as an external student with the School of the Air, meaning I was able to supervise his studies and use the same program for the brighter Aboriginal kids.

The kids would be waiting each morning, ready for school at 6 a.m. They showered, changed into their clean school clothes, had breakfast—porridge, toast and milk. That was supervised by Rae and an elderly Aboriginal couple, Elsie and Duncan. School started at 8 a.m. Phys ed was always first session, followed by a comprehensive day where I taught four separate groups of various age levels. While I did specific work with the seniors (Group One), reading or writing lessons were undertaken by Group Three, while Group Two was required to supervise the activity allotted for Group Four, the juniors. The day saw rotations like that. So the older pupils became the teachers. That is the strength of one-teacher education. My mum's brother,

Uncle Gus Brennan, spent twenty years in one-teacher schools; in my judgement, it is the ultimate approach to education, and its principles are transferable to bigger schools. There are no discipline issues.

Our first six weeks at Newcastle Waters taught me the meaning of the word *isolation*. Our house, the school and the cattle station were all on the western bank of Newcastle Creek. It began to rain in torrents and the creek ran, slowly but surely, six feet deep and a mile wide. That meant that the north–south Stuart Highway was blocked at the crossing, so there was no road traffic of any kind, between Darwin and Alice Springs, for six weeks. And we were on the *wrong* side of the track! Fortunately, we had a good supply of basic tinned food, but the principal shortcoming was that we were unable to get any meat. On a cattle station the size of Belgium!

The owner of the cattle station, Roy Edwards, did not like the idea of outsiders having influence in the lives of 'his' Aboriginal station workers. Although I had known him quite well in Darwin, he totally ignored my presence. They slaughtered their own beef at the station, but he would not sell or give meat to the few other local families—mine, the local PMG technician, or the handful of mixed-race people—who lived in the 'township'. Some township!

So I had to resort to driving westward on the Murranji Track, a couple of times each week, in my Peugeot, to shoot either a kangaroo or, more easily, a plains turkey—a bustard. The country generally had dried out, but the flooded creek still made access to anywhere east of us impossible. The poor old turkeys are very easy to shoot, but they are a protected species for anybody other than First Australians. Fair enough. The local Territory joke is that if you're caught shooting a turkey, you proffer the defence that 'the turkey attacked me'. I've never shot one since that time, and my fond recollection is that Rae did a magnificent job as she served turkey curry, turkey soup, sweet-and-sour turkey, roast turkey and turkey sandwiches for six weeks.

I have often thought I should have rolled one of Roy's prize bullocks; I was a skilled butcher, after all. How does the song go?

Dig a hole and bury the ears
We'll be back another day . . .

'Wee-ai Quee-ai, Kapramunda' (1968)

Straightaway, government funds were provided for the George Redmond Crossing, which nowadays provides a three-kilometre causeway over Newcastle Creek.

13

THIS YOU ISLAND?

I anticipated something like five years at Newcastle Waters. Imagine my shock at the end of my first year, when I was told that in January 1966, I would be principal at Angurugu, Groote Eylandt.

I was no stranger to Angurugu. Recall my visit in 1958. Now, in 1966, the government had decided to take control of all former 'missionary schools'. Fortunately for me, although I was to assume control over a school that would still be staffed by its former five female missionary teachers (now paid government salaries), I had established in 1958 strong relationships with Judith Stokes— former principal—and Deaconess Norma Farley, in charge of religious instruction. We now had six teachers and 150 pupils. I took over the senior boys and shared the senior girls with Judith.

My teachers were marvellous, but the pupils engaged us in daily warfare. I have never been so exhausted at the end of a day.

Twelve-year-old boys would confront me: 'This you island? You born here?'

'No.'

'This my island. I born here. I am soldier. You not boss for me.'

'Good to hear it. So can we work together? I get paid a lot of money to be here. I want to make sure you can read and write and be a good soldier like your dad.'

I eventually won them over by treating them as soldiers. I taught them marching, drumming, gymnastics—they were fearless at pyramids. Every second week I took the boys camping at Amagula River—Monday to Friday—for their school lessons. They delighted me by working relentlessly on their schoolwork, so they could get on with their own aggressive 'war games'. Additionally, I taught them footy and basketball. I was assisted by two very tough First Australian men, Nanind-jurrpa and Nandabida, whom I had befriended in 1958.

I once read *Tom Brown's School Days* to my Groote boys. Their reaction? They set up a fagging system! 'Good idea,' they said. 'We are soldiers.'

The senior girls were with me for two weeks in every four. They were colossal students, ready to learn at all times, taking on board my every word. But no individual girl would ever contemplate eye contact. Remember the *inugwamba*? The minute I spoke directly to a girl, or named her, she would hide behind her mental shield, eyes downcast—but always very alert.

The girls were like a flock of parrots. They did everything as a group. They spat out instructions to me: 'You teach us singing, Mistegan.' Or: 'We do science experiment, Mistegan.' They were brilliant.

They knew my nickname—'O Mariana'—from my 1958 days, but the girls always called me Mistegan.

Their mastery (or should it be Misstery?) of the many songs I taught them was an experience in itself. Different languages? That's okay. *'Isa Lei'*? *'Pokarekare Ana'*? 'La Marseillaise'? As I sang, they would watch me intently. You could almost see them learning the words. Sometimes they'd write a phrase in their books. Then I would say, 'Let's do it together.' I sang, they'd turn their backs to face the wall, and then sing with me. Word perfect. They were so admirable.

Poor buggers. Life is tough on Groote Eylandt; the accident of birth. I consider it ten times a day, every day, as I lead my privileged life.

Because it was impossible to have a direct conversation with any individual girl, I hit upon a novel idea. As part of the Art and Craft syllabus, we made excellent papier-mâché masks—ducks, horses, elephants, monkeys, you name it. The girls painted them beautifully. When they put the head masks on, it was like the *inugwamba*. Protection. It enabled genuine conversation.

'How are you today, Mrs Duck?'

'Not too bad at all, Mistegan. How's yourself? How's your wife? What's her name?'

'Rae.'

'She drink rum, Mistegan? Your wife? She smoke cigarette?'

'No, neither of those bad habits. She leaves me to do those things. But how's your husband, Mrs Duck?'

'Oh, the poor old thing. He's got a fever. *Marndiala*.'

Marndiala translates as 'poor bugger'. Conversation—first time in their lives. They would even laugh. Occasionally.

It was a fascinating twelve months. Again, I was looking forward to subsequent years. We went to Darwin for Christmas, but I was called to Harry Giese's office and told that there would be no Christmas break for me. I was to be transferred immediately to Yirrkala, in Arnhem Land, as district officer. Nabalco, a Swiss company, had been granted licences to mine bauxite there, and it was crucial to have an experienced government official who could negotiate between the mining company and the local Aboriginals.

14

GOLD NUGGET

The government anticipated problems after granting mining licences on an 'inviolable' Aboriginal reserve to Nabalco, a company that was part of the worldwide Alusuisse mining corporation. It didn't take long for problems to develop. In 1963, when bauxite mining was first proposed, an astute Methodist missionary named Edgar Wells heard the news and discussed the implications with the local Yolngu people.

Yolngu is not the name of a tribe or clan. The word basically translates as 'we who belong here'. The clan owners of the immediate country allocated to Nabalco were the Gumatj and the Rirratjingu, but many other clans were present at Yirrkala and would be affected by mining in the region. Collectively, the First Australians of Arnhem Land referred to themselves as *yolngu* and to white people as *balanda*—derived from the Macassan reference to 'Hollanders' in the old Dutch East India Company days.

As a consequence of those talks with Edgar, the Yolngu residents of Yirrkala Methodist mission station presented the famous Bark Petition to the federal government. Beautiful bark paintings were mounted, with an attached typed statement, signed by appropriate elders. Basically, it said: 'This is our country and we want to know why we weren't consulted.'

I arrived in the area in December 1966 and immediately sensed the tension.

The stance of the federal government, through its agency, the Northern Territory Administration—my employer—was that the Aboriginals were not the owners of the land. It was Crown land. However, the government acknowledged the *occupancy* of the land by the First Australians; it was determined that, because the government would be deriving hefty royalties from Nabalco, a percentage of that money would be placed in the Aboriginal Benefits Trust Fund, for the benefit of *all* Northern Territory Aboriginals. That, too, was a point of contention for the Yolngu. If royalties are payable, they argued, pay them to *us*.

The usual garbage about jobs and benign outcomes was advanced by the mining people, but the stance of Nabalco from day one was that any meaningful talks should only be with the government. Fair enough.

My job was to be alert and report the details of all happenings and opinions, and keep things on an even keel as best I could. At the outset, that seemed fairly straightforward, as I knew and liked the leaders of both Nabalco and the Yolngu.

Slowly but surely, I came to realise that the government was very much on the side of the miners. As fast as I organised for various contractual opportunities to be offered to competent bodies established by the missionaries and involving Yolngu workers, the government would allocate those contracts to companies who then brought new white workers to the region.

Also, after many long talks with the Yolngu elders, I began to shift my stance on the general question of who owned this land. By 1969, after three years in the region, I did a volte-face. Previously I had subscribed to the notion of Crown land, as long as there were safe reserves for First Australians, but here was a challenge that I had never contemplated.

Traditional ceremonial life at Yirrkala was conducted at a level I had never experienced before, revealing a dominant, comprehensive alliance with nature that existed deep in the psyche of every Yolngu person. Nothing else really mattered in life, as long as they fulfilled their prescribed social requirements to the land and to one another.

The Methodist missionaries were, not unexpectedly, engaged in ongoing discussion in their own ranks and I was not surprised when told that a legal challenge was to be mounted, questioning the government's right to impose mining contracts against the will of the real owners. This was a first in Australian history.

I was in a dilemma. I seriously contemplated resigning from the Territory Administration. But I was thrown a lifeline.

In 1968 I was advised that, as a consequence of the 1967 referendum, a Council for Aboriginal Affairs had been established by Prime Minister Harold Holt. The chair of the new CAA was Dr

Nornie, my grandmother,
Joe's mum, c. 1910.

My parents, Joe Egan and Grace Brennan, 1922.

My mother's brother Bob and sister Mary, London, 1917.

Me with sister Sal
(Shirley), Coburg, 1946.

My mother's brother Jack. A stretcher-bearer at Gallipoli, he died from wounds he sustained saving another man's life.

My mother's brother Bob was wounded on the Western Front. After the ship he was being repatriated on was torpedoed, he spent 3 days at sea on a raft.

My mother's brother Martin was captured and held as a POW by the Turks in World War I. He escaped, but was left badly shell-shocked for the rest of his life.

My mother, Grace. She was left behind by three brothers who all went off to World War I. I captured this tragic chapter in her life in 'Song for Grace'.

Welcoming baby Tim
as a family in 1939.
I'm on the left.

Uncle Martin,
with my sisters
Pat (left) and Peg,
Coburg, 1945.

My sisters Pat, Sal (Shirley) and Peg (left to right) on Sal's wedding day, 1951.

My brother Tim (left) and I, in 1956. I was on holidays from Darwin and attended the Melbourne Olympics.

St Mary's Football Club Darwin, Premiers NTFL 1955. I helped to establish the club in 1952 and was captain of their first Premiership team. I am centre, middle row.

Right: Aloysius Puantulura in traditional ceremonial Tiwi headdress. My face was painted thus for his funeral.

Left: Aloysius in 'everyday wear'. He taught me to speak Tiwi, so I could talk to the players in their own language.

Left: My mentor Bill Harney was Protector of Aborigines. In 1959 he became the first ranger at Uluru.

Ted Evans, another mentor to me in the Native Affairs Branch.

Galarrwuy Yunupingu. He and I have shared some groundbreaking experiences. (Northern Territory Archives Service, Dept. Chief Minister, NTRS 3823/P1, BW 478.)

Vincent Lingiari, who led the walk-off at Wave Hill Station, regarded as the beginning of the Aboriginal land rights movement.

Actor David Gulpilil.

Painter Albert Namatjira. Historic Collection/Alamy Stock Photo.

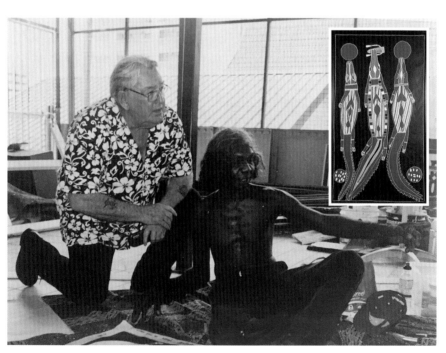

With David Gulpilil. He painted 'Maradila: My Mother's Dreaming' as a gift for saving him from drowning as a child in 1957.

Teaching at Newcastle Waters, in 1965.

My fine family: (left to right) Greg, Margie, Mark and Jacki, at Sinkatinny Downs, 1989.

My sort of audience. At the Stuart Arms.

Presenting *The Ted Egan Outback Show* at Uluru for a coach group.

Robin Jabananga Granites and 'Lofty', in 1978.

With Miss Australia 1975, Kerry Doyle.

'Forget the Sex Pistols—here's Ted': enthusiastic students from MacRobertson Girls High School (Melbourne) at my show, 1976.

With Gus Ntjalka Williams, country singer from Hermannsburg.

Bloody Good Drinker's Passport holder Kenny 'Colie' Coleman.

Thomas Anzac Burrows: 'The Gamekeeper'.

Jimmy Herreen (Shim Reen), a great character around Alice Springs.

Herbie Marks, my musical director on
eight albums.

Bruce Simpson, Brunette
Downs, 1999. A wonderful poet
and a man of sound principles.

Playing bush cricket in 1988. I was a useful leg-spin bowler and fairly
effective as a slogging batsman.

Bloodwood: (clockwise from top left) Barney Foran, Scott Balfour, Dave Evans, Bob Barford.

Members of Wongawilli Band posing as Fosterphone virtuosos at our big party in 1994.

Eddy and Greta Quong, Darwin, 2004. 'What would I know about rice?'

With Ronald Chin, 'The Flying Chinaman', outside Chung Wah Temple, in Darwin, 2007.

Bob Cook presenting me my gold album for *Bangtail Muster*, in 1975.

Riding on the Carlton United Brewery float in the parade at the Tamworth country music festival, 1995.

We never ended up using the movie sets we built for my film *The Drover's Boy* at Ooraminna Station in 1998.

H.C. 'Nugget' Coombs, better known as the illustrious economist who had headed up the federal Treasury, the Commonwealth and Reserve Banks, and the Department of Postwar Reconstruction. I had seen his signature on the new bank notes.

I was told by Harry Giese: 'Coombs is coming to your region for a visit. He's a tricky little bastard. I've known him since university days. I want you to watch his every movement and report to me every meaningful comment he makes.'

Well, what a surprise! I escorted Dr Coombs for four days and found him to be attentive, a great listener, intelligent and very much on the side of the Aboriginals, even though he worked for the same federal government as me! He made several later visits to the region and on each occasion, as events unfolded and preparations for the legal challenge were developed, he confided in me that he was at 'bitter odds' with my employers, the Northern Territory Administration, and with the Department of the Interior, which was in control of the Territory. His CAA was attached to the Prime Minister's Department.

'Would you consider taking a job with me?' he asked.

'My oath,' I replied.

'Keep your eye on the Government Gazette,' was his response.

Sure enough, three weeks later the job of research officer at the Commonwealth Office of Aboriginal Affairs, Prime Minister's Department, was advertised. I applied and in November 1969 I was appointed to Canberra. I was still a federal public servant, but my life was about to change dramatically.

* * *

I had never been to Canberra before. Rae and I bought a house in Hackett, and the kids settled in fairly well. Greg was now at boarding school at Rostrevor College, in Adelaide, and was able to travel by train to Canberra for all school holidays. Margaret, Mark and Jacki went to Canberra schools.

I was rarely home. I saw more of the Northern Territory over the next four years than I'd seen in the previous twenty when I lived there, for Dr Coombs wanted to be briefed adequately concerning all NT Aboriginal issues. In addition, I was expected to familiarise myself with some very involved matters in Queensland and Western Australia.

The 1967 referendum had empowered the federal government—in this case, advised by the Council for Aboriginal Affairs—to 'make laws in respect of various races', with the understanding that this meant legislation in respect of the Aboriginal race. Very contentiously, that so-called right had been vested in the various states in Australia's 1901 constitution; the outcome was a series of laws that purported to be protective, but actually and very deliberately denied any Aboriginal claims of sovereignty. They were sinister, in fact.

Consequently, there were rumblings, especially from the Bjelke-Petersen government in Queensland. They were happy to accept federal money, but they would protect to the last the stranglehold they had on 'their blackfellas'—the Aboriginals and Torres Strait Islanders.

I joined a compact team in the Office of Aboriginal Affairs. There were ten staff, including four talented First Australians: Major Reg Saunders, Margaret Lawrie, Phillip Roberts and

Charlie Perkins. My old patrol officer mate from Darwin, Jeremy Long, had joined the OAA six months previously. (Harry Giese was very angry with both of us.)

I was closely involved with the impending Yirrkala court case—*Milirrpum* v. *Nabalco Pty Ltd and the Commonwealth of Australia*—that was about to be heard in the Supreme Court of first the Northern Territory and then the Australian Capital Territory. I also spent considerable time at Daguragu (Wattie Creek), where the Gurindji Aboriginals—aided by trade unions and the Students Union organisation, Abschol—were holding out against Wave Hill Station, in the longest strike in Australian working history. The Gurindji were the first to bring the term *land rights* into the Australian vernacular. They were led by a dignified old stockman, Vincent Lingiari.

In both those cases there was the incongruous situation where two federal agencies were toe-to-toe opponents. The Department of the Interior, under its formidable minister, Peter Nixon, fiercely took the stance that the government owned the land. At the same time, the Office of Aboriginal Affairs, led by 'Nugget' Coombs and our magnificent director, Barrie Dexter, was paying the legal fees and supporting the arguments of both the Gurindji and Yirrkala First Australians that their traditional ownership should be recognised.

Well, the Yirrkala Yolngu lost their court case in 1969. The Gurindji sort of won their battle eventually, when given the 'title deeds' to their land in 1975, but all First Australians were given some hope in 1973. The new Whitlam government, acting on the recommendations of Dr Coombs, set up the Aboriginal Land

Rights Royal Commission, led by Justice Edward Woodward. As a consequence, the Fraser Liberal government passed the *Aboriginal Land Rights (Northern Territory) Act 1976*, which started the long, tedious examinations to establish connections to land that would enable Aboriginals to be declared the traditional owners of their land. Many years later, the *Mabo* and *Wik* judgments recognised traditional land ownership on a national level.

It all sounds good, but the real issues—sovereignty and identity—have always been too formidable for federal governments to tackle. The so-called 'traditional owners' have fancy pieces of paper, but no power over their land. Maybe one day there will be a prime minister game enough to look at the big picture.

15

I HEREBY RESIGN

I'm driving from Wave Hill to Katherine, outback Northern Territory. It's 1974. I've stopped the car for five minutes on impulse, grabbed a biro and a sheet of paper. On the bonnet of the car, I've written a three-line letter of resignation. I'm a level one public servant with over twenty years' experience. Department of Aboriginal Affairs. I'm the Director of Special Projects. 'I hereby resign . . .'

Life is complicated. I'm 42 years of age. I've walked away from a marriage that most people considered the ultimate. I have four kids, two still at school. I need a regular source of income. There are responsibilities that I am determined to honour, but I'm about to give up a hefty salary plus the superannuation package, in place since 1950.

I knew that the 1973 acknowledgement by government of traditional Aboriginal rights to land ownership was a major milestone in Australia; I had played a vital, if minor, role. I decided at Daguragu—the base camp for the Gurindji strikers—that it was time for a white bloke like me to get out of the way and let Aboriginals sort out their own lives, on their terms. All this was running through my mind as I drove the long haul from Wave Hill to the Katherine post office, where I posted my letter of resignation.

A major component of my midlife crisis was my extramarital affair with Sheila Shelvey. Although it was never obvious to any other person, I was desperately unhappy and unfulfilled in my marriage to Rae: I don't seek to apportion blame. I became attracted to Sheila, who was a stenographer at the Office of Aboriginal Affairs, when I was a research officer there. A lively, London-born blonde, Sheila was recently divorced and lived with her daughter, Claire, in a house she owned in Canberra. She was a sparkling personality around the office. There was intense chemistry between us.

Rae was still in our house in Canberra, with Mark, aged fifteen, and Jacki, ten. Greg, now twenty, had finished school in Adelaide, spent a year at Nhulunbuy saving up to finance his university studies and was now training to be a teacher in South Australia. Margaret, aged seventeen, was also in Adelaide, working as a waitress.

I still had my roving commission with the Department of Aboriginal Affairs, travelling within the Northern Territory most of the time. I'd just spent a week at Daguragu with Vincent Lingiari, the admirable old Gurindji stockman who took on the combined wrath of the Commonwealth government and the Vestey empire, based in London. To everybody's amazement, Vincent was about to win this David and Goliath battle: the new Whitlam government had announced that it would take up Lord Vestey's offer to surrender half of the Wave Hill lease to the Aboriginal claimants. I had just broken the news to Vincent; there was rejoicing all round.

I thought back to 1966, when the Gurindji went on strike. I was at Groote Eylandt then, principal at the Angurugu school, when the news came through on the wireless. People in Darwin laughed their heads off: 'Blackfellas on strike! What a joke! They'll be starved back into submission in a week.'

But Vincent mounted the longest strike in Australian history. Organised by Brian Manning, Dexter Daniels and Robert Tudawali in Darwin, subsistence rations were delivered to Wave Hill; funds were provided to enable Vincent, Captain Major and Donald Nangiari to go to southern cities, where their dignity and the sheer fairness of their claim enabled them to get hefty financial support from the big trade unions and university students.

The Gurindji claims had blossomed from a single demand—that they be 'treated as human beings, not like dogs'—into a broader quest for better wages and working conditions, and then into a demand to be recognised as the owners of the land in question, which was officially recognised as the property of Lord Vestey of London!

In September 1969, I wrote my song 'Gurindji Blues'. I had heard that day a minister of the Crown say, in parliament in

Canberra, 'If these Gurindji people want some land, why don't they do what any decent Australian would do? Why don't they save their money and buy some land?'

I thought: *Hang on, Minister! You weren't at the Wave Hill Races in 1953!* I had been, and I'd seen all the Gurindji stockmen being lined up by their employers. They, their parents and grandparents had for 80 years worked on the white men's cattle stations. In 1953, each of them was given a £5 note. It was the first time any Gurindji person had touched money. So even if they *should* have saved their money and purchased some land, I didn't see how they *could* have done that. I wrote the song at 3 a.m. on 9 September 1969.

> Poor bugger blackfella Gurindji
> S'pose we buyim back country
> What you reckon proper fee?
> Might be plour, chugar and tea
> From the Gurindji to Lord Vestey
> Oh poor bugger me.

'Gurindji Blues' (1969)

I began to sing the song to friends and acquaintances in Canberra and the Territory: there was immense support for the Gurindji in the south, as well as much animosity towards Lord Vestey in the north, so many people thought I should record the song. How did one go about that? My mind went back again, ten years this time.

In 1959, I was 27 years old and in my physical prime—fit as a Mallee bull, three times as dangerous and twice as ugly. I was superintendent of the Yuendumu Aboriginal Reserve, in Central Australia. In June 1959, with a few mates from Alice Springs, I had attended the famous ABC (Alexandria, Brunette, Creswell) Races at Brunette Downs Station.

What a time we had at Brunette! The big greeting in 1959 was: 'Good luck in the buckjump.' The two days of horseracing were to be followed by the rodeo and campdraft, so we had all nominated one another for the open buckjump. Let 'im go in the big yard!

There was no sleep for the entire weekend. We drank rum, rode buckjumpers, bet on the races, frolicked the night away with the dashing ladies each night at the dance, then sat around our campfires, drank more rum and sang our songs until dawn. As the ABC Races had always been held on the full moon in June, it meant that, each dawn, we witnessed, on the vast treeless plain, the enormous sun coming up in the east as the full moon disappeared simultaneously on the western horizon. It was breathtaking. Then it was time to have a few 'phlegm-cutters'—rum and black coffee—as we watched the horses do their track trials for the day's races.

One night, around the campfire, we had a visit from Sam Hordern—a member of the famous Anthony Hordern family, who had a big financial interest in Brunette Downs. Nice bloke, Sam. He had a tape recorder—none of us had ever seen such a device. Sam taped me singing some of my own songs that night. Three months later, I received a letter at Yuendumu. It was written on fancy letterhead, from a chap named Ron Wills of the record company RCA Victor, saying that he had heard a tape of my songs. Would I like to call on him the next time I was in Sydney, with a view to recording?

I promptly chucked the letter into the wastepaper basket. I was 200 miles north-west of Alice Springs and much too busy for anything like that. In any case, surely he was joking?

But ten years later, in 1969, we needed a studio if we were going to record 'Gurindji Blues', so I rang RCA at Ryde in Sydney. Tentatively, I asked the receptionist if I could speak to 'the recording man'. She responded: 'I'll put you through to Mr Wills.' That was him—what a stroke of luck!

Ron Wills had a good laugh. 'Well, you certainly took your time getting back to me!' Fortunately, he was still interested in my songs, perhaps even more so than when he wrote his letter ten years earlier. He explained: 'I was once at EMI, a member of the team that encouraged Slim Dusty early in his career. Then I moved to RCA and produced a group called The Snowy Mountain Settlers. They were massive sellers—still are. So I'm always on the lookout for genuine Australian talent.'

I had heard of The Settlers. They were very good, very Australian, although their leader was an Irishman named Ulick O'Boyle. Their excellent songs were based on the multinational nature of the workforce at the Snowy Mountains Hydro-Electric Scheme. I subsequently met Ulick. We shared a 'drop of the crayther', as he called it.

Ron politely heard my request to record my new song. He liked the 'Australian-ness' of 'Gurindji Blues'. Ron was a very shrewd man and a good listener. He said: 'Hmmm, I think you might be onto something here . . . Tell you what, Ted, let's do the

Gurindji song, but I want you to sit with a bloke named Herbie Marks and run some of those songs I heard on Sam Hordern's tape past him.'

The two major land-rights groups were the Gurindji of Wave Hill, led by Vincent Lingiari and the Yolngu of Arnhem Land. My song brought them together, and they remain united to this day in their ongoing quest for justice.

When we recorded 'Gurindji Blues' in October 1969, I asked Vincent to provide a spoken introduction. This is what he chose to say: 'My name Vincent Lingiari, come from Daguragu, Wattie Creek Station. *Yalangulu yanana Wattie Creek ngulung murayani. Mula ngura ngurayani jaragabgu, jangagani gadiyawu. Mula ngura yangana milanga jaragabgu.*' He continued in English: 'That mean that I come down here to tell all this parliament for the land, the land right. I got word from my father and my old grandpa, that land belonging to me, belongin' to Aboriginal man, before the white man, the horse and cattle comin' onto this land. That's what I got on my mind. I still got it on my mind.'

The recording session was easy and enjoyable. Vincent recorded his statement. Galarrwuy Yunupingu then laid down a musical 'bed' with his didjeridu, accompanied by the legendary George Golla on the guitar. (I am confident that this was the first time in Australia that the didjeridu—*yirdaki* in Galarrwuy's Gumatj language—was played in a Western recording session.) Then Galarrwuy and I sang the song.

Galarrwuy is the son of Munggurrawuy Yunupingu, one of the plaintiffs in the *other* issue that I mentioned earlier, where the Aboriginals from Arnhem Land participated in *Milirrpum* v. *Nabalco Pty Ltd and the Commonwealth of Australia*. Galarrwuy was very well educated in the Western sense; additionally, he was a member of one of the great traditional Gumatj families. He was the interpreter in the court case, first in Darwin and later in Canberra. He had also spent the previous month in Sydney, getting rave reviews as the star of a play I had written, *No Need for Two Blankets*. Produced by Amy McGrath, the play was presented at the Australian Theatre, Newtown; again, Aboriginal land rights was the theme.

The 'Gurindji Blues' recording session was enhanced by the fact that, on that very day, Fred Hollows also operated to remove the cataracts on Vincent's eyes. The old chap was joyful, saying, 'I'm right for hunting kangaroo again!' The next day we took Vincent on a tour of Sydney. He pronounced that it was 'a bigger place altogether—more big than Wattie Creek'. He was also amazed that traffic did not go 'over the top' of Sydney Harbour Bridge.

On this same day, at Black Inc Studios, we recorded and mixed an album of fourteen of my songs, titled *Outback Australia*. I was under the direction of Herbie Marks, a musical genius who had called in George Golla and the eminent cellist Lal Kuring to help him sort out this 'crazy bush bloke'.

They sat me down and were extremely—and genuinely— impressed by my percussive device, the Fosterphone—an empty cardboard beer box (24 cans size), which I tapped and stroked, bongo-drum fashion. I was gratified that three top musicians accepted, with approval, my innovative way of establishing a beat for my songs, given that I could not read or write what I called 'dots on lines'.

I did not tell them that I had developed my Fosterphone skills as a means of deterring the many bad guitarists who thought I would need 'accompaniment'. The world is full of inferior guitar players, people who often can't see that their limited instrumental skill is a handicap when they are trying to write songs: they are restricted to the inadequate number of chords they know. That's their problem.

It was fascinating being in the presence of Herbie, George and Lal. They started out by asking, 'What key do you sing in?' I knew what they were talking about. I looked at the Foster's box. 'If I play this carton, I sing in the key of F. If we are drinking Victoria Bitter, I sing in the key of VB. In Queensland, I occasionally lapse into XXXX.' Undeterred, they said, 'You sing; we'll follow you.'

'Gurindji Blues' was well received, and Chicka Dixon sold thousands of copies to help finance the Aboriginal Tent Embassy in Canberra. In the meantime, twelve months later *Outback Australia* was a gold album. Not bad for my first and only day in a recording studio. I don't think even Slim Dusty had a gold album at that stage.

All of this was on my mind in 1974 as I drove to Katherine. I knew that there were customers in outback Australia who liked my songs. I had gold albums (plural by this time) to prove it. Could there be a livelihood in all this?

16

GOLD ALBUMS: GOLDEN DAYS

In Australia in 1969, gold-album status was achieved after net sales of over 30,000 copies. RCA was impressed that *Outback Australia* sold so strongly; only a few of their staff knew that it 'went gold' largely because of my initiative.

It is essential to know that the things that set me on the road to recognition were, first, the title *Outback Australia* and, second, the song 'The Drinkers of the Territory'. I vividly recall the debate at RCA when I proposed the title *Outback Australia*. 'What do you mean by *outback* Australia?' I was asked.

My reply: 'The real bushies will know that I am singing about people and attitudes *beyond* the Black Stump. People in the south are used to songs about Gundagai and Snake Gully, but this is OUTBACK AUSTRALIA. More further, as the blackfellas say.'

'The Drinkers' was well established, since the 1950s. It was my party piece. This was the song recorded by Sam Hordern in 1959 that had attracted Ron Wills at RCA. Many bush people knew the chorus, they knew that VRD stood for Victoria River Downs, the biggest cattle station in Australia, and they knew that the word *Territory* was pronounced *terra-tree*, not *terra-tory*. To this day, only Yanks and imbeciles say *terra-tory*.

> We've got some bloody good drinkers
> In the Northern Territory
> From Darwin down to Alice Springs
> We're always on a spree
> Out on the Barkly Tableland
> Across to VRD
> We've got some bloody good drinkers
> In the Northern Territory.
>
> 'The Drinkers of the Territory' (1969)

Seasoned fans also knew that the chorus was sung with appropriate 'Here's cheers' hand movements, around the shape of the stars of the Southern Cross—north, south, east, west—as appropriate. They would join in the chorus after each verse I wrote on the given day, as events unfolded:

> At the Beer Can Regatta in Darwin
> The Murphy girls, Carmel and Jo,
> Were drinking their stubbies, watching the boats,
> And suddenly, wouldn't you know?
> A streaker ran right through the crowd

As they were sitting on the beach.

Poor old Carmel, she had a stroke,

But Josephine couldn't reach!

Anyway, back to how I managed to sell so many copies. I simply grabbed a pastoral map of Australia and posted letters to 'The Manager' at Such-and-Such Downs, asking if they'd like to buy an LP with songs such as 'The Drinkers of the Territory', 'Down on the Daly River O', 'Wee-ai, Quee-ai, Kapramunda' and 'The Reluctant Saddler'. Would they ever! Bushies are very familiar with mail order. Send in a cheque for $6.50 and the goods are in the mail. I paid the postage. The orders rolled in— gold album! I purchased stock at the artist's rate from RCA and made a good profit on the mail-order sales.

I never signed a recording contract with RCA, but Ron Wills and I agreed, with a handshake, that we would do an album a year forever. So for the next eight years I rang Ron to say, 'Ready.' I'd spend a couple of days in Sydney with Herbie Marks and then a day—always just a day—at the studio. Eight albums with RCA—all gold. 'Mail Order Ted', they called me.

George Golla was a regular at our recording sessions. I am sure George didn't need to look for work as a 'studio muso'. He was world-famous as a guitar virtuoso, but he really enjoyed the incongruity of my songs. On the first day of our acquaintance, he and Herbie were talking together in the studio, unaware that I was behind a screen collecting some notes I had left there. I overheard this conversation:

Herbie: 'What do you think of this bloke, George?'

George: 'Well, I've never seen anything quite like him. You need a bloody black tracker to follow him, but I'm loving it.'

George said to me one day, 'Ted, don't ever let anybody try to explain the fundamentals of music to you. You don't know the rules and you break most of them, but it works.'

All of these things were on my mind in 1974, as I wrestled with the question of how to make a living. Yes, I knew my songs were popular, but how to turn it into dollars on a predictable level? Royalties were a dismal percentage of the sales, and were only paid quarterly. I had kids to educate, bills to pay.

Late in 1974 a promising commercial opportunity presented itself. I had announced that I was going to drive around Australia with my son Mark, who was having 'issues' at school. We were going to meet 'characters' around whom I knew I could base future songs, as I covered the ground of some of my old songs and exploits. We would travel in Matilda, my faithful old Peugeot 403, towing behind us a trailer with Mark's motorbike on it.

A chap named David Roberts approached me. 'If I can get some sponsorship, may I film your trip?'

'Go for your life,' I responded. Sponsorship would entail a fee for Mark and me.

David obtained generous support from Reg 'Mophead' Harris, an old mate of mine, the enlightened director of NT tourism in those heady days, when thousands of people accepted the challenge to experience the real outback, the Northern Territory.

Another generous backer of David's film was Richard Lim, of the well-known Darwin Chinese family. 'Ricco' was one of George and Lorna Lim's sons, who manned the bar at the

Victoria Hotel in Darwin, where I had cut my drinking teeth twenty years earlier. The boys—Arthur, Richard, Alex and Gerald—were all great mates of mine and loved it when I sang my songs in the bar. Their dad, George, was not too keen—'Tell that bastard to shut up,' I heard him say one night in the early 1950s. By 1975, Ricco was paying me $1000 a night to sing the same songs at his Rapid Creek Pub!

Mark and I travelled around the outback with David Roberts, who fortunately had engaged a camera wizard, Geoff Burton, to film the action. Geoff was amazing, whipping in and around horses, camels and assorted drunks attending the outback carnivals, festivals and pubs. He would feign filming drunks, urging them to have their 'moment on camera'; they would be unaware that he had no film in the camera as he encouraged them: 'And . . . action!' But Geoff was always on the spot when the vital moments occurred. He later enjoyed an illustrious career as the director of photography on films such as *Sunday Too Far Away* and *Storm Boy*, and on TV series such as *Bangkok Hilton*.

David produced a magnificent film, which we decided to call *A Drop of Rough Ted*. It was a 45-minute 'commercial hour' documentary that took in the Beer Can Regatta, the Camel Cup, the Alice Springs Rodeo, plus some magnificent traditional Aboriginal dance sequences featuring David Gulpilil, Tjoli Laiwanga and my mentor Aloysius Puantulura, who led the Tiwi dancers in the *Bombing of Darwin* dance. We visited Kakadu, Uluru and cattle stations, we hunted dugong with Musso Harvey at Borroloola, we talked to old prospectors and soared the cultural heights with the barmaids and Bill 'Spoonbill' Easton—renowned buffalo hunter and the last man to go about Tennant Creek with six guns holstered, the man who was so well endowed he didn't dare wear shorts—at Sexy Rexy's Piss Parlour at Tennant Creek.

It was terrific, during the filming, to meet up with old Aboriginal mates and see them dance again. In 1954, I'd been the coordinator for the NT Aboriginal dancers chosen to meet the Queen at Toowoomba. Aloysius and Tjoli were the star performers on that occasion. Later—in about 1969, I think—a mercurial young dancer named David Gulpilil, a protégé of Tjoli, made his debut at the Darwin Eisteddfod. What a performance. He had us spellbound. It was a further joy that, after his performance, David reminded me that he was the 'drowning little kid' I had pulled out of the Liverpool River in 1957. I gave him a bit of the old Schaefer's resuscitation on that occasion, and he was soon okay.

In adulthood, I have watched Gulpilil's tremendous career develop. There is always such an aura about him. His performances in *Walkabout*, *Storm Boy*, *The Tracker*, *Rabbit-Proof Fence* and *Charlie's Country* brought him great acclaim. In recent years he has done a few traditional paintings as well; his beautiful *Maradila: My Mother's Dreaming* adorns our living room wall. When he presented that painting to me, he said: 'Thank you for saving my life.'

Reg Harris was thrilled with David Roberts' film. He demanded that it be screened regularly at Alice Springs, for we had covered the ground that was the basis of his tourism promotions. That was the spark I needed. I suggested to Bede McKenna—'The Venerable Bede', manager of the famous Stuart

Arms Pub—that I do shows at the pub, singing my songs, telling yarns and screening the film. Great idea!

With the assistance of David Roberts, I had a book published, also, titled *A Drop of Rough Ted*. We sought to follow in the footsteps of Bill Peach and Harry Butler, who had done film work for the ABC and then reaped a fortune from the companion book. David offered our film to ABC TV, but was staggered when they knocked it back, on the grounds that there were 'too many blackfellas'. The unsurprising paradox was that all viewers of the film were unanimous that it was 'good to see somebody presenting Aboriginals as fine human beings'. The ABC's rejection of the film meant that sales of the book were very limited. I still have hundreds of copies in my shed, 40 years later.

It was the start of almost 30 years of *The Ted Egan Outback Show* in Alice Springs. Thirty years? I keep saying 30, but it was 1975–2003 inclusive. For most of that period, according to Reg Harris, I was 'the only night entertainment in Alice Springs'. I must have entertained around a million tourists in that time, and the delightful factor was that every night was opening night for me. I just loved it—an audience paying to see me perform! I had discovered my market—outback tourists—for my songs were based on the environment they had chosen to tour. My promoters/sales managers were the coach drivers, for in those days hundreds of coaches were on the outback roads, bringing eager visitors to Alice and The Rock. It has changed drastically these days, I'm sad to say.

I used to hand out free cassettes of my albums to the coach drivers. They in turn would play different songs as they travelled to various destinations, to the point where, when they arrived in Alice, the passengers were familiar with my songs and, indeed, purchased the tapes themselves. The cassette tape became a unit of currency for me. How much is so and so? 'Oh, eight cassettes'—$50.

At my show I paid the coach captains 10 per cent of gross ticket sales to their passengers. That was hefty commission money for them, but 10 per cent was the order of the day, and more often than not the hostie would hand me the total sales money on arrival, less commission, of course. Often I would get four or five coaches at a show. I baby-sat their passengers while the hosties and coach captains had a relaxing drink in the adjacent Bull Bar, so they, too, loved my show. I paid the Stuart Arms $2 per patron, and Bede McKenna enjoyed the immense bar sales that my show generated. I received the balance of the admission price and I took the entire merchandise money. Life was good.

I performed in the back bar at the Stuart Arms. I'd start the show at 8 p.m., sing for fifteen minutes, show the 45-minute film, have an interval and then sing and tell yarns for about 90 minutes. At 10.30 p.m. I'd sell merchandise, and then we (me plus anybody) would adjourn to La Casalinga for pizza, drinks and merriment. It became known as 'Ted's shout' and I later did an album with that title. Then to bed, to be up at 6.30 a.m. for my morning run. I was the fittest bloke in Alice Springs.

I was assisted by a faithful helper named Allan Howard, who ran the film projector, looked after my sound gear and drove my car whenever I was involved in 'serious drinking', which was most of the time. Allan was a fine photographer. I paid him well, but he made great pocket money through sales of the portrait shots he did of patrons as they arrived at the show. While the film was running, he developed the photos in his darkroom. At the end of the evening, he'd have individual copies of the portraits mounted in a 'Ted Egan's Bloody Good Drinkers Passport', which accorded status, privileges and diplomatic immunity for life to the recipients. Just $2. 'Thank you, sir, thank you, madam—yes, Ted will sign your passport.'

Writing two particular songs was one of the cleverest things I did: 'Our Coach Captain' and 'The Hosties and the Cooks'. Usually the coaches were full (about 50 people per coach) of happy, laughing passengers, totally under the control of 'the skipper', who invariably set up a very professional rivalry with 'the hostie' to determine who was really in charge.

> Our Coach Captain, he's a very nice bloke to know
> Our Coach Captain, he runs the outback travelling show
> But he's certainly not a driver, he's a Captain, for sure
> We're very bloody lucky that he's taking us on his tour
> The funny thing about it is, we'll all be back for more
> Of the same travelling game with Our Coach Captain.

'Our Coach Captain' (1982)

Corny stuff, but the coach drivers established absolute control and got away with it. Most coach captains asserted that I had written the song about them; I never disagreed. They had various techniques: some were effusive, others would not talk to the passengers for the first few days, to keep them guessing. But by the time the coaches arrived at Alice, passengers were invariably having the best times of their lives. In the days before bitumen roads, the most memorable trips were the ones with the greatest issues to overcome. Bring on the bogs, breakdowns, rain—the passengers loved it.

I could predict the drinking habits of the passengers from the bookings each night for my show. I'd say to the barmaids, 'Chester's group tonight; they'll all be on the Bundy rum,' or 'Val Mack and Margie are booked: plenty of white wine for the ladies, and piercingly cold Foster's beer for the chaps,' or 'Ray and Bev . . . their people will ask you twenty questions each and drink light beer.'

I lived at the Stuart Arms, and during the day I was able to keep in touch with local people and issues. I had known all the Central Australian cattle families and station workers for many years, and drank regularly with them when they came to town.

I was apprehensive about Aboriginals and alcohol, so I generally avoided Aboriginal drinkers. In Alice, there was never any satisfactory middle ground. They either wanted to buy me a drink or borrow $20. I gave up going to the local football matches: I would meet an Aboriginal mate and buy him a beer, only to see it taken from him by some 'relative' who felt they had the right to do so. I continued to meet my many Aboriginal friends and associates through visits to places such as Yuendumu, Willowra and Hermannsburg, where there was no booze. Country music was always the thing that brought together my old First Australian mates. I loved and still love to spend time with them.

Not that I thought I belonged to any musical genre. Privately, I thought rock and roll was repetitive electronic garbage, where the exponents thought that the louder the sound, the greater the quality and impact. Just keep screaming: 'I lerve you, baby!' I was aware of both country- and folk-music scenes in Alice, but felt that most country singers wanted to sound like Yanks and most folkies wanted to sound like Poms. My attitude didn't change for quite a while.

For the big festivals in Alice and during the Victorian school holidays, we would have up to 50 coaches in town at a time, and I used to get most of the passengers along to my shows. In those days a trip to the Centre meant a week at Alice, plus two or three days at Uluru and Kata Tjuta.

Three or four times a year we had campfire concerts at Simpsons Gap. We would have up to 5000 people in the dry riverbed. Huge campfires were lit and we put subtle lighting on the rock face—not too much as we didn't want to upset the rock wallabies. We had a great local folk group named Bloodwood, and they, Gus Williams and I shared the entertainment. Gus was a delightful Western Arranta man and a good presenter of Aussie-style country music. He didn't try to sound like a Yank. One night Gus had the huge audience enthralled. This was his speech:

'Ladies and gentlemen, welcome to my country. Here you are, sitting in this lovely dry riverbed. This is the spot where my old tribal grandfather encountered the first white man he had ever seen. My grandfather was standing on the rocks . . . up there [he points] . . . dreadlocked hair, clutching his woomera, spears and a boomerang. Coming towards him was this strange creature. It was the explorer John McDouall Stuart, riding a horse, but my grandfather thought that he was seeing a single being. Grandfather came down, walked forward and John McDouall Stuart got off the horse. They walked towards one another . . .'

The huge crowd was spellbound, and Gus continued:

'And John McDouall Stuart said to my grandfather . . .' Here Gus took up his guitar and sang Kris Kristoffersen's well-known song 'Take the Ribbons from Your Hair' to tumultuous applause.

At the end of those concerts, we used to say to the audience, 'Please leave nothing here but your footprints.' The next day, invariably, there was not a single cigarette butt to pick up. Just shows you, doesn't it? Oh, I loved those nights.

The tourist season ran from April to the end of October. I'd then head south—to attend as many cricket matches as I could, to see family, and usually to record an album of songs. Eventually, by 2003, I had recorded 30 albums, indicating that I had written over 300 songs—mainly about the 'real people', as I called them.

In 1976 Sheila had moved to Sydney, and over each summer I shared her rental payments for a unit, first at North Sydney and then at Bondi. I would spend much of the summer with her and her daughter, Claire. In 1977 I had a very good year, and Sheila, Claire and I went to the United Kingdom to meet her rellies.

Ours was always a volatile relationship, as we alternated between tons of fun and storming rows for the silliest of reasons. She was a Cockney, used to saying her piece if anyone or anything upset her. I found that I could return the vitriol, and that did not impress me, for I always prefer the easy life. But Sheila was an independent type who did not seek to lay claim over me, so the relationship drifted on, fairly aimlessly.

When I was in Sydney, I always rang the theatrical agent June Evans; she would get me a few gigs at clubs, or occasionally an appearance on TV. I always got on well with Mike Walsh and, later, Ray Martin when they ran *The Midday Show*. Early in his career I met John Williamson, who did a TV show called *Travellin' Out West* in Newcastle; I did a few performances with him. He had not yet started his Australiana career and he used to do covers of songs such as 'Streets of London'. A few years later, John Singleton urged JW to write more Australian songs like 'Old Man Emu' and 'True Blue'. Eventually he did an album called *Mallee Boy*; he ascended great heights musically, under the management of Phil and Chris Matthews.

As well as recording eight albums with Herbie Marks as musical director, I used to watch Herb when he did gigs at the big Sydney leagues clubs, opulent palaces that were financed by poker machines. Herbie was a top drawcard, and taught me much about stage technique and the marketing of merchandise. He was ever so proud of his Jewishness—'One of God's chosen,' he would laughingly say of himself. He was huge, weighing well over 25 stone (159 kilograms), but he had been a virtuoso from age six, when he played first the mandolin and then the piano.

The piano accordion was always Herb's favourite instrument; he had a number of these, from huge to miniscule, which he interchanged during his performances. One day he went through the entire list of instruments that he could play; we totalled over 50. He was a colossal pianist; one of the best recordings I ever did with him was my song 'That's a Camel'.

> A camel is a horse
> Designed by a committee
> With features rather coarse
> You'd never call him pretty . . .

'That's a Camel' (1970)

Herbie played the most amazing piano accompaniment and then overdubbed another piano part—like duelling pianos. I play the track every now and again and always shed a tear as I recall my dear old mate in action.

Unlike me, Herbie was a consummate reader and writer of sheet music. There's a big repository of his music in the famous Mitchell Library. One of the boxes is labelled 'Ted Egan stuff'.

The big Sydney clubs had bands of five to ten top-line resident musicians; artists were always given just a short time to distribute their charts to the musos and talk through their routines. Speed was crucial. The club musos all loved Herbie because he was so brilliant in these 'talk throughs'.

I'll never forget one day when I was listening to him briefing the various musicians. It went something like this: 'Now, you come in with the sax at bar fifteen, we do five bars together. I'll bring in the trumpets and trombones, then the audience will start to clap in time. I'll let them clap for four bars and then I'll go into my solo . . .'

You'll let *them clap for four bars?* I thought to myself. But sure enough, in the actual performance, in came the sax, the trumpets and trombones. Right on cue, the huge audience picked up the beat and began to clap—in time, would you believe! Herbie counted the four bars, waved his arm dramatically. They stopped instantaneously and he went into a searing solo of '*Hava Nagila*'. What a joy! We had a quiet laugh about it later, as he shared a few beers with the band.

'Must have been that lovely *gefilte* fish I had for lunch,' said the maestro.

Herbie wrote the charts for my songs—he was like a stenographer taking shorthand, he was so fast. Harmonies came automatically to him, but he broke down and shook with laughter every now and again as I sang and he transcribed.

'My God, Ted, you can't put a 5/4 bar in there, but you just did and it works! Bloody marvellous,' he'd say. And he would roar at some of my outrageous rhyming, such as 'With the incredible speed of insatiable greed . . .' Another one was:

When we get to Camooweal,
We won't give a damn and we'll
Go riding along into Queensland.

'Matt Savage: Boss Drover' (2000)

And:

We'll take a walk to China Town
At the Roebuck Pub we'll knock one down
Broome's a place of great renown

The people are black, white, yellow and brown

It's Technicolor in Broome.

'Taking You Back to Broome' (1988)

Herbie Marks died on stage, eight bars from the end of his club act. I'm told there was absolute chaos as 25-stone Herbie went crashing into the drum kit; it was what Herb would have called 'a meaningful finish'. *Vale*, my dear friend.

17

CHARACTERS OF THE OUTBACK

In 1975, when I started doing *The Ted Egan Outback Show* at the Stuart Arms, I wasn't sure which nights would be the most suitable to perform, so I put out the word that I was available seven nights a week. Then, with ten patrons as the minimum, I did the show just about every night for two years. After that, I had established—for numerical reasons, obviously influenced by the coach tours—that Tuesday, Thursday and Sunday were the best three nights. So that was my pattern for the next 27 years—Tuesday, Thursday and Sunday. Mind you, there was often a request for a show on another night, perhaps another day, even a weekend out of town somewhere. It was always easy to do the show at the drop of a hat, or the lure of a quid.

It also meant that I had plenty of time to myself. I began teaching Aboriginal Studies at Alice Springs High School, mainly to kids of mixed Aboriginal descent. It was great fun. My best pupil was Gilbert McAdam, later a champion footballer and a credit to his fine family. I taught the kids local history, the kinship system and basic Arrernte language. They thought I was a genius; in fact, I was just one lesson ahead of them!

I am a good parrot with languages, and I've heard people say that I am 'very fluent' in Aboriginal languages (plural). The reality is that I can do small talk impressively, but I cannot claim fluency, or anything approaching it, in any First Australian language. I am the same with Latin, French and German. I can, especially, sing songs accurately, to the point where people assume I am the full bottle. I wish I was better, and I would love to be forced to learn another language properly, but it probably won't happen. I always urge parents, when they have another language in their family, to pass it on to their children, for I firmly believe that we can all handle five or six different languages. When we do, we are more likely to have greater levels of tolerance and understanding, as well as enjoy the cultural richness achieved.

The last Irishman of my ancestors who came to Australia was Peter Brennan, my maternal grandfather. He arrived here in the 1860s with four brothers and a sister. They came from Galway, and when they were together they spoke exclusively in Irish. I regret that I cannot speak a word of Irish. It is on my bucket list to go to Ireland and sing 'Amhrán na bhFiann' ('The Soldiers' Song'), which is the Irish national anthem—in Galway. In Irish! Give him room!

People are my fascination, as I keep saying. I love observing folk with something unique to them. To me, they register as 'characters'. Back in 1968, I wrote a song with that as its theme:

I asked an old Aboriginal bloke
Why they called him Galloping Jack?
He told me a buffalo chased him
One day on the Jim Jim Track.
The lowest limb, on the only tree,
Was fourteen feet from the ground.
Jack jumped for the branch—and missed!
But he caught it on the way down.

'The Characters of the Outback' (1968)

I'm always on the lookout for characters who have talent of whatever kind. I inherited from my beloved Pop a talent for wordsmithing and a propensity to bestow sobriquets—The Reluctant Saddler, The Yellow Peril, Disaster Dick, The Whispering Baritone, The Horizontal Oriental, The Davenport Lounger, Rigor (Mortis), The Man from Humpty Doo and The Gamekeeper are a few I have launched over the years.

The Gamekeeper, aka Tommy Burrows, is a case in point. People keep saying to me: 'They don't make characters like "The Gamekeeper" anymore'—and they're right.

Tom Burrows was born on Anzac Day, 25 April 1939, at Atherton, North Queensland. His father, Mervyn, came from the Rhondda Valley in Old South Wales; his mum was an Australian girl. Appropriately, they had their new son baptised Thomas Anzac. The family were battlers with problems; Tom, his brothers and sisters often found themselves in foster homes for varying periods. At fourteen years of age, Tom left school and worked in various rural occupations. He must have become a good horserider, for at sixteen he was working as a stockman on cattle stations in the Camooweal region of western Queensland.

At nineteen years of age, Tom had a terrible accident. He was working on Morestone Station; a horse lost its footing at full gallop and fell, rolling onto him in the process. He was knocked unconscious and remained in that state for three months. When he regained consciousness, he discovered that he had been taken to the Mount Isa hospital.

When the staff saw that Tom was conscious and able to hear them, one of the doctors said, 'Well, you're going to live, young feller, but you probably won't be able to talk, or walk, ever again.' The story goes that Tom shook his entire body; in a frenzy, he threw himself off the bed, onto the hospital floor. The doctor reconsidered: 'Son, if you can do that, maybe you'll be okay.'

Well, Thomas Anzac was never quite okay, but he could walk eventually, with a list to port. He also got his speech back—a bit slurred, but functional enough. He was an extremely handsome young man, but one eye was a bit lazy for the rest of his life. Fortunately, he had spirit.

Slowly he recovered, and he returned to Camooweal, where he came under the care of the legendary drover Bruce Forbes Simpson. For the rest of his life Tom expressed gratitude to Simmo, who 'gave me a chance in life, after my buster'. That was typical Tom, he established his own vernacular; on a daily basis he would deliver precise, idiosyncratic Australianisms. His favourite farewell was: 'I'm off, like a fart from a goose.'

* * *

Some people assumed that Tom was always drunk. Many years later, I was with him at the Alice Springs Casino. I ordered two beers. The barman said to me: 'You're okay, sir, but your mate has obviously had too much to drink.' Tom walked over, gave him a filthy look and said to me, 'Do you want me to jar this prick?'

Bruce Simpson was not only a famous drover, but an eminent bush poet as well. He gave Tom a job as cook and horsetailer with his droving plant the next season. Tom never forgot that; for the rest of his life, he said: 'Nobody can take it from me: I was a drover.' Simple as that.

Given his physical issues and balanced against his determination never to be 'a bludger', Tom became adept at manipulating anyone who came into his jurisdiction. He was a charmer with the ladies, he was kind to old folks and he became a superb raconteur—although he constantly reminded people: 'If you think I'm slow, I won't say you're wrong.' He learned many of Bruce Simpson's magnificent poems; around bush campfires or in the bars of pubs, it was always a good idea to get Tom to 'do us a poem' or 'spin us a yarn'. When he went into one of his regular 'dissertations', you never knew whether he was delivering fact or fiction. And his timing was impeccable.

One day he was talking to a young lady friend, Jody Compton. I was having a drink with them. Slowly, Tom lit his pipe, took a speculative puff and said, 'Jody, did I ever tell you about the time I was working at Groote Eylandt?'

'No, Tom,' said Jody, wide-eyed. She loved Tom.

I thought to myself: *Groote Eylandt? He's never been to bloody Groote Eylandt . . .*

Tom continued: 'Yes, Jode, I was working on the manganese mine, living in the big camp there . . .' Puff, puff . . . 'Christmas came around and, at the Christmas party . . .' Puff, puff . . . 'there were 85 blokes and only two girls.'

Jody was taking in every syllable. I was waiting.

'Do you know what, Jode?' Puff, puff . . . 'I looked across the room and there were two blokes, under the mistletoe, kissing one another . . .'

Jody couldn't believe it. There was a meaningful pause.

'And the fellow dancing with me said, "Isn't that disgraceful?"'

Straight face, puff, puff, not a blink, take it or leave it. That was The Gamekeeper at his best.

Following his 'buster', Tom was a drover for a few years, then worked on a few cattle stations as the cook; he also filled the role of 'yardie' at the pubs at Barrow Creek, Aileron and Ti Tree, where he was a delightful source of information to passing travellers.

Tom was always 'gunna' go places and do things:

I was gunna go down to Sydney,
Gunna do the things a man needs to do,
But a very fast woman and a very slow nag
Brought on an attack of 'fiscal drag'.

So I'm having a Jimmy Woodser
Before I head on out,
I've got enough left to buy you one
This is Burrows' final shout.

'Tom Burrows' (1985)

I met Tom many years after the 'buster'. I had heard about him and his exploits around the traps and one day in July 1975 we met at the Alice Springs Show. We got on famously. At that time he was 'sitting down' at Canteen Bore on Yambah Station, about 80 kilometres north of Alice Springs. Tom lived in a little caravan; he used to check the water bore, maintain the windmill and report on the cattle numbers to John Gorey, who owned Yambah. No wages, but Tom had somewhere to camp, and he received the invalid pension.

I occasionally visited Tom at Canteen Bore, taking other friends with me for a night of drinking, merriment, poetry and songs. We took our swags and Tom cooked both an evening meal and a hearty bacon-and-eggs breakfast next morning.

Tom loved a drink, but was unsteady on his feet in any case, so if he imbibed too freely we had to watch that he didn't fall in the fire. He used to say: 'Call me "The Moth"—I'm attracted to flames.' Indeed, one night, as he was cooking the steaks on a hotplate over the fire, he did lose his balance. He stuck out both hands to break his fall and his hands went onto the barbecue plate.

I dived at him and grabbed him by the waist to pull him backwards, but his hands were stuck on the hot steel plate; as

I pulled him away, the entire barbecue plate came with him. Eventually we freed him and he said, 'Don't be worried, folks, I've got hands like steel.' Sure enough, the next morning when we checked him, thinking of applying bandages, there wasn't a mark on his hands, just calluses.

Tom had an old Army Jeep, which he drove erratically around the bush. Whenever he came into Alice Springs, he parked the car about fifteen kilometres out, in the rocky hills, hid it and then walked to the outskirts of town where there was a public telephone. He used to call me 'Dad'. The phone would ring at the Stuart Arms Hotel and Tom would bellow: 'Tell Dad to come and pick me up! I can't drive in the city.'

Tom would do his shopping and occasionally camp with me at the Stuart Arms. He loved to attend my show and enjoy the hospitality at the end of the night. In those days each of the banks had a lot of staff, mainly young blokes, who were absolute terrors on the booze in their leisure hours, and they all loved my show. They all loved Tom, too, so occasionally, instead of going to La Casalinga after the show, we'd repair to the Bank Mess for drinks. Tom would recite a poem, and there was always a game of snooker or eight ball, with everybody participating. The bank johnnies used to place their drinks—usually cans of beer in stubby holders—on the edge of the snooker table while playing. They were all adroit, alert young fellows, and they didn't spill their drinks.

One night, Tom was in an expansive mood and announced that he was going to join in the game. He grabbed a cue for his shot, surveyed the table, swung his cue in a swirling arc to take aim at the white ball, and proceeded to knock about ten now foaming beers onto the immaculate green table.

He was all apologies. 'Jesus, fellers, I'm sorry. A man's a complete fucking idiot. I'd better sit down quietly.'

So he did—on a cocktail cabinet that had about 50 wine glasses inside. The flimsy legs of the cabinet collapsed under Tom's weight and every glass was shattered.

'Take me home, Dad,' he implored me. 'I'm a walking disaster! Call me "The Bent Unit".'

* * *

One day Tom approached me. 'They tell me you've bought a block of land out near the winery.'

I had. My mate 'Diddy' Smith had sold some five-acre blocks of land about 15 kilometres from the Alice post office. *A perfect rural setting for a bloke like me*, I thought. 'That's right, Tom,' I replied.

'Dad, what you need is a gamekeeper.'

We had read one another's minds. Tom actually moved onto the block before I did, taking his caravan. That was his home for the next 24 years. The Gamekeeper.

I once took Tom to Adelaide, to see the cricket. One evening we decided to have dinner at an Italian restaurant. We sat down, I ordered a bottle of Chianti, and Tom surveyed the menu. He was bewildered. 'Christ, Dad, I'm no good at this wog tucker. You'll have to order for me.'

I ran my eye down the list. 'Mmm . . . Tom, you're a meat man—I think I'll order you a veal parmigiana.'

We sipped on our drinks and chatted away. Eventually the waiter brought us our meals. He was Italian, crisp white shirt, red bow tie, clipped pencil moustache. He placed the parmigiana—smothered in exotic Italian sauces—in front of Tom and took a pace back, obviously anticipating an appropriate comment from 'sir'.

Tom took on a baleful look, gave the waiter a withering glance and said, 'By the Jesus, you'd walk around that if you saw it on the footpath!'

Tom died on Valentine's Day in 1995. He left enough money for his cremation and a sizeable donation to Palliative Care. His ashes are buried under the tree we planted on our block, in honour of 'A Drover', with one of Simmo's poems inscribed on the headstone:

Down the river we go, steady but slow
Feed them along and we're right
Store cattle for town, we're walking them down
And we sing them a song every night.

'Down the River', Bruce Simpson (1975)

* * *

Another great character around Alice Springs was Jim Herreen, known to all and sundry as 'Shim Reen', which was how Aboriginals pronounced his name. Jim had come to the Territory in the 1930s, for the Tennant Creek gold rush. He knew something of minerals then and became an expert, eventually being employed by the Mines Branch until he was in his late seventies. He had a break away when, from 1942 to 1945, he served with the AIF in New Guinea.

Jim was a confirmed bachelor, but at the same time a real dasher with every woman who came into his orbit. He was a beautiful ballroom dancer; it was fascinating to see how easily, how adeptly, how quickly Jim would have a new female acquaintance joining him in a few dance steps. He had a neat little cottage on the outskirts of Alice, and it was not unusual to visit him and find three or four young female tourists oohing and aahing as Jim plied them with drinks and cooked simple but tasty meals. Then he would produce his violin. I am not sure whether he really could play the violin, but he would tune it, play a scale or two and then say: 'Enough of this nonsense—I want to hear the story of your lives, girls.' He would charm the socks off women, and enjoyed his fair share of horizontal dancing, as well as the vertical.

After the war, Jim went mining at Hatches Creek and did well, mining mica. While he was at Hatches, he had an old Aboriginal chap named Friday working for him; they mined an underground shaft quite successfully. Jim was away from the mine quite a bit for various reasons. He was a great horseman and a famous bush jockey: his services were in high demand for the various bush race meetings. Occasionally he went to Adelaide for the big events there.

On one trip to Adelaide, he attended an Army disposals sale and purchased a plunger detonator—the type of box you see in the movies, where they press the plunger and blow up the bridge.

When Jim got back to Hatches Creek, Friday emerged to help unload the truck. Supplies, tools, drums of petrol. Friday looked at the strange little black box. 'What that, Shim?' he asked.

'Friday, I'm going to give you a big surprise. Watch closely.'

Jim set the box up on a concrete block and assembled dynamite, detonators and a roll of fuse wire. He connected the fuse wire to the box and walked towards their mine shaft. Friday was curiosity itself.

Jim reached the entry to the shaft and carefully checked the goods in his hands—ten sticks of gelignite, detonators. He climbed down the ladder to the bottom of the shaft. There he excavated a hole in which he packed the dynamite and inserted the detonators, ready for the big bang. Steady . . .

He carefully exited the shaft, climbed up the ladder and walked back to Friday and the plunger. He prepared to do the deed.

'Stand back, watch closely, and listen,' he said to the old bloke.

Jim pressed the plunger . . . and nothing happened.

Back he went to the shaft opening, hopped inside, down the ladder—careful—check. Dynamite, fuse wire, detonator. He climbed back to ground level and walked confidently to the plunger box. 'She'll work this time,' he muttered.

He was just about to press the plunger, when Friday stopped him in his tracks. 'No more, Shim, no more—stop! He still buggered,' said the tribal elder.

Jim turned on him. 'What are you talking about? What would you know about this?'

'He still buggered, Shim.'

'And how would you know?' roared Jim.

'Well, I'm pushim coupla time while you down the hole!' said Friday.

Jimmy Herreen always said that he gave up chasing Friday ten miles from Hatches Creek, so he kept walking to Barrow Creek, where he drank five schooners of beer and decided to buy the pub. He spent the next five years as 'Mine Host' of Barrow Creek, blissfully pulling beers for thirsty travellers. He put up a big sign outside the pub: 'OPEN 25 HOURS EACH DAY'.

When a tourist lady queried this, Jim said, 'We're so busy here, we don't have an hour for lunch. Will you be staying the night, madam? We can run the jukebox and have a bit of dancing.'

After Jim sold the Barrow Creek pub, he was employed by the Mines Department as a consultant, for his knowledge of mining and minerals was vast. He was a very experienced bushman and often, quietly, would espouse the dos and don'ts of outback life—what he called the Rules of the Bush. Often he was serious, but sometimes it was nonsense. I recall him saying, one night, as we each drank a pannikin of rum, apropos of nothing: 'Ted, you *can* kiss an emu on the arse, but you've got to be moving fast at the time.'

One day he returned after a visit to a few prospectors out bush; he came to our place a bit subdued. I poured him a rum. 'What's the problem, Shim?'

'Well, Ted, you're aware that I'm always quoting the Rules of the Bush? As we all know, you never camp in a dry creek bed at night. Never! A flash flood five miles away and your dry creek bed is a swirling torrent of water, mud and debris in ten minutes.

'The other night, I'm out bush—it was so cold, not a cloud in the sky, and there's a biting south-easterly wind. I thought: *Hang it, it'll be much warmer down in the creek bed.* So I parked the Toyota on the riverbank, took my swag down into the warmer sand, unrolled the swag, lit a fire, cooked two johnny cakes, which I had with a lovely bit of salt beef. Delightful.

'I opened my brand new 40-ounce bottle of Bundaberg OP Rum and had a good nip. Then I took out my false teeth, put the lid on the Bundy bottle and placed the teeth and the rum on top of my little tuckerbox. I hopped into my swag and in five minutes I was sleeping serenely.

'Two hours later, I heard it! The roaring flood, coming my way—fast. I jumped out of the swag. Must get out of danger. I had to make a split-second decision. What do I grab, the choppers or the rum?'

'What did you choose, Shim?'

Only at that point did I realise that he had been talking with his hand over his mouth. He revealed a forlorn, toothless grin.

'My dental appointment's on Thursday.'

* * *

I mentioned 'The Yellow Peril' earlier. That was Eddy Quong, one of the great identities of post-war Darwin.

> I've got a Chinese mate in Darwin
> By the name of Eddy Quong.
> We call him The Yellow Peril

And that's why he's in this song.

Quongy says that he never eats rice—

Fair enough, I suppose.

He said: 'I only ever had one bowl

And look what happened

To my eyes and my nose!'

'The Characters of the Outback' (1968)

True story. I wrote that verse of 'The Characters of the Outback' after I had asked Eddy's opinion about various types of rice. He looked at me and said: 'Rice? What would I know about bloody rice?'

After you live in the Territory for a while, you relax when people offer politically incorrect or racial comments like the one in the song, about themselves in particular. Among intimates, the utterances are based on an easy acceptance of our various differences. Mind you, there's a need for sensitivity, awareness and absolute familiarity before you risk making such statements. But Quongy got on famously with everybody, and was accepted totally in all situations. He had an admirable connection with the many Aboriginal people who had mixed with and worked for his family over generations.

In his younger days, Eddy ran Quong's Bakery in Darwin; it was the hub of the little town of around 5000 people when I arrived there. Eddy and the rest of the Quong family did their baking at night, so many Darwinites would adjourn to Quongy's after the pubs shut at 10 p.m., for merriment. You either took your own beer or Quongy had some; there was always the delight of hot bread rolls as they came fresh out of the oven at midnight. Songs were sung; drink was taken.

A beautiful young nurse from Brisbane named Greta Yow came to work at Darwin Hospital. Eddy was entranced and delighted when Greta accepted his marriage proposal. They went on to raise a wonderful, talented family who grace Darwin with their style and inimitability. The ABCs of Darwin—Australian-Born Chinese—do it so well.

Like many Darwin Chinese, Eddy was into gambling, although it never took over his life. When Greta's dad, Frank Yow, came to visit Darwin, Eddy and his brother, Lester, took Frank to a big gambling picnic we had organised at Rapid Creek. It was 1954, and we were raising money to send away our first NT representative team to the Australian Basketball Championships. Joey Sarib, Ron Bridgett and I were the fund-raisers. We had approached the police and they agreed to look the other way for six Sundays straight, so the word went out to all the big Darwin gamblers that there would be a *pai kew* game under the big trees at Rapid Creek Beach, with no chance of police intervention.

Out came the big gamblers, mostly Greeks and Chinese, all bringing Gladstone bags full of £10 notes. I am not kidding—Marilyn Paspaley once told me that her Sunday mornings as a child were spent ironing beer-sodden £10 notes. Around the large table that day we had reserved seats for the big gamblers such as Mick Paspalis, his brother Nick Paspaley—although they both spelled their surname 'Paspali' in those days—Jackie Byrnes, Scotia McGowan, Charlie On, Leo Fortiades and

'Tiger' Lyons, a solicitor. The players sat around the table and we plied them—and anybody else who turned up—with free drinks and food.

The clerk runs the game of *pai kew* (the local name for *pai gow*), which is played with dice and dominoes. The clerk invites any one of the players to be the banker. The banker puts up a bank—he announces the sum and is required to put the actual cash on the table—and the next round is played for that stake. As with pontoon, or blackjack, you have to beat the banker. Players put forward their allocated wager, usually keeping in mind the size of the bank: it would be silly to bet £100 if there's only £50 in the bank.

When the money is on the table, the clerk mixes up the dominoes, face down. He invites the banker to throw the dice, which determines who gets which set of dominoes. Then the clerk gives each player, including the banker, four dominoes each. The players read their dominoes and arrange them in various combinations, two in front and two behind. It was always much too intricate for me, but I sometimes bet a small amount and the clerk would arrange my dominoes.

The banker may ask the clerk for assistance; the banker's hand is declared, and the clerk then turns over the other players' dominoes, announcing 'Winner'—he pays you the equivalent sum from the bank, or says 'Go back' if you have equalled but not beaten the banker. If you lose, the clerk takes your wager and adds it to the banker's money.

Importantly, this routine happens twice for each bank. You can get great dominoes the first time around and double the size of your bank, but then you might draw badly for the second round and blow the lot. Or vice versa.

After the second round, either the clerk counts the winnings or the money has been reduced accordingly. The banker is paid whatever stake remains, less commission (called a *tong*).

'Who neck [next] banker?' Robert Chin, one of the clerks, would ask, and the game would continue.

As part of the routine, the clerk deducted one shilling as a *tong*, which was 5 per cent for every £1 won on the table by both bankers and punters. That commission went to the proprietor— in this case, the basketball fundraisers.

Tiger Lyons had to leave the picnic, so Eddy and Lester Quong sat Frank Yow in the vacant chair. 'Will we take a bank?' asked Lester.

'Why not?' said Eddy.

Frank was unfamiliar with the Darwin game but felt he was in safe company, so he nodded his head. 'Yes, I'll be the banker.'

There is a Chinese expression, *sart sai*, which means 'I will cover any bet of any size'. The banker does not have to put up any actual money, but is liable to cover whatever bets ensue. Out of the blue, Eddy announces *sart sai* and the gamblers reached under the table for their Gladstone bags. Out came the rolls of tenners. The bets were placed, and Frank Yow's face registered his apprehension as he saw about £10,000 on the table. But they were committed.

On the first round, Frank, Lester and Eddy had the lowest possible combination of dominoes, 2–3. They were up for ten grand at least. Indeed, given the *sart sai* call, some of the punters increased their stake for the second round.

I can still remember the combined shout of 'Yes!' from the three comrades. The clerk turned over their second set of dominoes and announced 'Nine Kong', which is the highest score achievable. Unbeatable.

Well, didn't we celebrate? The boys had won about £12,000 net, after the hefty *tong* commission. The basketball tour was guaranteed. In the end we raised well over our £5000 target in six weeks. *Sart sai* indeed.

One of my great memories of Eddy Quong is that he is buried head-to-head with Leo Fortiades in the Greek section of the McMillans Road cemetery. Eddy won the burial plot from Leo in a bet. It could only happen in Darwin. May they both rest in peace.

* * *

From the 1950s until about the 1980s, Alice Springs was very much dependent on two factors: the cattle industry and tourism. Black and white stockmen were seen on a daily basis, in the shops, in the streets, in the pubs, dressed in standard Aussie 'ringer' gear—big hats, moleskins or jeans, check shirts, elastic-sided boots.

Tourists wore mainly T-shirts and shorts, cloth hats and sturdy shoes. In the winter months, windcheaters were the best-selling garments, for tourists usually had no idea just how cold it can be in the Centre between April and August.

The bars at the Stuart Arms and 'Uncle Ly' Underdown's Alice Springs Hotel were always crowded; people drank rum in the winter and beer in the hotter months. From 1975, I spent time pretty well every day drinking with one school or another. Tourists, locals, ringers, drillers, truckies and station workers tended to drink with their peers; stock and station agents took their briefcases to the pubs at 10 a.m. and drank five-ounce beers, while the cattle-station owners and managers drank schooners. The town's business was done thus, every day.

It was all reminiscent of 'Duke' Tritton's poem 'Shearing in the Bar'. The tallies got bigger, the number of calves branded were hard to believe, the horses bucked higher, the drillers talked of the footage they had achieved with their mud-punchers. I heard one bloke shout out to a bunch of drinking drillers one day, 'I wish you bastards would hit water in that bore; I've got the contract to put the windmill on it.'

One of the great raconteurs was a bloke named Charlie Hosking, better known as 'Charlie Like'. He always put the word *like* on the end of every sentence. 'Howyer goin', like?' 'Christ, it's hot, like.' 'Could you handle a rum, like?' And he always seemed to have an alternative word. He had an operation on his eyes 'to remove the Cadillacs, like'. He complained about the bush roads: 'The congregations, like! They're dreadful.' I was talking to Charlie one day and an attractive girl in culottes walked past. 'Ted, what do you reckon about them curettes, like?' he asked me.

Charlie had a road train named The Gold Seal Cattle Transport Company Like. He had that painted on his truck. Charlie always said: 'Gold Seal is the epitome of class, like.' He regularly transported cattle from Mount Doreen to Alice Springs when I was living at Yuendumu in the late 1950s.

One morning, about 6 a.m., bitterly cold, I heard the big truck rolling through. I got up to greet Charlie, who stopped the truck and immediately poured two full pannikins of OP Basket Rum—immensely powerful stuff. He handed me one.

It was a bit early for a phlegm-cutter, even for me. This is the verse of 'The Drinkers of the Territory' that I wrote as a consequence:

In the Alice, there's a feller,
We call him Charlie Like
He poured me a pannikin of OP Rum
That would make a champion pike
When I asked old Charlie for water
To break it down, by gosh
He said: 'There's a waterbag on the truck
If you want to have a wash—like!'

'The Drinkers of the Territory' (1969)

One winter in Alice, Charlie was talking to a group of us at the Stuart Arms. He said, 'Boys, I must tell you about last Tuesday, like. I'm carting cattle from Brunette Downs on the Tableland, into Alice. It's freezing outside, frost everywhere. And as you all know, like, they're having a dreadful drought on the Barkly.

'Well, I get caught short for a shit, like. I feel it comin' on, like, and I know I'm not gonna last until Tennant Creek. So

I stopped the old Gold Seal Cattle Transport Company truck, like, and I hops out into the freezing cold. The wind would cut right through you, like. I divested myself of the old combination overalls'—Charlie always wore these—'had my shit and looked around for something with which to wipe my arse, like. I had no paper, like, but there's not a bloody blade of grass, not a twig, not a stick, like. Then I spots a pebble, like . . .'

A pause, then Charlie reflectively held up his thumb and forefinger, as though he was holding the Hope Diamond. 'Boys, have you ever wiped your arse with an ice cube?'

18

BIRDSVILLE RACES: I'LL WALK BESIDE YOU

Me and me mate, we just come into Birdsville
We come in at 'Races Time' each year
Me and me mate, we just come into Birdsville
But we're only interested in the beer!

'The Birdsville Races' (1964)

In 1975, RCA rang and said that my album *The Bangtail Muster* had gone gold. Where would I like the award ceremony to take place?

I had been in dialogue with Tim and Ros Bowden, by now old friends. We first met when Tim did a memorable radio program titled *The Top End: It's Different Up There*. Tim's cousin, Dr John Hawkins of Alice Springs, had introduced Tim to my music, so Tim used a few songs as background to the interviews he did with various Territory characters; indeed, he had even interviewed me. We put the program together in a delightful Sunday night session at the ABC studios in Sydney, with the one and only Margaret Throsby. Tim, his wife, Ros, and I got on famously and a lifelong friendship developed.

Tim had always been impressed by the authenticity of my performances, especially when singing in outback pubs, where I could get the attention of the noisiest crowds without need for a microphone, a band or any gimmickry. Tim often expressed concern about the sterility of some studio recordings he had heard, where there was obviously no relationship between artist and audience at the time.

So I suggested to Barry Forrester of RCA: 'Why not present me my gold album at the Birdsville Races? At the same time, RCA should finance Tim and Ros Bowden to record an album of my songs in the bar at the Birdsville Pub—warts and all, crowd noises, fights, dogs barking, you name it.'

Barry thought it was a great idea, so the arrangements were made. I would drive from Sydney to Birdsville, taking Sheila and ten or so mates in their vehicles, including the Bowdens and their two boys, Barnaby and Guy. Barry Forrester and the RCA personnel would fly to Birdsville, take in the races, present the award and stay a couple of nights with us in my bush camp.

I was very experienced in that respect. We loaded trailers with swags, cooking gear, a portable dunny, a bush shower, plenty of food, beer, wine and spirits. I sent a telegram to my mate Jimmy Evans at Durrie Station, near Birdsville, asking him if he would have a 'side of beef' ready for us. Jim selected a neighbour's best bullock, slaughtered it and hung half the carcass for us in a bough shelter that we erected on arrival. We set up camp on the Diamantina River, five miles out of town.

We had two blissful days prior to the races, organising our camp, feasting, swimming, singing and drinking around the campfire at night. The night before the races, when I rang Barry Forrester, still in Sydney, to check his ETA and arrange to meet the RCA party when they landed in their charter aircraft, he told me: 'Ted, great news. A Yankee bloke named Bob Cook, a legend in RCA, has just been appointed general manager of RCA Australia. We told him about you and he insists that he wants to come to Birdsville and do the presentation.'

'Terrific,' I responded.

'Yes, Ted—and Bob Cook's world-famous. He's the bloke who spotted and signed ABBA for RCA, and that deal has made billions for the company.'

Well, they duly arrived and we recorded a few songs in the bar that day after the races, with hundreds of drinkers milling around, sometimes singing along. Barry was thrilled at the obviously genuine outcome of the recording session, which was done by Tim and Ros with a couple of little Nagra recorders. Bob Cook was enthralled; he also had a good laugh, which is still a highlight on the 'Marsupial Joe' track on my *The Bush Races* album.

That night we adjourned to the ball, which was attended by happy, joyful people. We really drank hard, mostly rum and beer chasers. What we didn't know was that Bob Cook was an alcoholic. He proceeded to get terribly pissed and began to abuse anybody and everybody.

'Let's get him out of here, Barry,' I hissed. Much to Bob's chagrin, we bundled him into a car and headed back to our camp, where, I thought, he might quieten down.

But he didn't. He found fault with everyone and everything, so I thought: *Bugger you, mate, you'll keep.* I hopped into my swag, very angry, but listening to the rampage still going on around the campfire.

'What sort of a place is this you've brought me to?' Bob demanded of his three RCA staff, Barry, Keith and Murray. 'Here we are in this godforsaken place, on a goddamned riverbank, no tents. Is this some sort of joke? I was going to ask John Laws to come on this trip. I'm glad I didn't. What would Lawsie think of this abomination?'

The RCA boys tried to appease him, but he wasn't having any of it. 'We make this Ted Egan a star and this is his way of saying thank you?'

Barry intervened on my behalf. 'Bob, this is a very remote location and Ted has gone to a lot of trouble setting up this camp. A lot of people would say it's ideal; no tents, because you don't need them—and we are camped out, in this beautiful weather, under these magnificent stars.'

'Barry, you are fired! Do you hear me? You're fired.' When Keith and Murray entered the conversation, he sacked them also. 'The three of you! You're finished with RCA!'

At that point they took him to his swag, put him to bed and all was quiet.

I lay there, simmering.

The next morning, I quietly eased out of my swag at sparrow's fart. I showered, shaved, clean moleskins, shirt and R.M. Williams Santa Fe boots. I walked quietly across to Bob's swag. I placed the chisel toe of my boot gently in Bob's ribs and gave him a nudge, which woke him. He looked at me, his bloodshot eyes slowly achieving focus.

'Get up!' I ordered. 'You and I are going for a walk.'

Everyone else was asleep. I quietly woke Barry, Keith and Murray, and signalled for them to follow Bob and me. Bob shuffled along beside me, obviously suffering. It was about to get worse.

'Bob,' I said, 'you have committed the serious sin of abusing hospitality extended to you in the bush. You have insulted the leading citizens of Birdsville. You have offended me. I never think of myself as a *star*, but RCA has, in fact, done very little towards my sales. I cost you nothing in the recording studio, and then I get out there and sell the product. Now, I want you to apologise—not so much to me, but to your three very valuable staff members, who are to be reinstated on this walk. Do I make myself crystal-clear?'

Bob stopped, shoulders slumped. He looked me in the eye. 'Ted, I am so sorry. I have this condition with alcohol, and it got me again. How can I redeem myself with you?'

Further words were unnecessary. Bob and I had a big hug and a wry smile. Then he turned and, to his eternal credit, hugged each of the lads. Their reinstatement was silently achieved.

For the next two days at the Birdsville Races, indeed for the rest of his several years in Australia, Bob Cook drank only light beer and joined in the fun. He had a terrific time at the races. We took some great photos of him presenting me with my gold album.

Every time I went to Sydney thereafter, Bob, Barry, Keith, Murray and I would have lunch. Bob would have just the one light beer, and would relate to any other guests at the table the story of 'my bushwalk with my old buddy Ted Egan'.

The *Bush Races* album went gold, I add immodestly. Thanks, Ros and Tim.

19

THE FACES OF AUSTRALIA

Every time I visited Sydney, I went to the RCA offices at Ryde. There would be minimal business matters to sort out, then we'd all adjourn somewhere for the monumental long lunches the music industry is renowned for.

It always seemed to me that the real work in recording companies was done by a few very smart women, who stayed at their desks and slogged away while the men were out, day after day, drinking enormous amounts of booze all afternoon. Not that I complained, for I was never required to pay a cent. My recording career was always positive, as I was a hot seller. After twelve albums with RCA and EMI, I knew how to produce albums myself, so I went it alone, with a much better financial outcome. I have never accumulated any money—probably never will—for there is always a new project to finance, but it is good, clean fun and I keep telling myself that the next one will be the big one. Occasionally I organise a long lunch these days, just to show that I can.

I've mentioned Barry Forrester and the famous walk at Birdsville in 1975. Barry was the A&R (artists and repertoire) manager for RCA, a fine guitarist himself and a good songwriter. He and I got on famously, for he, too, loved a drink and a singsong. One day he showed me an American magazine. A group was doing the History of the Wild West via albums of songs. Barry said to me: 'Ted, this is the sort of thing you could do—cover the history of Australia with your songs. You write songs about real people. What do you think?'

My reply was instant: 'What a great idea. The *Faces of Australia*.'

I was fairly well informed about many aspects of Australian history. I had always been impressed by Russel Ward's book *The Australian Legend*, which often referred to songs and poems alongside the details of history. The ultimate challenge for me, as a songwriter, was to get a story across in the three to four minutes of a song. People had always been my particular interest. I can't take great photographs or paint fine portraits, but I do like to compose songs about people—especially those who are unlikely to capture the attention of the academic historians.

I selected ten *Faces of Australia* topics and set out to research the background that would enable me firstly to acknowledge and use any appropriate songs in existence, and secondly to write new songs where necessary.

It was at that point that I realised just how few songs there are in Australia with a genuine historical base to them. The purported classics, such as 'Click Go the Shears' and 'Lachlan Tigers', are sung to traditional Welsh tunes. All the footy songs are parodies, most of them abysmal. (As a Tigers supporter, I am pleased to announce that Richmond has the best song— 'Yellow and Black'—but it's nonetheless a parody.) 'Moreton Bay' is a steal from the famous Irish 'Boolavogue'. Even the tune of 'Waltzing Matilda' is based on a Scottish melody, and the song has nothing to do with dancing but is based on the German tradition of *auf der Walz*, where apprentices went on the road seeking employment, rolling along aimlessly like barrels (*walz* means 'barrel'), clutching 'Mathilde'—their overcoats, their surrogate female companions—to keep warm in order to survive the long winter nights on the road.

I estimated that I would need to write at least a hundred new songs to cover the ground adequately. At the same time, I knew that there *are* a few great songs and poems—written in Australia by Australians—that *do* cover the right ground. I knew I must get permission from the writers of those songs to allow me to use them under my various headings.

My ten proposed album topics were, in something resembling chronological sequence: Aboriginals, convicts, explorers, immigrants, gold-diggers, bushrangers, shearers, overlanders, Anzacs and children.

Somewhat incongruously, I did the children's album first, with the title *The Urapunga Frog: Australian Songs for Children*. A good songwriter, Bryan Clark, came to me with ideas for a song called

'The Urapunga Frog'. We worked on it together, made a few changes and now Bryan is happy to have us listed as co-writers.

My son Mark did the lovely artwork for the album's cover, and we recorded seventeen songs with Herbie Marks and a new friend, Terry Walker, a fantastic guitar and banjo player, and just the best sound-effects man. Terry's frog calls are amazing, awe-inspiring. We did some songs in Aboriginal, Torres Strait and other languages.

Keeping in mind my intention to use other people's songs, as long as they were good and appropriate, I did a cover version of John Williamson's 'Old Man Emu'—it's such a great song. My daughter Jacki and I performed 'I Wonder Why?' together. Jacki was always asking questions, so I wrote that song especially for her. Nowadays she and I still sing the song, with Jacki's daughter Jess making up a trio. Jess's own daughter, my great-granddaughter Tiahna, will be next to join us.

We recorded this kids' album in 1974 and it is still a good seller. Regularly, I get letters along these lines from Australian grandmothers: 'Great to hear some real Aussie songs for kids. I learned the songs as a girl, I taught my kids and now I'd like a copy of the CD so I can teach my grandkids.'

* * *

In the years between 1975 and 1980 I found time to plan and research the various other albums that I hoped to record as the *Faces of Australia*. Daunting stuff. Big task, big financial outlay, almost certainly slow sales.

149

I decided that I would prepare to do *The Overlanders* next. I had met a stimulating historian named Peter Forrest, who had come to the Northern Territory from western Queensland. Peter gave lectures in Alice Springs on a regular basis, and he put an exciting touch to his stories, as they related to the biggest movements of cattle the world has ever known. It didn't happen in the United States or South America or Asia. It happened right here in Australia.

Before 1972, any rights to and ownership of this land by the First Australians had always been denied in Australia. The government—in the 1870s, following exploration journeys by people such as McDouall Stuart, Burke and Wills, the Forrest brothers—threw open huge areas of Crown land in the remote north and north-west regions of Queensland, Northern Territory and Western Australia. Arbitrary lines were drawn on maps. Leases were issued by the Crown to establish cattle and sheep stations, often the size of European countries. Victoria River Downs (known as VRD) in its heyday was 50,000 square miles in area—that's 130,000 square kilometres. In order to fulfil the requirement for stocking these allocated properties, hundreds of thousands of cattle and sheep were walked overland from the southern regions, in huge mobs that were often years on the road. The drovers travelled slowly and carefully, establishing one depot after another, with access to water always dominant in their minds.

With Peter Forrest steering me in the appropriate direction, I wrote songs about Nat Buchanan—the greatest cattle drover the world has ever seen—and Harry Redford, who stole 1000 head of cattle in western Queensland, walked them across 'unknown' Australia and became the model for a fictional hero, Captain Starlight, in the book and film *Robbery Under Arms*.

I thought back to my days as a young cadet patrol officer with the Native Affairs Branch of the Northern Territory Administration. In 1952, I had been listed in the Commonwealth Government Gazette as a 'Protector of Aborigines'. My mother Grace, in Melbourne, was ever so proud of me. I was always mystified by the term *protector*, as in all my many experiences with Aboriginal people it was always me who needed protection and tutoring.

I always got on well with Aboriginal people, as I did not patronise them; instead, I was always anxious to be 'one of the mob', so I'd ask many questions and accept their usually wise responses, which they imparted so generously. I played footy and basketball with my Aboriginal peers and I was always coaching kids. I loved being taught many songs, most lighthearted, some serious. I always marvelled at being paid to do my exciting job.

By the mid-1950s I had visited many of the big cattle stations, checking the conditions for Aboriginal workers. Always interested in the cattle game, I closely observed the activities around the stockyards. I noticed that on the really big runs, such as Wave Hill, Inverway and VRD, there was invariably a group of old Aboriginal women sitting around a campfire in close proximity to the action. They all wore big hats, and most smoked pipes. Methodically, they cooked damper and boiled tea buckets for 'dinner camp'. In the same fire they heated branding irons, if they were required. The women readily shouted encouragement and advice to the stockmen performing the various tasks such as branding, earmarking, castrating and drafting the cattle and riding rough horses.

I often sat with the women and asked lots of searching questions. They certainly knew the ins and outs of the cattle game. The women often used the expression: 'We born in the cattle.' My friend Dr Ann McGrath subsequently wrote a book with that title: *Born in the Cattle*, a lovely description of the many and varied experiences of those same women. Great book, Ann.

One day at Mt Doreen station, around 1960, an old Aboriginal woman said to me: 'Hey, you the bloke sing the song, ain't it?'

'That's me,' I responded.

'When you gonna make a song about we fellers, we womans? We only hear songs about white men, but we born in the cattle. We stockmen, olden days.'

Over the many years since my first contact with Aboriginals in the 1950s, I had picked up details of the women's experiences, and marvelled at the fact that they had obviously been involved in the phenomenon that Peter Forrest kept harking back to: when Australia had witnessed the biggest movement of stock ever known in the world. Here were some of the actual participants.

But the women confused me when they began to talk of trips to New South Wales, Queensland, South Australia and Western Australia, speaking with obvious familiarity. They mentioned specific places such as Gepps Cross (South Australia), Goulburn (New South Wales) and Midland Junction (Western Australia), formerly famous destinations for the cattle drovers from the north who walked the big mobs down.

'How come you know of those places?' I asked.

'Well, when we delivery the cattle, we camp there little bit. Our white bosses got on the grog, but we still had to look after the horses.'

'But you know that I work for the government? There's a government law that says Aboriginal women and girls are not allowed to work as cattle drovers.'

'That right,' was the response, 'but you not here, this country, when that law come in, were you?'

'Correct.' These old campaigners were talking about the 1920s.

'Well, we was here. And when that new law came in, the white men who owned us had our hair cut short and they gave us new names . . . Geoffrey, Tommy, Peter, that kind of business.' They identified one another thus and had a good laugh as they reminisced.

The women used language like that—'the white men who owned us'—with no rancour or vitriol; it was simply a statement of fact. They explained that they were wearing 'trousers, shirts, hats, same as man', but insisted: 'We better than the men. Track cattle better, better even than Aboriginal men. We never got on the grog like the white men. We looked after the cattle. We were kinder to horses. And we worked all day in the saddle and all night, jig-a-jig, in the swag.'

They would go into showers of mirth as they discussed the sexual talents or shortcomings—pardon the metaphor—of the various white men who 'owned' them, and who had enjoyed them in their swags on the cold nights. One old lady said to me: 'You know, Ted Egan, we all Mrs Johnson here, before that white Mrs Johnson come along.'

Over many years, a song about the old Aboriginal women kept eluding me. I knew basically what I wanted to say, yet it wouldn't gel.

In 1981, I was having lunch with Peter Forrest at the Overlander Steakhouse in Alice Springs. It was very pleasant, as Peter is always stimulating company. We shared a delightful bottle of Peter Lehmann Stonewell shiraz.

'What are you writing these days?' Peter asked, aware that I was trying to put *The Overlanders* album together.

'Oh, I've done the Nat Buchanan song—I called it "King Paraway". "Captain Starlight" you've heard . . . but there's a song in my mind somewhere that won't come out. You'll know the background—the old Aboriginal women who were taken as girls and masqueraded as males when the new law came in.'

'Oh,' said Peter reflectively. 'The drover's boys.'

That's it, I thought. *'The Drover's Boy'—yes!*

'Peter, I'm going to leave you to polish off Mr Lehmann's fine shiraz. I'm just going to whip around to the Stuart Arms.' It was only a block away. 'I'll see you at your motel, later, with a song for you.'

That afternoon I handed Peter a cassette tape. 'There you are, mate—"The Drover's Boy".'

Isn't it silly? All I needed was that tiny prompt. I think it's the best song I have written. Thanks to Peter Forrest.

They couldn't understand why the drover cried
As they buried The Drover's Boy.
For the drover had always seemed so hard
To the men in his employ.
A bolting horse, a stirrup lost,
The Drover's Boy was dead.
The shovelled dirt, a mumbled word,
And it's back to the road ahead.
And forget about . . . The Drover's Boy.

'The Drover's Boy' (1981)

The Overlanders album was coming along, but not quite ready to record. I wanted it to be a milestone, a concise history, the highlight being the contribution made by hundreds of unknown Aboriginal girls and women—The Drovers' Boys—whose unheralded participation had done so much to enhance Australia as a nation.

It was 1981, and my good mate Tim Bowden was visiting Alice. After recording *The Bush Races* in 1975, Tim and I had done a very successful tour of the Top End, recording songs and interviews at places such as the Torres Strait, Bathurst Island and Wattie Creek. Tim, Peter and I agreed to record a series based on Northern Territory history, titled *The Territory Story*. We chose six headings: *The Top End*, *The Centre*, *The Explorers*, *The Overlanders*, *The Aboriginals* and *Those Blinking Bods in Canberra*.

We finished up with a highly acclaimed, but poorly supported, box set of six cassette tapes, each running for an hour. I commissioned Jeanette Cook to do six portraits for the covers. I cherish them to this day. For *Those Blinking Bods in Canberra*, she had to portray Harold 'Tiger' Brennan, the voluble, pith-helmeted, cigar-puffing miner, parliamentarian and one-time mayor of Darwin.

Tiger had been one of the leaders of the movement towards NT self-government, finalised in 1978. His principal claim to fame is that he drank through Christmas Eve in 1974 at the NT Brewery, emerging at 7 a.m. to find that Darwin had been devastated by Cyclone Tracy.

20

TURNING POINTS

By 1978, Sheila and I had been in a relationship for four years—she living in Sydney and me based in Alice Springs, but travelling extensively around Australia, including time with her in Sydney. Sheila always insisted on her independence; as she was a qualified stenographer, she always had highly paid work.

In 1979, I invited her to spend a weekend at Alice, to stay with me at the Stuart Arms. She loved the place, proposed that she sell her Canberra house (which she was leasing out) and suggested we share a deposit on a house in Alice, to enable her to live there permanently. That seemed a good idea. Indeed, during the same weekend, we agreed to get married.

Thus we went halves on a deposit for a house in Pedler Avenue, Alice Springs, and I took out a mortgage for the balance. Sheila moved to Alice and we were married by Wendy Kirke in a simple ceremony at the Old Telegraph Station.

The marriage was a disaster and within six months we separated, but quite amicably. I paid back her share of the Alice house and Sheila returned to Canberra, where she bought another house and got a job at Parliament House. We never saw one another again. In 1982, we were divorced. Sheila died in Canberra in 2014. She was a fine woman, just not the right one for me.

In my ongoing teaching role at Alice Springs High School, my boss was Alison Garnett. We got on well, and I knew that Ali was the wife of Barney Foran, a member of a local folk group, Bloodwood. Other Bloodwood members were Bob Barford, Scott Balfour and Dave Evans.

Bloodwood had travelled the world promoting NT tourism, and were very popular in the Australian folk movement. You might recall my earlier assertion that most folk singers tried to sound like Poms—Bloodwood was a notable exception. Scott was born in Scotland and Dave in England, but they were very Aussie in everything they did.

I was having a cup of tea with Ali in the staffroom at ASHS one day early in 1980, and she said, 'Ted, the National Folk Festival is to be at Alice this year. Why don't you do a workshop?'

'What's a workshop?'

'Well, you select a topic, talk around that subject and sing relevant songs. Usually about 90 minutes duration.'

By that time I had done more than ten albums.

'Tell me more,' I said.

There would probably be 500 to 1000 people at the festival, she said, from all around Australia—and she reckoned they would be interested in some of my songs about local characters. So we agreed that I'd have a go at a workshop. Bit of fun.

Easter 1980 came around and the festival was on at the Alice Springs Youth Centre over the entire weekend, with a couple of big open-air concerts on Anzac Oval.

On the Saturday afternoon I presented my workshop, called 'Be a Good Listener'. The title came from my mother's advice back when I left Melbourne, aged fifteen: 'Wherever you go in life, Teddy, keep sweet with the cook and be a good listener.' I am, when necessary, a very good listener, so in the workshop I explained my songwriter's technique: posing what I hoped were relevant questions to interesting people and listening intently to their responses. You never know, I told the audience, when the gem phrase or sentence is going to be delivered.

The workshop went very well and I was thrilled at the generous applause that followed each song I sang, accompanied by my 'different' instrument, the Fosterphone. When it came to an end, I thought: *That's that. That's the end of my career as a folk singer.*

But I had nothing to do that night, so I decided to attend the outdoor concert at Anzac Oval. It was a delightful setting, a thousand people under the stars, listening to very pleasant music. Bloodwood were especially good. But the highlight of my night was a Pommy bloke named Tony Miles. He was a good raconteur, played nice guitar and sang a wide range of songs. Halfway through his act, he said: 'I, like many of you today, had a very interesting experience. We listened to this local bloke named Ted Egan, who apologised at the start of his workshop, saying that he did not belong to the "folk movement". I don't know about you, ladies and gentlemen, but I have never heard a more consummate folk singer in my life.' Warm applause came from the assembled audience.

Sitting alone in the darkness, I felt a real buzz of pride.

I did not attend more of the festival, but a few weeks later I received an invitation to attend the New Zealand National Folk Festival, to be held in Wellington. My fares would be paid, and I was offered a $200 fee. Yes, please! I had never been to Aotearoa.

I was in for a few surprises. I thought there'd be a lot of Maori people in Wellington, and that there would be an emphasis on Maori songs. So I brushed up on my Maori repertoire, '*Poka-rekare Ana*' and '*Po Atarau*', two lovely songs that I was taught by my mate Prince Peta—he is indeed a member of Maori royalty—who sang at Papa Luigi's restaurant in Alice Springs. Peta and I used to drink a lot of beer together and I helped him produce a nice album of his own songs, together with a magnificent poster to advertise it.

Not a single Maori person attended the festival. Almost everybody there was a migrant from the United Kingdom, and most of them had *The Bushwackers Australian Song Book* under their arms. It was quickly obvious that they saw me as a good leader of 'colonial' songs such as 'Lachlan Tigers' and 'Click Go the Shears'. I went along with that for a bit, but then I concentrated on presenting my own songs about outback characters, wondering why there seemed to be no New Zealand counterparts.

I must acknowledge that my brand-new song 'The Drover's Boy' and my versions of the two Maori songs were enthusiastically received; I got thunderous applause when I sang a few Aboriginal songs in traditional Australian language. I was confused but very happy with my contribution.

It was a lovely, if mystifying event, my first trip 'across the ditch'. I was saddened that I had nil contact with Maori culture, for I always reminisce about a wonderful experience of my boyhood.

I was selling newspapers in Coburg—I was about eleven, so it would have been in 1943, during the war—and I swung onto a tram one day. '*Herald* . . . Get your *Herald* . . . Read all about it!' But I was stopped in my tracks, because there were two New Zealand soldiers on the tram and they were singing. Were they singing! One was a Maori, the other a Pakeha. They had obviously been fighting in New Guinea; they wore jungle-green uniforms and the famous New Zealand 'lemon-squeezer' hats. Their skins were identically yellow; all Aussie and New Zealand soldiers took Atabrine tablets to guard against malaria. They both obviously spoke the Maori language and loved the songs that they were sharing with us, harmonising exquisitely. I stayed on the tram, transfixed, until they got off at the Sarah Sands Hotel in Brunswick and headed for the pub, for more beer, more singing. Then I swung onto another tram heading back to my stand at Bell Street. Unforgettable. '*Herald* . . . Get your *Herald* . . . Read all about it!'

It was one of the great experiences of my life. I still have great admiration for New Zealand and Kiwis generally.

I could tell that the feller was a Kiwi
As he danced the Maori Haka
Sang '*Pokarekare Ana*' all night long
We were hevin' a drunk togither
In a pub at Bondi Beach
And as he dodged a flying jug
He sang thus song:
I've come over here from New Ziland
The Land of the Long Wide Comb
Then he sang the Kiwi national song
I stull call Australia home!

'Kiwis I Hev Mit' (1989)

Back in Alice, I resumed my 1980 season at the Stuart Arms, and then came another surprise. I had a telephone call from a bloke named John Minson of Tamworth, asking if I would come to the Tamworth Country Music Festival the following January. 'We want to induct you into the Hands of Fame,' he told me.

'Are you talking to the right bloke?' I asked. 'I'm not a country-music singer.'

'Mate,' John replied, 'I run the biggest country-music radio program in Australia, from station 2TM; it's called *The Hoedown*. I've been a fan of yours since about 1970. Your songs are ever so popular. You are the second-highest gold album holder in Australia, after Slim Dusty.'

That was news to me. But January was always a free month, so I said yes. I drove to Tamworth, through some incredibly wet weather, and arrived at the big festival. I was staggered at the sheer size of it. Every pub and club had music going. There were buskers galore in Peel Street and I had a whale of a time taking in the various acts. I did not have any gigs lined up, but I determined that I would be back the following year: I think I attended every January festival for the next twenty years. I have only missed three or four Tamworths since.

The Hands of Fame was good, in that I met a bloke named Terry Gordon, who was also being recognised for a long career, so we did our handprints in wet cement together. I often go back to the park at Tamworth and slot my hand in the original mark. And Terry and I have had a ton of fun over nearly 40 years of friendship, including a memorable tour of New Zealand together. Terry is one of the absolute gems of country music. He is without doubt the best-organised artist I have ever met, and his generosity is boundless. We all had a good laugh when, for his 60th birthday, Terry shaved off his beard. He was a dead ringer for Robert Trimbole, a famous crook, so he quickly grew the whiskers again.

The year 1981 turned out to be a very good one for me. A good tourist season at the Stuart Arms, good record sales, and I was in good health. I started to go to a few Folk Club gatherings, when they didn't clash with my own show. In about June I had a phone call from a fellow named Dave Hults, an American who was on the committee of the Western Australian Folk Federation. Would I like to be a guest at their folk festival in Toodyay, at the end of September? My word I would. I was starting to enjoy this.

My entire life was about to change. I was picked up at the Perth airport by a bloke named Greg Hastings, who drove me to Toodyay, a lovely little country town about 85 kilometres from Perth. I was accommodated at the Freemasons Hotel. Greg saw me to my room, and at about 7 p.m. we headed to the bar. It was quite crowded, so we sat on stools back from the action, under the dartboard. Greg introduced me to quite a few people, some of whom were on the festival's organising committee.

'And, Ted, I'd like you to meet Nerys Evans.'

I turned. Here was this tall blonde.

'Hello, Nerys . . . nice to meet you.'

'Good to meet you, too,' she responded. 'May I buy you a drink?'

We both laughed as I took a pace backwards.

Wow, that's a good intro, I thought, and looked her over. *She's tall, wears glasses, has a great set of tits, an impressive laugh . . . and she wants to buy me a drink—my kind of woman.*

'Well, I think I should buy *you* a drink,' I said. 'What'll it be?'

'Brandy and dry ginger ale,' she replied.

'That's interesting,' I said. 'I'm drinking Bundaberg Rum and dry ginger. Like to try one of those?'

'What's it taste like?' Nerys asked.

'It's like kissing a sailor,' I told her.

'Well, I'd better have one.'

We clinked glasses.

'Cheers! Humpty Doo, digger! That's the Territory toast,' I told her.

'*Iechyd da*!' she responded. 'I'm Welsh.'

On that memorable evening, Nerys and I attended a couple of concerts and joined in some terrific folk dancing and community singing—she also had a colossal singing voice, I noted. We spent that night (and the rest of our lives) together.

The Toodyay experience was an eye-opener in many other respects. Again, most of the attendees were migrants from the United Kingdom and Ireland, but they were quickly Australianising themselves. Yes, there were lots of *rol-de-diddle-fai-dol-day* songs, and strange phenomena such as morris dancing, but there was also a thirst for Australian material, so my concerts and songs received rapt attention. There was a band called Mucky Duck, and were they any good? They had a mixed repertoire, and when they did songs such as 'The Overlanders' I pricked up my ears, for they were singing my type of song and they were just so gutsy.

The standard of the performers at the festival was astonishing, and Nerys and I began searching discussions about engaging these singers and musicians for recordings. In particular, I loved what the folkies called 'the sessions', where everybody sits or stands in a big ring and you join in the chorus of songs that everybody seemed to know, word for word. Some of the leaders in these sessions seemed to have thousands of songs at their disposal. I began to understand why singing at British soccer and rugby matches is so spontaneous and impressive; to this day, Australian-born people don't seem to be able to do it, no matter how hard one tries to encourage it. I once tried to get a group together to take on the Barmy Army, but found I was wasting my time.

Nerys and I had the Friday, Saturday and Sunday at the Toodyay festival, then on Monday morning (a public holiday in Western Australia) they had the Chorus Cup, a competition based on ribald songs. It was good fun. Nerys then drove me back to Fremantle, where she had a small home.

On the drive, we got to know each other better. She was a teacher, born in Wales, but resident in Australia since 1964; she had been on the Western Australia Folk Federation committee for several years. Nerys had actually been at the National Folk Festival at Alice Springs in 1980, and had attended my workshop and established that I was 'the same bloke' whose songs on the ABC had interested her, because they seemed 'so Australian'. Being Welsh, she was aware that most Welsh people—including herself—sang mainly in Welsh, whereas Irish and Scottish singers usually sang songs in English, as did English folkies. She said that she had been on the lookout for authentic Australian material and she had heard me sing in both English and Aboriginal languages, often with Aboriginal themes to the songs. She had said on the Friday night that her favourite song of mine was 'Poor Fella My Country', which I had recorded many years earlier.

She asked: 'Have you written anything as wonderful as that since?'

'I think I have,' I said. 'It's called "The Drover's Boy".'

In fact, Nerys had been talking about my music in Perth for a long time, so Dave Hults, along with the WA contingent, at Nerys's urging, had attended my workshop at the 1980 Alice Springs festival. Hence Dave's phone call. When she knew that

I would be going to Toodyay, Nerys decided to attend to hear me sing.

'Don't you have good ideas?' I said to her then, and many times subsequently.

We spent a tremendous Monday night together, and the next day I flew back to Alice. We had agreed to meet up as soon as possible, and had decided that we would record *The Overlanders* in Perth, as quickly as possible.

21

RECORDING IN PERTH: THE OVERLANDERS

I kept in touch with Nerys in Fremantle, on the phone and via letters. I continued presenting my shows in Alice, then set off on a tour—in my Land Cruiser—of north-western Western Australia. Kununurra, Derby, Broome, Halls Creek. Nerys and I had arranged for her to fly from Perth to Port Hedland so she could join me for the remainder of the tour, which eventually would head down to Perth.

It was great introducing Nerys to camping out, in the swag, doing a bit of bush cooking and sharing the wonderful conversations that are inspired by starry skies and campfires.

In Perth and Fremantle I teamed up with many of the excellent musos and singers I had met at Toodyay, for I was determined to engage them for *The Overlanders* recording. I explained to

Nerys that I would need to find an equivalent of Herbie Marks as my musical director, given my inability to read or write sheet music, and my absolute ineptitude in discussions about keys and tempos.

To her eternal credit, Nerys said: 'I think you need to meet a chap named Erik Kowarski—he's frighteningly good.' She had known Erik for many years. He is a lovely combination of a consummate musician, recording engineer, musical arranger and good fun bloke. Erik is classically trained, but elects to move in the broad genre of folk music. Like Herbie, he found me 'interesting', in that I was the absolute opposite of him, yet I turned out good-selling albums of original songs. We embarked on yet another of the lifelong friendships that music inspires.

I mentioned the band called Mucky Duck earlier. Mucky Duck is a Barmy Army–type shot at the black swan, Western Australia's emblem, which is on the state flag. The Perth-based band had seen quite a few members coming and going over the years; Erik Kowarski and Greg Hastings were foundation members who had moved on but still remained in contact.

I came to realise that all Perth musos knew one another, so I was confident we would be able to engage the best talent available. Eventually, through Nerys and Erik, we hired Soundwest Studios at Subiaco. Dave and Will Upson, talented musicians themselves, were the owners, and Ric Curtin was their engineer. On 6 July 1982, during *The Overlanders* recording, I turned 50: we had a good night at the Briar Patch, an Irish pub that served a memorable Guinness.

For the proposed *Faces of Australia* albums, I decided to get an authoritative voice to do a linking commentary: commercial me envisaged the albums eventually being placed on schools' curricula. I also proposed, in each case, a companion songbook, with sheet music, historical notes and appropriate maps and pictures. I could see that Erik was going to be important, not only in providing charts for the recording sessions, but also in organising sheet music for the songbooks.

Who better, I thought, than Dame Mary Durack to be the authoritative voice for *The Overlanders*? The writer of *Kings in Grass Castles* now lived in Perth; she and her sister Elizabeth had lived among tribal Aboriginals and managed one of their famous family's cattle stations in the Kimberley. One of the Folk Federation members, Jeff Corfield, knew Mary well and introduced Nerys and me; it was the start of another wonderful friendship. I was thrilled to discover that Mary knew and liked some of my songs.

We had a lot of fun recording *The Overlanders*. As musos, we had the Mucky Duck members and Erik, plus the Upson brothers (Dave on double bass, Will on piano), three guitarists and an American girl, Louisa Myers, on violin. As singers, we had all of the above, plus many more and Nerys and me. A highlight was my song 'Further Out', featuring all singers and instrumentalists. Dame Mary did a beautiful job on the links to the songs; she even recited one of her own poems, 'Ben Hartigan', confirming my view that, if there was in existence a definitive song or poem relevant to the topic, I should seek to use it, to cover the requisite historical ground.

Before coming to Perth, I had written a song titled 'Matt Savage: Boss Drover'. I had known Matt for many years. He was married to a typical 'Drover's Boy' wife, a Mudbara woman named Ivy. They had three daughters and the family was a formidable droving team, often confusing the so-called experts by using horses and camels together. Matt and Ivy often 'swam the rivers' to prevent the police from taking their mixed-race daughters away from them.

> He's a legend in the outback, he's a man among men,
> Matt Savage the Boss Drover and he's riding again.
> Two thousand store bullocks, wild ones at that,
> That's the mob that he's taking into Queensland.
> Matt Savage the Boss Drover, he'll take a mob over,
> Taking the bullocks to Queensland. Ah ha!
> Matt Savage the Boss Drover, he'll take a mob over,
> Taking the bullocks to Queensland!
>
> 'Matt Savage: Boss Drover' (1981)

The Mucky Duck lads did a great job with the song, and I'm thrilled that it has become a regular for sessions at folk festivals throughout Australia.

I had also been recommended to include a poem named 'A Drover's Life'. I read the poem and considered it very appropriate. I was told that it had been written by a famous WA cattle drover named Wally Dowling, and I credited it accordingly. We got a popular old chap named Bert Vickers to recite the poem; Bert was a good choice, and it is indeed a terrific poem, with its repetitive, cynical line:

171

Oh yes, the drover's life has pleasures
That the townsfolk never know.

It also had wonderful laconic lines such as:

When you eat the babbler's brownie
It's best to shut your eyes
For it's hard to tell the difference
Between the currants and the flies.

After all the so-called 'pleasures' are listed, there's a punchline:

The drover's life has pleasures
That you wouldn't want to know.

Two years later, I discovered that the poem had, in fact, been written by Bruce Simpson. I met Bruce, apologised and sorted out the royalty issue. Typically, Bruce was not offended that another person had laid claim to his original works; I came to realise that many of his wonderful poems had been similarly appropriated by various people. A good outcome was that, in later years, Bruce very willingly gave me permission to put a tune to some of his poems. He thinks I'm smart, but it is he who has written bush poems that match those of Paterson, Lawson and Ogilvy; in fact, because he was a famous and very accomplished cattle drover, Simmo brings an authenticity to his work that nobody else, to my knowledge, can match.

You may rub your head on my coat, Old Chap
As you stand by the gate in pain

I'll loosen the knot in this greenhide strap

You won't need to wear it again

Nudge my hand, as you've done so oft

In the days that are now far away

For we'll never again be together on watch

Round the mob at the break of day.

'Goodbye Old Chap', Bruce Simpson (1950)

Eventually, I recorded two more tracks for *The Overlanders* album—'The Goanna Drover' and 'King Paraway'—with the Bushwackers in Melbourne. The Bushwackers had a terrific line-up—as they always have, over 40 years.

Artwork for the cover was by Robert Wettenhall.

The results of *The Overlanders* speak for themselves. I was eternally grateful to Peter Forrest for the directions in which he had led me; Peter agreed to write the text for the songbook. The album and book sell well to this day, just on 40 years later.

22

THE UK, TAMWORTH AND LAGU 2

In 1982, Nerys came to live permanently in Alice Springs. We went to the United Kingdom late that year, and stayed there over Christmas and New Year. I met Nerys's mum in Wales; we got on famously.

'What do I call you?' I asked. 'Mrs Evans?' I knew that her friends called her Sallie.

'Well, nobody ever calls me by my real name, which is Sarah.'

'Is it okay if I call you Sarah?'

'I think it's an excellent idea.'

Sarah was a fascinating woman. She had been a teacher all her adult life and was now retired, but she remained very busy, giving lectures on Welsh history, Welsh heraldry and Pre-Raphaelite art. She lived at Barry, near Cardiff, but was immensely proud that she had been born within the walls of Caernarfon Castle, in North Wales.

Sarah and Nerys sang beautifully together. Later, during visits to Australia, Sarah liked to say: 'This is my daughter, Nerys. She is Welsh. I am *very* Welsh.' We were there again in Barry for her 80th birthday, in 1988, so we had some presents made for her, inscribed '*Sarah am byth*', which translates as 'Sarah forever'.

For my 80th birthday gift to Sarah, Nerys had taught me the Welsh national anthem, '*Hen Wlad Fy Nhadau*'. I sang the song, assisted by the wonderful four-part harmonies of the friends who spontaneously joined in. Sarah and the many others at her birthday party kindly said I had done a 'good job'. Ten years later, in 1998, for her 90th, I learned '*Ar Lan y Môr*'; for her 100th birthday in 2008, I sang '*Ar Hyd y Nos*'. She lived to 102. Every morning, to this day, Nerys and I say: '*Bore da, Sallie fach*' (Gooday, dear Sallie).

I loved Wales from my first visit, and still do. Especially in North Wales, where their language and culture are so strong, the Welsh are adamant that their language was spoken and written centuries before English developed. It seems to me that, additionally, most of them speak English better than the English.

Speaking of the English, Nerys and I were in a pub in London one day and a very drunk Pommie bloke took exception to my Australian accent. He said, surlily, 'Why don't you go home to all the other convicts?'

I contented myself with the smart retort: 'What was the cricket score today?' Australia was giving the Poms heaps. But Nerys stood up, took on a statuesque pose and said: 'I was in this land before Boadicea!' That shut him up.

After my first visit to the United Kingdom with Nerys, we left Wales and the bitter winter weather and returned to Australia in time for scorching hot Tamworth at the end of January 1983. I was still unfamiliar with the big country-music festival, but everybody made us welcome and I was given a few concert spots at various pubs and clubs. I met up, again, with Terry Gordon and John Williamson, who had both hired venues at The Workers Club. Nerys and I were invited to ride in one of the floats in the parade; when Nerys almost fainted in the heat, John Minson kindly came to her aid. Lovely chap, John.

We attended the Golden Guitar awards, where my song 'The Drover's Boy' was a finalist; I did not win, and that was the start of a long and somewhat interesting connection with the awards. To the present date, I have been a finalist nineteen times at Tamworth with my songs, but have never won a Golden Guitar for Best Song. I subsequently won a Golden Guitar for Best Video for 'The Drover's Boy' many years later. And, in 2014, I was given another one as a Life Achievement Award, so I can't complain too much.

I actually *own* a third Golden Guitar. John Williamson did a cover version of 'The Drover's Boy' in 1990, and he won the Golden Guitar for Best Heritage Song! At the awards, JW announced, 'This should really go to Ted,' and he proceeded, the next day, to present it to me at The Longyard. Thanks, mate— let's share the honour.

Nerys and I returned to Alice, where, as well as doing my shows, I began to organise a festival, in four months' time, in Broome, Western Australia. Yes—Broome! To say I was apprehensive is to diminish the reality.

It happened like this. On a previous visit to Broome, in 1982, I had been approached by the local council to organise a second festival for the town, to celebrate the town's centenary the following year.

I was aware that in August 1983 they would have their annual Shinju Matsuri Festival—the Festival of the Pearl. As the name implies, there is a focus, in Broome, on the Japanese involvement in the pearling industry. I decided, for a second theme, to approach the Malay community, as there has been an equally strong participation by Malay workers over the 100 years of recall. There is a strong Malay influence in the very cosmopolitan population of Broome to the present day.

I asked for a Malay name that would equal 'lots of music', and the unanimous choice was *lagu lagu*, which they wrote as 'Lagu 2'. So we decided to set May 1983 for the first Lagu 2 Festival. Six months previously, I had given the local council the details of my requirements: venue, ticket sales, transport, catering, stage, sound, lighting, three-phase power, etc. While I was holidaying in Wales over Christmas, because I had never had any response to this request, I sent Broome Council a long—and very expensive—telegram from Wales, listing again my requirements and asking for a progress report. I received this telegraphic response the next day: 'TED EGAN ST OSYTH COURT BARRY SOUTH GLAMORGAN UK NO PROBS SJ'.

No probs? When I returned to Australia, I rang Broome and went through my list yet again, item by item. There had been a general decision that the festival could be 'at the racecourse', but that was it. No probs? No action, more like it!

So in February 1983 I set to—on the phone from Alice Springs. Nerys and I knew that we could anticipate support from the strong Folk Federation in Perth, so we dealt directly with FF committee members Ann Fitton and Eleanor Carney, and the word went around there. *Happy to come*, said a couple of hundred people. I also knew there was a strong interest in a visit to 'exotic' Broome among Alice Springs people, especially the folkies. I tipped that there would be Broome people keen to visit Perth—and, better still, Alice—to see the local scenery, so I did an accommodation deal with the newly opened Alice Springs Casino. A flutter on the gambling tables was likely to pull punters, I thought. I intended to charter aircraft to make all this travel possible—a monumental task.

First up, I asked Elizabeth Durack if she would be the patron of Lagu 2. The famous artist was delighted at the prospect of visiting her 'home country'—Broome—and readily accepted. That gave us a big-name endorsement.

Following our recording of *The Overlanders*, Nerys and I had forged a lovely friendship with Mary Durack and her sister Elizabeth and we often lunched together in Perth. They delighted in sharing bush experiences and their wonderful overview of Western Australia was unsurpassed. They once drove overland to Alice Springs, where we were able to return the hospitality.

On that occasion, Elizabeth attended one of my shows at Alice Springs. I knew she was in the audience that night, and I knew she would understand 'The Drover's Boy', which she hadn't heard. But as I sang it, I looked down and saw she was crying. After the show, I said to her: 'Sorry, I didn't mean to upset you with my song.'

'Ted, you didn't upset me at all,' she said. 'On the contrary, I was thinking of Stockman Biddy, a wonderful Aboriginal woman who worked for us at Argyle. She always presented as a male—stockwhip, trousers, shirt, hat, smoked a pipe. She is a treasured memory.'

I immediately asked Elizabeth to paint Stockman Biddy for me. I will enjoy the lovely painting forever; Stockman Biddy became the face on the cover of my album *The Aboriginals*.

For the weekend of Lagu 2, I booked out all the motels in Broome. I asked a Perth company to drive their truck to Broome, delivering stage, top-quality sound, lights, plus the technicians and engineers required for the concerts. And then, the masterstroke. I approached Ansett Airlines to see if we could hire a jet to be placed at our disposal for the weekend. They agreed and we began to organise how to fill the aeroplane to best effect. Ansett allocated us a Fokker Friendship.

We took bookings from people in the three towns. We finished up doing Perth–Broome–Alice Springs–Broome–Perth–Broome–Alice Springs–Broome, on both the forward and return legs. All in all, we transported over 500 people, giving them cheap return flights to their various very acceptable venues. Nerys and I went on the first flight from Alice to Broome with our treasured assistant organiser, Ursula Balfour. As I expected, the Broome locals had done nothing additional, but we had covered the ground so we didn't need them. Although they had made the racecourse available, they had made no effort to clean the showers and toilets there, so we had to sort that out as well. Theirs was a strange attitude, but you get that on the big contracts.

Elizabeth Durack was in her element. She was such a gracious woman, and she was accompanied by her charming daughter, Perpetua. They both knew Broome inside out. Very soon after they arrived, Elizabeth wryly commented: 'The city fathers are noteworthy by their absence?' I heartily agreed. But the audience was thrilled to have such a celebrity among us, and Elizabeth and Perpetua settled in for what turned out to be a terrific festival. All the arrangements, which we had orchestrated from Alice, worked out well.

We had budgeted soundly; there was enough money to pay appropriate fees to three bands, Mucky Duck, Bungarra and Bloodwood, plus leading artists such as Eric Bogle, Bernard Carney and Margret RoadKnight. So we had concerts all day and into the early evening, then we finished up with bush dancing at a level that Broome had never seen before—or since.

An ironic twist occurred on the Saturday night. I had hired a car and was driving Margret RoadKnight from her motel to the racecourse, which is a couple of miles out of town. Oh, no! A police siren. *Pull over, driver.*

I stopped the car and this quite dumb policeman said: 'Do you know you were doing 70 in a 60-kilometre zone?'

'Sorry, mate,' I responded, 'but I hope you'll let it pass. I'm taking Ms RoadKnight to the festival. She's due to sing in about twenty minutes.'

'I'll have to charge you under Section 17 of the *Traffic Act*, sub-section (iii).'

He pulled out his infringement book and took at least ten minutes filling out the form, with questions such as: 'Ted? How do you spell that?'

He finally concluded, tore out the notice, gave it to me and warned me: 'Watch your speed. You're in Broome now.' I noticed that I was up for a $50 fine.

I got Margret to the festival, a bit late, but she went on stage quickly and did her normal wonderful set.

The bush dancing then started, and I repaired to the bar to have a drink with my mate Eric Bogle, who had also given us a lovely concert earlier. We were on our second schooner when along comes the policeman! I had already told Eric about the traffic offence and we had shared a laugh.

'Excuse me, sir,' says the policeman, 'but when I filled out your infringement form I forgot to put a sheet of carbon paper in the book. I gave you the original, but I don't have a copy, so I'll have to go through the procedure again.'

I thought Eric would explode, he laughed so loudly. He was even more amused when I politely complied, saying: 'Ted—now, that's T . . . E . . . D . . .' I thought I'd really give Eric something to remember, so I spelled out every word: 'Alice . . . now, that's A for alpha, L for Lima, I for item . . .'

I certainly didn't pay the fine, and I don't recall getting any further correspondence about it. I'd better be careful here, for if there's no statute of limitations I might be up for hundreds of dollars. But maybe the officer just forgot to press the charges?

Apart from my traffic offence, there were only a few minor hitches with the entire festival. Everybody who attended has the fondest of memories—but they only ever had *one* Lagu 2 festival in Broome.

23

GREENHOUSE AND THE SHEARERS

Two down—*The Urapunga Frog* and *The Overlanders*—in my proposed *Faces of Australia* series. The total recording and manufacture of stock for *The Overlanders* had cost around $50,000. I had limited money, although my shows at the Stuart Arms were still popular.

I was thrilled when Sally Milner, the boss of Greenhouse Publishers, agreed to do a companion songbook for each of the *Faces of Australia* albums. Sally had had tremendous success with the Bushwackers' songbooks and their dance book; these had become de rigueur possessions of anybody seeking out bush ballads and appropriate dance routines. Sally had a super staff, headed by the highly intellectual, incredibly perceptive Sue McKinnon and business manager Peter Steer, who also soared to cantorial heights as a chorus singer on *The Shearers*; Nerys dubbed him 'the Pavarotti of Bridge Road' (their offices were on Richmond's main road).

Sally assigned Marg Bowman as my editor. Marg and I shared a great relationship around the books; Nerys and I are still great friends with her. In fact, we subsequently enticed Marg to live in Alice Springs for many years, where she did superb work promoting traditional First Australian art.

Recording was ever so expensive in those days, pre-computers. You had to hire the big studio, with the huge multi-track desk, plus the engineer. We always engaged the best available musicians and singers, and paid them handsomely. After working with Herbie Marks, I made sure there was always plenty of food and drink available. We were very fortunate with our sound engineers.

We recorded three albums in quick succession between 1984 and 1987—*The Shearers*, *The Anzacs* and *The Aboriginals*. I had been working on the many new songs for those albums in the ten years since Barry Forrester's initial suggestion. Erik Kowarski was amazing, quick with the various arrangements, and I also enlisted the skills of Michael Harris when we did most of *The Shearers* with the Bushwackers in Melbourne. As Dobe Newton constantly reminds audiences at their concerts, 'The Bushies are deeply into sheep!'

Everybody in Australia relates to shearing in terms of cultural heritage. Many folk singers to this day regard the wool industry as the specific background to the political events that shaped our nation. The establishment of trade unions, the camaraderie of the shearing sheds, the attitudes to 'cooks, cuckoos and wilful murderers', the social rift between the squattocracy and the working class, the strikes of the 1890s, the establishment of the Australian Labor Party, the Wide Comb dispute—all of these are grist to the mill for historians, songwriters and singers. People who have never touched a sheep earnestly sing about 'tallies' and 'squatters'—and if the rouseabout doesn't respond at speed when they call for tar, the consequences don't bear thinking about.

> In the bar at Lazy Harry's mate
> They shore sheep big as whales
> And the bar was two foot deep in dags
> As the crutchers told their tales . . .

'Jackie Howe' (1980)

All of which is why, for many years, I had dodged shearing themes in my quest to write songs. I was inspired by people who lived *beyond* the shearing sheds, *past* the black stump. I had elected to sit down in the country that was further out. I was used to dealing with people contemptuous of sheep cockies and sheep generally.

> There's a place where I misspent my youth,
> Darwin is its name;
> The old town's getting bigger now,
> But the life is still the same.
> There's plenty of time for meeting
> Your mates around the town,

With the famous Darwin greeting:

'Do you reckon you could keep one down?'

'She's on Again in Darwin' (1972)

I hasten to add that I did not feel superior to the people closer to civilisation. Hadn't I been born to working-class parents in suburban Melbourne? Hadn't my mum's brothers been shearers? So I need to acknowledge here a truth that I constantly assert: I am *not* a great bushman in any respect. In fact, I don't stand up well to scrutiny in any assessment of talent or skill in outdoor activity. I'm better than average, but that's it. It's interesting to check out my life. There are no great feats of personal endeavour, in physical or mental achievement. If anything, though, I am an acute observer of people who *do* have talent that I admire. Be careful of Ted—he might write a song about you.

Getting back to *The Shearers*, my original attitude was: 'I'm not going to sing all those shearing songs that the coffee-shop folk singers bellow out. My songs are about frontier people such as Roger Jose, Granny Lum Loy, Matt Savage and The Man from Humpty Doo.' As Tom Burrows would say: 'Forget the coffee: get out the rum bottle.'

One of my albums is titled *Beyond the Black Stump.* No sheep out there.

But I knew that if I was to cover the *Faces of Australia* comprehensively and impressively, I must do *The Shearers*. Who better to do it with than the Bushwackers?

The problem was that the Bushies had already recorded every classic shearing song at definitively high quality. Or had they?

They had done the Australian equivalents of the traditional Welsh songs '*Bachgen Bach o Dincer*' and '*Twll Bach y Clo*', which, when adapted in Australia, became 'Lachlan Tigers' and 'Click Go the Shears'. The melody for 'Ryebuck Shearer' is Welsh also, but the lyrics are very Australian. It is a great song.

Reedy River was an Australian cultural and folk milestone, the first musical of consequence based in an Australian setting. It, too, centred around the wool industry. One of the great fair dinkum Aussie songs, 'The Ballad of 1891'—based on the strikes of the 1890s—was the highlight of *Reedy River*. I knew I must include that one, so I asked Doreen Bridges, who had originally set Helen Palmer's words to music, and she gave me permission to record my interpretation. She was most gracious.

But nobody in Australia had written a song about legendary shearer Jackie Howe. I did so. Nobody had considered the wives and families left behind as the shearers left for the big Queensland runs. I composed 'My Man's a Shearer' for Nerys to record, and she did it beautifully. I love writing women's songs in the first person:

And when he returns
I shall ride out to meet him
My pony will prance
As I leap off to greet him
I'll hold him and kiss him
We will be laughing
Winter will turn into spring.

'My Man's a Shearer' (1982)

Nobody had yet tackled the immense rivalry between Western Australian shearers and the 'wise men from the east'—the Australian Workers' Union. We had a lot of fun putting down 'It's Different in WA'.

In all of my research I was assisted by old mates Artie and Carol Byrnes. Artie was a shearing contractor, and Carol used to accompany him on the long tours into outback New South Wales and Queensland, filling the immensely difficult role of 'The Babbler'—which is to say, the babbling brook, or cook. Wow, what a job that is!

The shearers' cook is up before daylight, seven days a week, usually having to cook on inferior wood stoves in kitchens with minimal facilities, often not even having running water on tap. There may not even be electricity. The cook has to prepare three wholesome meals a day, plus morning and afternoon tea—always called *smoko*—then clean up after all of the above. In the big sheds, there can be up to 50 workers. The jokes in the shearing game are mostly centred on the cook and her/his drinking habits—not that I'd blame shearers' cooks for getting on the grog.

> The cook complains, he never stops
> Deserves the flak he always cops
> It's mutton stew and it's mutton chops
> Tea that's made from mutton slops
> The bastard's always on the hops
> As we shear the Golden Fleece.
>
> 'Shearers of the Golden Fleece' (1981)

Artie Byrnes was always patient with me. He took me to a couple of the old-time sheds, with stands for 40 shearers. He discussed the role of everybody connected with that incredible task of shearing, say, 30,000 sheep in a single shed. I decided to write a song covering all those roles: 'The Shearers of the Golden Fleece'. I mention the shearers, the rousies, the classers, the pressers, the squatters, the 'sweat extractors' (the contractors)— and not forgetting the women back home:

We are the women in the shearers' lives
The shearers of the Golden Fleece
Girlfriends, sweethearts, lovers, wives
Shearers of the Golden Fleece
As lovers we are never lax
We're deductions on their income tax
We are the ones who strengthen the backs
Of the shearers of the Golden Fleece.

'Shearers of the Golden Fleece' (1981)

Speaking of women in the shearers' lives, Nerys made her mark during *The Shearers*. She was recording the song 'The Rouseabout':

Oh I am just the rouseabout
They reckon I'm a dag
I'm eight stone, fly blown
A shearer's punching bag . . .

'The Rouseabout' (1983)

Unbeknown to us, she had slipped on her tap-dancing shoes. At the end of the chorus, she hopped up on a table and did a lovely little tap sequence. We kept the tape rolling and it's there on the CD. Ginger Rogers, eat your heart out!

I am ever so proud of my song 'The Union Way', which in three minutes gives a fairly precise appraisal of the struggle between the squatters and the shearers, where this nation almost saw civil war. Fortunately, sanity prevailed.

In 1991, at the centenary of the establishment of the Australian Labor Party at Barcaldine, Queensland, Hazel Hawke and I led the Trade Union Choir as we sang 'The Union Way' outside the Globe Hotel at midnight.

Hazel, what a gal! She had put Bob to bed a couple of hours earlier—'He can't stand the pace,' she told us—but she was just starting to hit her straps. She had played 'The Ballad of 1891' beautifully on the old piano in Pat Ogden's pub earlier that evening, and we had lustily joined in the final lines of that mighty song.

For the 'authoritative voice' for *The Shearers*, who better than Brian Morrison, the gun shearer from Euroa, who in 1972 established yet another world record? There are, of course, many claims to 'world's best' tallies, often created under very different circumstances, but I would argue that Brian's best effort is still the most astounding day's work of sheep shearing that has ever been achieved.

Brian Morrison shore 410 fully grown wethers in eight hours, using the old Australian 'narrow comb' shears, under work conditions, which meant that the sheep had to be shorn cleanly. That means he averaged about a minute per sheep; his fastest was 43 seconds! He shed quite a few kilograms on the day, but the interesting outcome was that he couldn't piss for three days afterwards, so there were obviously medical outcomes following such extreme physical output.

I couldn't help reflecting on the sheer speed that Brian had attained. Forty-three seconds to shear a sheep! When I had a go, I had to tie my half-shorn sheep up and finish shearing it after smoko. I wanted to demonstrate Brian's speed in one of my songs, but in a novel way. I asked Artie Byrnes to shear a sheep methodically for me, explaining the sequential routine as he did so. I applied each movement of the shearer to one of the verses of my song 'Jackie Howe'.

In the time it takes to sing that verse, Brian Morrison could have shorn a fully grown wether! A delightful outcome is that Brian and Judy Morrison are lifelong friends. When I hosted *This Land Australia* for TV, my wardrobe was supplied by Morrisons of Euroa, the clothing store the two of them established. As a shearer, Brian asked Judy to design clothes to suit his particular requirements. The outcome was a highly successful outdoor clothing range for men and women.

There was a delightful and unexpected outcome to *The Shearers*. In Wales—that's Old South Wales—Nerys's mum, Sarah Bryn Evans—*Sallie fach*—was justifiably proud of her daughter's singing of 'My Man's a Shearer', particularly as we had employed the old practice of harp accompaniment by Huw Jones, a Welshman now resident in Australia. Sarah had the song played on BBC Wales many times; subsequently, it has been registered in the National Welsh Library Archive at Aberystwyth.

For my version of 'Lachlan Tigers' I wanted to create a unique sound, for I was conscious that the Bushwackers had done what is considered the definitive version. Although I had Michael Harris, Lou McManus, Stephen Cooney and Dobe Newton— all Bushwackers—playing various instruments for me as I sang the song, I also incorporated Rob Flynn on the didjeridu, to give it that driving force that is the thrust. I won't say my version is better than the Bushies', but it's as good!

We had a lot of laughs as we recorded *The Shearers*. Louis McManus was one of the greatest of guitarists; he also played mandolin and fiddle in his inimitable way. He and Nerys always liked to discuss 'the goss'. As they exchanged notes on the various scandals, drug-taking, who's up who and the general mayhem in music circles, Lou kept announcing: 'I'm going to deck that bastard' or 'If he doesn't watch out, I'm likely to deck him.' You had to know Lou to appreciate such threats: he was about four-foot-eleven in high-heeled boots, and weighed about six stone wringing wet. A strong fart would have blown him over. We respectfully called him 'Decker', though.

Lou died, much too young. His music will never be forgotten, nor will he. He used to growl at me: 'I know where you're coming from with your songs, Ted.' He played on ten of my albums. I often play one of my old tracks, just to remind myself of Decker's contributions.

24

ANZACS AND ABORIGINALS

Recording *The Anzacs* is still the most stimulating experience of my career in music. And the most challenging. I was aware of the immense level of knowledge held in families that had a connection with World War I, in New Zealand and Australia; I knew I must prepare meticulously.

My own family is a good example. My mother had three brothers who were Anzacs, members of the Light Horse. I painstakingly researched the Anzacs for around ten years, but my interest had developed years earlier, via Mum.

As a child, I certainly knew the war was on. World War II, that is! World War I was supposed to have been the war to end all wars, but the world had lost the plot somewhere. Certainly a madman named Hitler had gone astray, and he had a mate named Hirohito giving him a hand. Australia was in jeopardy.

I mentioned that we were quite a poor family when I was a kid. My parents were standard Depression victims. My mother was a typical housewife, caring for the home and our family. To augment Pop's income, she took in ironing from various families in our neighbourhood. She was invariably ironing when I arrived home from school at around 4 p.m., and she would give me my chores—chop the kindling, fill the woodbox, light the fire, peel the spuds, shell the peas, set the table for tea. Sometimes I'd cook.

Or else Mum and I reversed roles. Before she prepared tea, she would set me on the routine ironing—tablecloths, handkerchiefs, sheets (yes, sheets). I am a good ironer to this day, but I don't do sheets! At these times, we always had our chats.

One day, when I came home from school, Mum was ironing away, but crying her eyes out. I had never seen her weep previously.

'What's wrong, Ma?'

'Oh,' she responded, 'sorry, Teddy.' She wiped her eyes. 'It's Anzac Day and I always cry on Anzac Day.'

I think I was eight years old at the time, making it 1941. I knew that 25 April was Anzac Day and there was some connection to 'the war'—the old 1914–18 war, that is—but I had no detailed knowledge. During World War II, there wasn't any huge observance of Anzac Day. Our forces were too busy—at the front again, fighting Hitler and Hirohito.

So Mum sat me down and told me the story of the involvement of her family in World War I. I cried with her. Forty years later—by which time she was dead—I put her story, word for word, into my 'A Song for Grace'. It is perhaps *the* vital component of my album *The Anzacs*. I am pleased that it is often presented as 'an anti-war song'. Grace would have approved.

> And I, I'm just an old lady who watched them all go
> But I am the one you should ask about war, for I know
> That all of these years have gone by and I know the grief yet
> Yes, I will remember them, I can't forget.
>
> 'A Song for Grace' (1985)

As with all the other *Faces* albums, I had a lot of ground to cover, with new songs that I had to write. Nobody else had ever covered the ground.

I am particularly proud of my song 'De Profundis'. It tells the poignant story of the Army careers of the three Elder brothers. Eric, Ken and Colin Elder were all classically educated. In 1915, Ken had won the medals for Latin and Greek at The University of Sydney. They enlisted together and somehow contrived to fight together on the Western Front. On 20 October 1917, Colin, aged nineteen, was killed by a shell, right alongside brother Eric, who had to bury the young boy. Ken Elder, in a trench nearby, wrote his diary entry that night in Latin.

With my friend John Elder—who had told me the story—we searched the Elder family archives, but could not find the diary. I have always loved Latin, so I wrote 'De Profundis' as my tribute to three brave men.

Why is this, my brother, slain?

Gone to death on Flanders Plain?

Why will he not smile again?

Lord, hear my voice.

De profundis clamavi, ad te, Domine,

Domine, exaudi vocem meam.

'De Profundis' (1985)

Perth was the best option to record *The Anzacs*. I wanted a 'big brass band' feel for some of the songs. I also wanted a string section to accompany Nerys, who had agreed to record 'A Song for Grace'. So I needed Erik Kowarski more than ever!

Good old Erik! He had never worked with a brass band before, but he rose to the challenge superbly. Given his innate instinct for harmonies, he purchased the Boosey handbooks on brass band music and went to work. If nothing else, *The Anzacs* is a tribute to the musicianship of Erik Kowarski.

I knew that for every category we could bring in the best available musos and singers. Dave and Will Upson were both engaged again at Soundwest Studios. We approached players from the best Army and brass bands in Western Australia. Erik and his dad, Stan, who was principal violinist for the West Australian Symphony Orchestra, got together a fine group of strings. All of the best 'folkie' singers came along, so we had a good drink and a series of singing sessions that are typical of the better folk festivals.

To cover adequately the participation of New Zealand and Australia in the dreadful, unnecessary carnage of World War I, I sought permission from my old friends Eric Bogle and Judy

Small to use their versions of their iconic songs 'And the Band Played Waltzing Matilda' and 'Mothers, Daughters, Wives'. Alan Ralph gave permission to use his wonderful song 'Men of the Tenth Light Horse'. My album is suitably enhanced.

Amazingly, we had *The Anzacs* done and mixed in three days. My 'authoritative voice' was a wonderful old World War I veteran—an original Anzac from day one on the beach at Gallipoli. His name was Jack Nicholson, and he gave the album a powerful sense of authenticity; his recitation of 'The Ode' on the final 'Troopship Medley' is, in my judgement, the best version ever recorded. Jack's family is eternally grateful that we have immortalised him in this fashion.

I wouldn't change a note of *The Anzacs*.

* * *

We recorded *The Aboriginals* in Melbourne. By this time it was 1987 and I was a regular performer at the Tamworth Country Music Festival every January. After Tamworth that year, I did a few gigs organised by Terry Gordon, and in March attended the Port Fairy Folk Festival. After that we booked Sing Sing Studios, Richmond, and our favourite engineer, Chris Thompson.

I had come to know some top performers in Melbourne, during and after *The Shearers*, and particularly wanted to engage them, along with members of my own family—my dear sister Shirley (or Sal, as I always called her) and her daughters Elaine, Kris and Annie were all good singers. We also brought in Sal's son Des, who was a popular performer on Daryl Somers' show *Hey Hey It's Saturday*—he was the drummer who answered to the nickname 'Animal'. We call him 'Banjo', and he played drums on all the tracks of *The Aboriginals*. Three of my sister Peg's daughters—Anna, Janine and Liz—were living in Melbourne at that time, and they were all fine singers, too. It was a happy family reunion.

I was thrilled when Lowitja O'Donoghue agreed to serve as my 'authoritative voice' to link the songs on *The Aboriginals*. Who better? Lowitja and I had been friends for many years, through many different stages of Aboriginal struggle, she as a champion of her people, me as a white bloke who cared. She was born at Indulkana, in remote South Australia, but like so many First Australian children of mixed descent, she was raised in an institution in Adelaide. She graduated as a nurse and worked to a senior level in Adelaide, but always missed family life. At age 30 she was reintroduced to her mother. As Lowitja says in her links on the album: 'The government thought that taking us away from traditional life would be good for us, but we were the ones who most yearned for our Aboriginality.'

Once again, there was a need to write many new songs if I was to cover the ground. I am very proud of my song 'Albert Namatjira'. I met Albert many times; he had stayed at our house in Darwin in 1954, when he was getting ready to meet the new Queen.

When I was young I walked this land
With wise old men who said
When we change you to a man
If you don't share, you're dead.

'Albert Namatjira' (1987)

197

What a tragedy that Albert was convicted for *sharing* with his sons. In 1954, he had been granted 'citizenship of Australia' by default. The sad outcome was that, legally, he was, thereafter, different from the other members of his own family, who were still classified as 'wards' within the meaning of the *Welfare Act*: among other things, they were not allowed to drink alcohol. Albert was sentenced to the mandatory six months' imprisonment for 'supplying liquor to Aboriginals'. A further indignity occurred when he tried to buy a block of land in Alice Springs—Arranta land, his own traditional country. His application was rejected. He died in 1959, a very disillusioned man. He had lost interest in painting.

I created songs about Bennelong—'Bennelong, the White Sea Eagle'—and 'Truganini'. I also wrote, of sad necessity, 'Teach the Blacks a Lesson', to cover the massacres and the various euphemisms used to justify the various 'dispersals'. It was crucial to include my best-known songs with First Australian themes: 'Gurindji Blues' and 'Poor Fella My Country'.

I had been recognised by the Khungarakung people for my song 'Alyandabu', about a wonderful old tribal woman of that name. I met Alyandabu—who was:

Straight as a spear shaft, wide-brimmed hat
Tall and proud and black

—shortly after my arrival in Darwin as a teenager. She was a much-loved woman there, the matriarch of the well-known McGinness family, as a result of her very atypical marriage to an Irishman named Stephen McGinness. Despite the many tragedies surrounding her life, Alyandabu is very positively remembered to this day in Darwin.

> If you were white they'd call you a pioneer
>
> Name a suburb after you
>
> You're forgotten by the ones who took your land
>
> But those who knew you, knew your worth,
>
> Cherish private thoughts
>
> And memories strangers wouldn't understand.
>
> 'Alyandabu' (1986)

I am proud to be called *Namiuk Kwaruk* (Singing Elder) by her descendants. Ted Egan AO NK, lucky to be alive.

I flew Erik Kowarski across from Perth to Melbourne for the recording of *The Aboriginals*; he was as invaluable as ever, writing the charts for the musos, participating as a guitarist and fiddle player, as well as helping with the many chorus songs. I particularly needed Erik as musical director for an extremely difficult song, 'White Man', written by Peter Knight, a member of the internationally famous group Steeleye Span. What a song! Nerys and I had heard Steeleye Span perform it the previous year in Perth. We exchanged a look that said: 'That's a must for *The Aboriginals* album.' While in the United Kingdom over Christmas, we visited Peter in Brighton; he was very happy for us to cover his song and make a couple of minor amendments to the words.

Erik explained to me that Peter's song was unusual, having a 12/8 beat. I had no idea what Erik was talking about, but the other singers carried me with them as we recorded 'White Man'. It is indeed powerful.

I wanted my album to be me presenting a personal, musical, historical overview of this important aspect of Australian history—the history of the First Australians—but I knew of one song and one singer who was a *must* for inclusion. I had known Bobby Randall since he was a lad at the Croker Island mission. Like Lowitja, Bob—the child of a tribal woman and an unknown white man—had been separated from his family and reared in the well-intentioned but unrealistic environment of a 'Methodist Mission for Half-Caste Children'.

As an adult, Bob did what so many others did: he sought out his tribal relatives, only to discover that his mother had recently died. He wrote the poignant, searing song 'Brown Skin Baby'. I wanted to have Bob sing the song himself, but he was in the United States at the time. He kindly gave me permission to record it. I was supported by guitar accompaniment from my friend Paul Ah Chee Ngala, and singing with me, on the album, is Paulie's wonderful mum, Kanakiya, herself a child of the Stolen Generations. Kanakiya sang the chorus of Bob's song in Luritja.

Another song written by someone else was also very suitable for *The Aboriginals*. I had come to know Ernie Dingo very well; I knew he was a fine didjeridu player and guitarist, but also a sensitive singer/songwriter. A famous old First Australian from the Kimberley region, a man known as King Wally, had died recently and Ernie had written a splendid song about him.

Ernie also recorded one of my songs, 'Bullocky's Joy and Jesus'. Many years earlier I spent some time on a mission station where Aboriginal people were issued food rations each week, augmented by a tin of golden syrup (popularly known as 'bullocky's joy') if they produced tokens to prove that they had attended church each day. A variation on 'rice Christians'.

> Bullocky's joy and Jesus, boy
> That's the only way to go
> Bullocky's joy and Jesus, boy
> The Bible tells me so.
>
> 'Bullocky's Joy and Jesus' (1982)

I had always been impressed by the great (and late, sadly) Hugh McDonald of Redgum. Hugh seemed the right person to produce 'The Hungry Fighter', a song I had taken years to write. I wanted to sing about the boxing tents that used to be a feature of every agricultural show in Australia. Hugh captured the spirit of the era beautifully.

'BOOMBOOM, BOOMBOOM' was the beat of the bass drum as the spruiker urged local pugs to 'step up and take a glove' against the boxing troupe's professional team. So many Aboriginal fighters had started—and finished—their careers in the tents of Jimmy Sharman, Roy Bell and, in recent years, Fred Brophy.

'The Hungry Fighter' tells of Ron Richards, a very talented Aboriginal boxer from Roma, Queensland, at one time the middleweight, light heavyweight and heavyweight champion of the British Empire. Typically badly managed, and fighting far too many times, Ron finished up a shuffling, punch-drunk wreck, looking for food scraps around the Sydney markets. I shook his hand there one day. 'Thank you, son,' he said, when he realised I had slipped him ten dollars. I shed genuine tears whenever I sing my song. What sadness. Nonetheless, I think it is one of my best five songs.

> He shuffled through the Sydney market
> Puffed-up face, no shoes upon his feet
> Checked out all the rubbish bins
> Then a kind old lady gave him a bite to eat
> He'd been bashed last night in Redfern Park
> By a gang of thugs, lurking in the dark
> One of these was heard to remark:
> 'That old boong was once a fighter, so they say
> That old boong was once a fighter so they say . . .'
> And the Hungry Fighter faces another day
> The Hungry Fighter faces another day . . .
>
> 'The Hungry Fighter' (1969)

Sadly, sales of *The Aboriginals* album have been mediocre. I still think that my album, and especially the companion songbook, provide a fair summation of the unfair deal that has been given to our First Australians in all walks of life. Perhaps one day we will establish the means whereby they have real sovereignty over some land and manage their own affairs in their own way. The sooner, the better.

25

THE CONVICTS

The Convicts was the next, and last, *Faces of Australia* album. I had at that point done six albums (if you count *The Urapunga Frog*, which I do) and four companion songbooks. I wrote the manuscript for *The Convicts* songbook, and the sheet music was to be included. It's filed away somewhere, but I can't see the songbook happening. Perhaps . . . ?

For the 'authoritative voice' to provide the links between the songs on *The Convicts*, I was fortunate in that two members of the 'First Fleeters'—descendants of the people who travelled to Australia in 1788 as guards or convicts—were working with me on the album. Judy Small, one of the most revered songwriters of Folk Australia, was there, along with Dobe Newton, chair of the Country Music Association of Australia (CMAA), who was our producer. Ironically, Her Honour—Judge Judy Small—holds an important position as a judge in the Federal Circuit Court. Rightly so. It is good to have such mates, descendants of convicts!

I felt I had to begin *The Convicts* album with Peter Bellamy's song 'The Green Fields of England', as it's such a comprehensive listing of the men, women and children who were transported to Australia. I sought and was given permission to record the song.

It was great fun recording 'For the Terms of Their Natural Lives', one of my tongue-twister songs. These songs regularly delight me, because very few people can sing them!

> They're awful, they're vicious, they're excrementitious
> They're scum and a damn they're not worth . . .
>
> 'For the Terms of Their Natural Lives' (1985)

Our magnificent pianist, Robyn Payne, gave us stimulating accompaniment. Send them away!

Judy Small recorded a beautiful new version of her celebrated convict song 'Mary Parker's Lament' for our album, and thereby enabled me to concentrate from the outset on women prisoners. For they suffered twice: they were penalised for their own sins (or misdemeanours or whatever), and they also had to endure sexual harassment, exploitation and the predatory behaviour of most males at every level. Nonetheless, we had a ton of fun recording my 'A Bunch of Damned Whores' with four magnificent women: Margret RoadKnight, Margot Moir, Geraldine Doyle and Nerys Evans.

We're a bunch of damned whores

We never wear drawers

They say we're the cause of dissension

But none of your fuss

Before you judge us

There's a few things that we'd like to mention.

'A Bunch of Damned Whores' (1985)

Nerys did an emotional rendition of my 'Mary: The Girl from Botany Bay', about Mary Broad (sometimes called by her married name, Mary Bryant), who helped her husband organise an amazing escape from Sydney Cove in 1791. Steve Housden from the Little River Band did some deadly guitar work.

Sail, across the dark and stormy ocean

To a destiny unknown and far away

Sail, across the seas to freedom

I'm Mary, the girl from Botany Bay.

'Mary: The Girl from Botany Bay' (1985)

The big mystery, of course, is the ultimate fate of Mary Bryant. She got back to England, was once again incarcerated at Newgate Prison, and then was pardoned—indeed, she was granted a stipend—after 'the kindly Mr Boswell' defended her. Mary certainly returned to her native Cornwall, still a young woman in her thirties, but the many efforts to trace her have been fruitless. The challenge is there.

I found myself compelled to write two songs after visiting the paradoxical Norfolk Island and researching its history. Norfolk is truly, in physical terms, as close to paradise as one can imagine. And yet the atrocities that took place there, in its second period as a penal colony, the 1830s, are unparalleled. Men and women were flogged to the point where the flesh was removed from their backs. To counter the brutality, it is alleged that convicts formed suicide pacts, whereby one agreed to kill a comrade in order to have the opportunity for repentance prior to hanging. It is hard to believe that such policies and practices were deliberately implemented by the authorities, on the one hand, and their prisoners accordingly.

My song 'Ne Plus Ultra' covers the monstrous era created by the inaptly named Governor Darling, and it's certainly the most gruesome song I have written. It was enhanced by the cello playing and the countertenor singing of John Napier, a very talented muso indeed. Sadly, I don't know of a single occasion when the song has had airplay. Maybe I should write something called 'I Lerve You, Darling?' (Gervernor Darling, that is.)

Nerys and I sat at midnight just outside the Norfolk Island cemetery, on the unhallowed ground that is known as Murderers' Mound, where the instigators of the mutiny of 1834 were buried after they were slaughtered. I had a specific participant, 21-year-old Dominic McCoy, on my mind at the time, and subsequently wrote 'No Tombstone for McCoy'.

Strangely, there were no ghosts at the cemetery. In fact, being there at midnight was a peaceful experience. And yet the next morning, when we walked through the crumbled gateway of the pentagon that was once the Norfolk Island cell blocks, Nerys burst into tears.

I wanted to include two established songs, 'Moreton Bay' and 'Jim Jones at Botany Bay', both standard convict fare. I planned to ask Dobe Newton to sing 'Jim Jones' aggressively—it is often sung mournfully and thereby insipidly—and I planned to sing 'Moreton Bay' on my own. Nerys suggested swapping the roles to produce the unexpected, so we did just that. Dobe combined with Joe Camilleri of the Black Sorrows and there has never been a version of 'Moreton Bay' to match it. I am very pleased with the version of 'Jim Jones' that I put together. I really wanted to make those chains rattle.

We rounded off the album with 'The Convict Stain' and 'Think of Me', then a final chorus of 'The Green Fields of England'. A lovely experience.

The Convicts has been a slow seller, but I think it might get up one day. I played the album for Barbara Tiernan, the director of the Araluen Theatre in Alice at the time. Barb has died since, but she was a fine woman, of vast theatrical background. She listened intently, and as the last notes of 'Adieu to Old England' faded away she said, 'You have the makings of a great opera there, Ted.'

I hope she's right. In recent years I have tried to create a musical titled *Balls and Chains* around *The Convicts* songs. It's a bit hard to get people enthused about new musicals. There are too many failures, and even one rehearsal costs a lot in money and time. Watch this space.

There are divided opinions about the cover painting I chose for *The Convicts*. During the recording, we were introduced, by Jonah Jones, to the well-known painter Caroline Williams. Jonah was connected to the Moët et Chandon Art Awards, which Caroline had won a couple of years before. She asked if she could attend our recording session, and particularly loved the song 'A Bunch of Damned Whores', especially after I had explained how a group of convict women called the Flash Mob used to bare their bums if clergymen or prison officials bored them. That's where the term *flashing* originated.

Caroline rang me a few weeks later to say she had painted the Flash Mob, based on the Three Graces—the mythical Greek goddesses Charm, Beauty and Creativity, beloved by sculptors. But Caroline's trio were the Harlot, the Whore and the Virago. I bought the painting from her and put it on the album cover, but not everybody approves of my choice.

26

MARREE: INSPIRATION FOR SONGS

There's something about the little town of Marree—in the middle of vast South Australia, 700 kilometres north of Adelaide—that keeps pulling me back there. It's certainly not a pretty place, but its rich heritage is still very apparent, both in the region itself and in the history books. Things such as the ongoing presence of Muslims who introduced camels to Australia, all the ongoing hazards of the Birdsville Track, and the internationally acclaimed film *The Back of Beyond*, which covered the journeys of mailman Tom Kruse. To get to Marree, to this day, you can bet you will encounter interesting roads; it's located where the kilometres end and the miles start!

It was originally named Marree, thought to approximate the Diyari word for 'possum'. Located near the town are important mineral springs, which were named Hergott Springs by John McDouall Stuart after Joseph Hergott, his botanist, who was shown the crucial source of water by the kindly local Aboriginals. So the little town also became known as Hergott Springs. During World War I, however, many South Australian towns had their German-sounding names changed, so the town and the railway station reverted to Marree.

Marree is on the junction of the Oodnadatta and Birdsville tracks, travelled by cattle and sheep drovers and latterly, by tourism operators. It also became a base for the cameleers who came to Australia with their wonderful beasts of burden in the 1840s. They were generally referred to as Afghans, shortened to Ghans, although most of them came from Baluchistan. They built the first mosque in Australia at Marree. When the Central Australian Railway line came through Marree in 1883, originally just from Port Augusta to Oodnadatta, it somewhat displaced the cameleers, and so the new train was called *The Ghan*.

This narrow-gauge rail link was extended to Alice Springs in the 1920s, but in the early 1950s the southern section was changed over to standard gauge, to enable the carriage of brown coal from Leigh Creek to Port Augusta, and passengers were forced to change trains at Marree. It was an ordeal, I can tell you, carting small kids and lugging old-fashioned suitcases from one long train to another, both on the single set of rails. We copped the hardships, for there was no greater experience than travelling on the 'old *Ghan*'. We played cards, drank to excess and sang our songs as we were served by the incomparable crew.

On three or four occasions since those days, I have driven to Marree and booked in at the Great Northern Hotel to spend time there writing songs. It works for me. It's a good place for thinking and drinking and I have rounded off a few albums there over the years. As a bonus, I have recorded four songs about Marree itself; more importantly, I have spent time in a place that just abounds with outback heritage.

On my first visit, I was on the lookout for a traditional 'Ghan' song, and I got it. Mind you, I had to pay $10 to get my worst-ever haircut; in exchange, the barber, Ali Khan, taught me 'Khala Khala'—he was 'short of a quid', as he put it. I reckon I got value for money, although everybody said I looked like Joe Frazier when Ali had finished with me. That's Ali Khan, not Muhammad Ali!

Khala khala
Di zanggi, zanggi
Zalpan droya
Oh oh oh oh
Takla shundra, shundra
Di zanggi, zanggi
Zalpan droya
Oh oh oh oh.

'Khala Khala', traditional, arr. Ali Khan

Ali Khan had 'no idea' what the song was about, but told me: 'The old Ghans used to sit at night, on the ground in a ring, outside the mosque and sing that song.'

Herbie Marks heard me sing it for the *My Australia* album. 'I know a little bit of Arabic, Ted,' he said, 'and *khala khala* means "my bride, my bride".'

211

Can't you see the cameleers, sitting in the dust, under the Australian stars, yearning for their homeland? They had been brought to Australia in the time of the White Australia policy, and were tolerated for their skills, but never allowed to bring their womenfolk to this land.

On another trip to Marree, I was having a beer in the bar and a little Cockney fellow sidled up to me.

'Wotcher, cock!' he greeted me.

'Why, is somebody pinching them?'

He was thrilled that I knew the standard response. I couldn't remember who had taught me. One of Sheila's rellies, I think. He did tell me his name, but sadly I can't recall that either.

He went on: 'I'm a Ten Quid Pom. Only been in Australia for three months.'

'So what are you doing in Marree?'

'I'm selling Hoadley's Violet Crumble bars.'

'I'll bet you're making a killing.'

'I am, as a matter of fact! But the barman tells me you're Ted Egan, the songwriter. What sort of songs do you write?'

'Well, if you want the scenario for the ultimate Ted Egan song, the little fellow takes on the big fellow and has an unexpected victory. And it would be good if there's a laugh in the final line.'

'Oh,' he mused, 'a bit like Marsupial Joe?'

You sense it, don't you? I caught the barman's eye. 'Geoff! Two schooners please, mate.'

I handed my Old Cock Sparrow a beer, and he took an appreciative sip.

'Tell me about Marsupial Joe,' I said.

He told me the story.

'Don't you move!' I responded. 'Geoff, give this joker as much beer as he likes. Ted's shout. I'll be back.' I raced upstairs to my room, switched on my cassette recorder and sang the new song, 'Marsupial Joe'.

Twenty minutes later—back to the bar. But he was gone.

'Where did the little Pommy bloke go, Geoff?'

'No idea, Ted. A couple of fellows started talking soccer with him and they went to some party.'

I never saw him again. If there's anybody out there who fits the description, a cheeky ex-Pom who reckons he was once a Hoadley's salesman at Marree, I owe him a modest royalty payment. There'll never be a better song than 'Marsupial Joe' to match the criteria: the little fellow has an unexpected win and there's a laugh in the final line.

My third Marree song has relevance for contemporary Australia. I changed the names for propriety's sake, but it is absolutely a true story; old-timers at Marree know exactly who the participants were. It is titled 'The Marree Line' and is based on the fact that, in the old days, the narrow-gauge railway went through the middle of Marree. The Afghans—so-called—lived to the east of the line; everybody else lived to the west.

Their parents had known one another for years
Got on very well, so it seems
Hamish McPherson had a big cattle station
Bijay Mahomet ran camel teams

213

But when their children grew up and professed their great love
The parents were shocked to the core
Miriam and Angus were both reprimanded
Strictly forbidden to meet any more
For the railway line runs through Marree
Star-crossed lovers are doomed to be
Forever denied their true destiny
By parents who know what is best.

'The Marree Line' (1988)

But the absolute best story surrounds my fourth Marree song. I had been staying in the pub for a week, finishing off an album. I'd got into the practice of going down to the bar around 9.30 a.m., before opening time. I'd have a coffee and a couple of slices of toast. If anybody interesting came in for a drink, I would join them in the bar; if not, I would disappear upstairs and work on my songs, usually well into the night. Sometimes I worked in the dining room.

On Monday morning, right on 10 a.m., opening time, in he came. He burst through the batwing doors, a tall, lean bushman with an air of authenticity to him. He chucked his hat and his 'cigarette swag' in the corner of the bar, sat on a barstool and pulled out his tin of tobacco, papers, matches and a hefty roll of notes.

'Rum and a beer chaser,' he snapped to the barman.

The barman tried to engage him in conversation, but he was having none of that.

'I didn't come here to talk, I'm here to drink,' he announced. Fair enough—the customer is always right. The barman stood back. I was watching intently from the far corner.

He stayed on that stool all day, then disappeared at about 6 p.m., taking his swag. I guessed he was camping out on the flat. But the next morning at 10 a.m., in he came. Same procedure. He drank rum and beer chasers all day, rolled cigarettes and puffed away contentedly. But not a word. I remembered the old bush maxim—*First one to talk loses*—as I watched him from the dining room. Leave him alone. Six p.m., he's gone.

Wednesday morning, same procedure. In he comes. Drink, smoke, look straight ahead. But he was to have company. An elderly Aboriginal couple came nervously into the bar. The husband escorted the wife to a corner table, where she sat demurely as he ordered two five-ounce beers. They clinked glasses and took an appreciative sip, probably reflecting on the fact that ten years previously they'd have been barred from the pub.

They were neatly dressed, the lady in a floral frock and wearing sandals and a white hat. The old Aboriginal chap's jet-black skin was gleaming—Johnson's Baby Oil—and he wore a spotless white shirt and pressed black trousers. I noted that he wore no socks, but was sporting a pair of those patent-leather shoes that ballroom dancers wear. Proper flash.

The man at the bar ignored them; he kept looking straight ahead.

But then in came a pair of local hoons. They'd already had something to spur their feeble spirits, but they ordered double rum and Cokes and announced that they were going to have a game of pool. I was still watching intently from the dining room. They set up the balls on the table and commenced their game. They weren't very good players, so they had cause for a lot of swearing and carrying on. The man at the bar took no notice. The Aboriginal couple watched them intently but said nothing.

After their third quick rum, the game continued, but then one of the hoons spotted that the old man was wearing dancing pumps.

'Hey,' he said to his mate, 'get a load of old Fred Astaire. We might get him to do a dance for us.'

That was okay, but when the old man did not respond to the attention, the hoon walked over to him, poked him hard on the chest with his billiard cue and said, 'Come on, Fred, let's have the rain dance.'

The old couple got to their feet and prepared to leave, but not before the man at the bar turned on the hoons: 'He'd fucking buy and sell you pair of bastards.'

The hoons left. The Aboriginal couple left. I thought: *It's time.*

I joined the man at the bar. 'How are you doing, mate?' I asked.

'Not too bad, Ted,' he responded.

So he knew me. He obviously knew something about the old Aboriginal bloke, too.

He opened up. 'Yeah, I know most of your songs, Ted.'

'Thanks,' I responded. 'Who was the old Aboriginal bloke?'

'Mate, that's Tommy Russell, the brumby shooter. Best bushman in this part of the country by a fucking mile.'

'Why didn't you say something to him?'

'Oh, I know him and he knows me—there's no need to talk.'

'But who are you?' I asked.

'I'm Lachie McKinnon—'

We spoke the next sentence together: 'The Last of the Pack-horse Bagmen!'

We laughed and shook hands. Ted's shout. 'Two rums with beer chasers, please, Geoff.'

Lachie McKinnon! This bloke was a real legend. But I had heard of him only in the Top End.

'What are you doing in Marree, Lachie?'

'I'm waiting to get a lift to Birdsville. I'm going up there to die.'

You don't often hear of packhorse bagmen these days. Up to the 1950s, there was a recognised group of people—mainly men, but a few women—who used to travel around the bush on horseback. They invariably rode quality horses—sometimes stolen—and led one or two packhorses. In their packbags they carried their tools of trade. You might meet a mechanic, a cook, a 'windmill expert', a fencer, a yard builder—as Lachie was. A very famous yard builder.

They would ride into a big station and announce that they had come for work. Their reputations preceded them, so they were always given employment, on their terms. They called nobody boss, but would work assiduously until they were ready to move on. Then they would front the manager, work out their financial entitlement, take a cheque and leave.

So what was Lachie McKinnon's reason for going to Birdsville to die?

When I have to carry pliers
To cut them fencing wires

The country's getting too civilised

So I'm giving the game away.

'The Last of the Packhorse Bagmen' (2006)

Lachie and I spent a noisy ten days together, then I waved him goodbye as he sat on the back of the Birdsville mail truck. My reward? The song 'The Last of the Packhorse Bagmen'.

Mind you, it often takes years for a song to find its way. That experience with Lachie occurred in the mid-1970s, and I thought no more about it. In 2006, I made a memorable trip up the Birdsville Track with Governor-General Michael Jeffery, organised by an old mate, Ian Doyle. I wrote the song as we planned that trip. We met the legendary whip-maker Monty Scobie, who also remembered Lachie McKinnon. We shared a few laughs about the Packhorse Bagman. I purchased one of the world-famous Scobie whips from Monty, who gave me a discount when I sang my brand-new song about Lachie for him.

Aftermath. Lachie did not die at Birdsville. He relented and returned to the Top End—where he belonged—and did die eventually. He is buried at Katherine. I found out subsequently that Lachie was the uncle of Colin Beer. Colin and Maggie Beer have been friends of ours for many years, and when we have our annual lunch in the Barossa I am invariably asked to sing my song.

27

SINKATINNY DOWNS

Between 1983 and 1989, Nerys and I lived in a mobile home on our five-acre block, fifteen kilometres from the Alice Springs post office. The first person to live on the block was Tom Burrows, 'The Gamekeeper' I told you about earlier. Tom graced us with his presence for the rest of his days. He said: 'This is the only real home a man's had.'

The mobile home was very comfortable, and while living there I was always busy researching and writing songs, and doing my show three nights a week from April to October. Nerys was always on the door at the shows and in charge of merchandise sales. During the days, we shared the task of handling my large mail-order sales. Then we travelled south each summer, attending various festivals, leaving The Gamekeeper in charge to 'repel all dole bludgers', as he succinctly put it.

From 1983, we also started to build our lovely home, which has come to be called Sinkatinny Downs (STD). I wonder why?

We started by erecting a big, modified shed frame, steel, with a high-pitched roof line that would give us seven-metre ceilings. The shed frame was 12 metres by 27 metres in area, and we planned to have a four-metre verandah right around, so it's a big house. We hired a crane and operator, put the shed frame up in two days; Ray Henry was in charge, organising my son Mark, a few of his mates and me. Ray showed us how to use 'podgie bars' when the hole and the bolt did not meet easily.

Nerys and I dug the first hole for the concrete footings. Then we constructed the cellar—an underground bar that became the centre of six years of merriment, enjoyed by the many paid workers and volunteers who helped us. For the next six years, building the house was a cashflow project—do a show, buy a door; do a show, hire the bobcat. Slowly we filled the various wall spaces with rammed earth, stone and stained glass.

There are hundreds of empty Foster's cans in the footings trenches: we usually drank two cartons at the end of each day, for there were often twenty workers around and building a house is thirsty business. I worked every day from 7 a.m. to 5 p.m., drank my share of the beer and then Nerys and I showered for the evening show, starting at 8 p.m.

The principal walls are made of rammed earth (*pisé*). We hired Tony Linn and his formwork; Tony is a tall, handsome Chinese chap who trades under the name The Great Wall Company. We dug a hole for the swimming pool and used that earth, fortified by 5 per cent cement, to ram into Tony's frames and make lovely thick walls that are thermally so good. My son Mark is a very talented bricklayer and stonemason and he and Tim Newland combined forces to build the beautiful huge fireplace that everybody admires; Mark also encased all the steel shed uprights with lovely clay bricks. Finally, he constructed a lovely subterranean (Coober Pedy–style) cave for his own dwelling at STD. Clever feller properly, my son!

We had great working bees on Sundays, to help us get the various wall sections rammed. These were fun days and we always had a keg of beer in the cellar. Nerys has photo albums of all the activities, our mates and their kids assisting. It's one of the terrific rituals at our house, to this day, to 'get out the photo albums'.

All our door and window frames are old jarrah railway sleepers, and we have a magnificent ten-seater dining table also made from jarrah sleepers; it was put together by a superb local craftsman named John Stroud. Anything that required a drawn plan was done by Nerys on graph paper. My role was all-round labourer; in my late fifties, I was never physically fitter— wheeling barrows of concrete does that for a chap. Our verandah is a welder's masterpiece, thanks to Billy Blyth. The roof fitter, Helmut Meier, pronounced our house 'the squarest in Alice'.

It is Australian colonial design at its best, huge bull-nosed verandah all around, the cellar (and bar) underneath, split roof-lines, and there is a 'separation'—with the kitchen, dining and living rooms on one side, a breezeway in the middle, and the bedrooms on the other side. Also involved was a genius named Robin Turner, who assisted his partner Cedar Prest—yes, the famous artist Cedar Prest—to install beautiful stained-glass sections designed by Nerys, as well as a window that Cedar created personally.

Robin Turner left his mark on our house forever. He was a giant of a man, so we called him Kurrkura, the local Aboriginal word for 'desert oak'. He looked just like a big tree. He wielded a chainsaw like a surgeon with a scalpel, and he would only use dead wood to make his incredible furniture.

The first thing visitors note in our living room is a huge ironwood tree, reaching the ceiling, slap bang in the middle of our dining area. That's Kurrkura for you! Come and visit us and try Kurrkura's chairs, hand-crafted from local ironwood; it's like sitting in the best saddle. You belong in them. Dear Kurrkura. He has left us, but such greatness must never be forgotten.

Nor will anyone forget our house-warming, in October 1989. We had 400 guests with us for ten days, many of them camped on the block in tents, swags, a couple of caravans. Others stayed in motels in town and came to us daily. Pam Holland did the catering as only she can. Three meals a day were served for all-comers, and we drank 48 kegs of beer and Guinness. There was nonstop music, singing and dancing each day, and a big concert on our floodlit stage every evening, with artists such as John Williamson and Pixie Jenkins, Margret RoadKnight, Robyn Payne, Bernard Carney, Bob Maza, Ernie Dingo, Gus Williams, Roger Montgomery, Phil Beck, Bloodwood, the Bushwackers and Eric Bogle.

Marrkilyi (Lizzie Ellis) one evening held 200 people spellbound for about an hour as she told ancient stories in her Yankunytjatjara language, using a sand tray and making intricate trackmarks with her fingers. The only non-Aboriginal word I heard in that entire, breathtaking performance was 'Hermannsburg'.

The Nuriootpa Brass Band came from South Australia. George Gund and Hal Cannon flew in from Nevada, United States. Dick and Pip Smith were there with their helicopter. Guests came from all over Australia and joined happy locals from Alice.

We had a major obstacle to overcome, as our opening co-incided with the notorious pilots' strike. We had engaged the Sydney Theatre Company to come to Alice to perform Louis Nowra's play *Capricornia*—based on Xavier Herbert's novel— for our actual opening night, 10 October 1989. But there were no airline services! Well, the artists came by bus, by train, by car; we organised a few charter flights—and we did it! Under the stars at Sinkatinny Downs. It was a breathtaking performance by all and sundry. People still talk about our 'ten-day opening'. It was so good that we had a repeat performance five years later, in 1994, and an even bigger group of friends attended.

* * *

Shortly after we moved into our lovely home in 1989, I had my master's degree to achieve.

Back in the early 1950s, as a cadet patrol officer, I had visited Umbakumba, Groote Eylandt, and met a famous man named Fred Gray, mentioned earlier. Fred was present in the 1930s, reporting a series of killings in the Caledon Bay/Woodah Island region of north-east Arnhem Land, which was fairly wild country at that time. Typical me, I had asked Fred many questions about those days. He was a delightful man, still very English, despite having lived in Australia since 1919. He was only too happy to show me his diaries and photographs and answer my queries.

In subsequent years, I was posted to various parts of Arnhem Land and had the opportunity to interview all the Aboriginals involved in the various incidents who were still alive. I researched the many issues for years, on and off. It was a series of events that subjected Australia to international censure. We were still under world scrutiny following the last police-organised massacre of First Australians, at Coniston in 1928. In 1932–3, after Aboriginals killed five Japanese, two derelict white men and a white police constable in Arnhem Land, there was apprehension when it was again proposed to 'teach the blacks a lesson'. Five Aboriginal men acknowledged that they had done the killings; they agreed to go to Darwin, but only for 'talks'—as they insisted they had the right to uphold their own law in their own country. They were promptly arrested.

The farce wound up in 1934, when a Yolngu man called Tuckiar—his correct name was Dhakiyarr Wirrpanda—was sentenced to death for the murder of Constable McColl. There was a subsequent appeal to the High Court by counsel for Tuckiar. He was eventually acquitted and released from Fannie Bay Gaol, but he was never seen again. There is speculation.

So I had done a power of research into these events and their ramifications, but I kept putting off finalising my project. *Next year, maybe*, I kept telling myself—for nigh on 40 years! In 1990 I thought: *I will never finish this. I am the best-informed person on these events, thanks to Fred and the many Yolngu I talked to. I am the only person ever to interview Djaparri, the wife of Tuckiar, the on-the-spot witness to three killings; not even Fred Gray talked to Djaparri, and she is now dead!*

I decided to apply to do a Master of Arts degree, writing a thesis covering these events. This meant I was required to bring my research to finality by a set date. So for the next six years, from 1990 to 1996, I had yet another project to keep me busy. I came home from my show each night, typed for two to three hours and then went to bed. Under the supervision of my great but tough mate Bill Gammage, a celebrated historian and author, I graduated with an MA from The University of Adelaide in 1996.

In June 2003, I was involved in a memorable event at the Supreme Court in Darwin. At the request of Tuckiar's relatives, the Chief Justice of Australia had invited the descendants of Constable McColl to meet the Wirrpanda family at a *wukidi* (peace-making) ceremony. There was spectacular dancing outside the building, and then the dancers came in, seemingly aggressively. They confronted the McColl family, spears were broken and the members of the two families embraced. Huge *yelmalandji* (six-metre posts, magnificently painted) were unveiled, and they remain in that spot to show the world that reconciliation is achievable, even under the most unlikely circumstances. To this day, members of the McColl family pay regular visits to Arnhem Land, and the descendants of Tuckiar often visit the McColls in Victoria.

I subsequently told the entire story in my book *Justice All Their Own*. As I write, in 2019, my book is being translated into Mandarin.

28

A BUSY BICENTENARY YEAR

The bicentenary of 1988 was observed by many Australians, celebrated by some, and pilloried by most First Australians. It was 200 years since the arrival of the British at Sydney Cove to found a penal colony.

It was a busy year for me. For one thing, I was asked to be a performer at the opening of the foolishly named Australian Stockman's Hall of Fame. A straight copy of the equally silly Cowboy Hall of Fame in Oklahoma, United States, our ASHOF was established at Longreach, Queensland, after hefty lobbying by Queensland National Party members. Ever since, they have needed to defend their dedication: 'It's not just to honour stockmen, it's about shearers, drovers, bush people, even women!'

Why they didn't simply call it the Pioneers' Heritage Centre is beyond me.

I had been involved in the various fundraising activities around Australia, so I was made an Inaugural Life Member. I don't mind admitting that it's good to have that fact on my CV. Nerys and I were invited to attend the opening, which was performed by Queen Elizabeth II, with my old mate (by now) Dame Mary Durack.

The launch was impressive: the Queen and Dame Mary obviously hit it off! After the speeches and the official opening, Eric Bogle and I were scheduled to do an interview together on national TV, airing our views about the outback. The props on the interview table were pannikins and a single 40-ounce bottle of OP rum. To our dismay, Eric and I watched the interviewees preceding us—Dame Mary, 'Smoky' Dawson and Reg (R.M.) Williams—as they reminisced about their long connections to the bush. They all settled in nicely, taking hearty swigs of rum as the interviewer kept topping up their pannikins. They knocked off the entire bottle in about fifteen minutes! Eric and I were given pannikins of water when it was our turn. We compensated later.

During the celebrations at Longreach, I met a chap named Hal Cannon, a tall, rangy American who ran the Elko Cowboy Poetry Gathering in Nevada, United States. He wore one of those stovepipe hats, making him seem about ten feet tall. Hal is fascinating: he knows more Banjo Paterson poetry than most Australians, and he was keen to establish links between the United States and Australia. He had come to Longreach with the express intention of looking for Australian poets, to promote interaction between Elko and Longreach, a cultural exchange between the American West and the Australian Outback.

The year 1988 also saw the launch of the TV series *This Land Australia*, with me as the host. I was invited to Sydney by a chap named John Mabey of Sorena Productions. John had seen me in the David Roberts film *A Drop of Rough Ted*, and was impressed. He did a few screen tests with me, submitted them to Channel Ten and we were away. The plan was to make thirteen one-hour documentaries, and a decision was quickly taken to use my song 'This Land Australia' as the theme and title of the series.

> Try to understand, this land Australia
> Take her as she is, her moods, her mysteries
> Mother of us all, beneath the Southern Cross
> In a frame of peaceful seas.
>
> 'This Land Australia' (1988)

It was a lucky break for me. John and Rhonda Mabey were most enlightened filmmakers. They had long-term vision. They were scrupulously honest. They were generous with staff. They paid us well and never stinted. If a helicopter shot was needed, we did it. They took the wise decision to record the series on film, rather than tape, so the footage from *This Land Australia* is still in very good condition, and of considerable historical interest. It is interesting that the DVD of one episode, 'Railways of Yesteryear', sold as many copies as all the others put together. People are intrigued by trains.

Rhonda and John employed top-level researchers, who meticulously plotted the thirteen episodes. They always sent the director to the different venues to do a trial run. Cameraman Gary Maunder and sound engineer Ralph Steele became great mates of mine. I introduced Gary to Morris dancing!

The episodes were titled 'The Snowy Mountains', 'Central Australia', 'Beyond Mt Surprise', 'Broome and the Pearl Coast', 'Discovering a Rain Forest', 'Gulf Country', 'Norfolk Island', 'Railways of Yesteryear', 'Hahndorf and the Valleys of Hope', 'Murray River Paddleboats', 'Islands of Torres Strait', 'Mysterious Australia' and 'Cape York Peninsula'.

What a thrill to get such a job, and to be handsomely paid for it. The major attribute required is patience. Directors and camera operators work from first to last light, and they expect the 'talent' to be able to 'do it again' even when you've done it perfectly ten times already.

What journeys we had! Places such as Norfolk Island, Broome, Port Douglas, the Snowy Mountains and the Barossa, staying in the best accommodation, meeting fascinating people, always in the knowledge that what we were doing was truly archival.

We were very good for Channel Ten, whose overall ratings at this time were otherwise abysmal. Each time *This Land Australia* went to air, Ten's ratings would go from 4 to 28 immediately, and then drop down to 15 at the end of our show.

Sadly, though, after being told by supposed experts that the attention span of Australian viewers was three minutes, Channel Ten axed our show. Pity—we could have gone on for another two years, in my opinion.

For a short time I was employed, again by Sorena Productions, on *The Great Outdoors*, catering for that three-minute attention span, but ultimately they phased me out in favour of better-looking talent such as Ernie Dingo. I was almost 60, and getting older and uglier by the minute, so I can't complain. Over to you, Ern.

29

THE LONGYARD: A NEW
TAMWORTH PERSPECTIVE

As I've told you, my first visit to Tamworth was in 1981. I must admit that I was not too impressed by the big country-music festival at the outset. It wasn't that it was too Yankified, because in many respects that was not the case. It just didn't turn me on. For quite a while, I couldn't work out why.

It was certainly commercial and, to this day, I love the patrons, who, by and large, are hardworking people who come to Tamworth during their summer holidays from work, determined to spend a good quid and enjoy their music.

My attitude started to change, slowly, after 1985. A couple of years earlier, I had met a redoubtable woman named June Mary Smyth at my show in Alice Springs; June, Nerys and I hit it off famously from day one. June told us she ran a pub in Sydney, the

Croydon Park Hotel and arranged for me to do a show there in the summer of 1984. That went well and June told me that her hubby, Donny Smyth, was related to people who were about to open a pub in Tamworth, which she and Don would manage. Was I interested in a connection there for festival time? My oath!

They decided to call the new pub The Longyard. That was a good start. Kelly Dixon had written his wonderful song 'Leave Him in the Longyard' and everybody was doing cover versions. The grand opening of The Longyard was to be St Patrick's Day, 1985. Nerys and I were invited and I was to cut the ribbon.

They were a great team, June and Don. Don managed the bars and the money, June organised the food and the staff rosters; at festival time, she and I would work out the concert programs.

The money for the new pub came from Don's uncle, Jack Smyth, revered in pastoral circles as the biggest cattle dealer since Sidney Kidman. Jack and I got on famously from the outset; he always had a list of my songs that he wanted to hear at my concerts thereafter. The word around the cattle industry was that Jack Smyth often signed off on million-dollar transactions with a handshake, so skilled was he and so highly regarded.

From our first festival together, June and I decided to put on very Australian artists at The Longyard. We courted John Williamson, Graeme Connors, Eric Bogle and the Bushwackers (all of whom, like me, identified with both country and folk audiences, presenting the same songs to both). We formed friendships with new young artists—Luhrs & Crawford, Greg Champion, Brent Parlane, Jane Saunders and Beccy Cole. A certain club flavour developed, particularly at late-night sessions out the back of the Goonoo Goonoo Room. A new group, the Dead Ringer Band, was given its first-ever gig at Tamworth at The Longyard, as was Adam Brand, a promising young singer who had come across from Western Australia looking for recognition. The Ringers went on to thrive, particularly through the solo careers of Kasey Chambers, her dad, Bill, and her brother, Nash, who produces for Kasey and many other stars these days.

At the request of a local bush poet called John Philipson, one Saturday afternoon at the festival around 1986, Donny and June put on a keg of beer at their home to test the idea of bush poetry becoming a feature at Tamworth. What intuition! A few of us sat on the verandah and listened to John and other poets strutting their stuff, and agreed that a Poets' Breakfast might work at The Longyard. Did it ever! From that humble start, bush poetry is now as strong as bush music at Tamworth, and indeed throughout Australia. The poetry fans are up and ready to start their day at around 7 a.m., earlier if you like! The sales of merchandise have to be seen to be believed.

Nerys and I invariably lived in with the Smyths at their home, which is across the road from the pub. My role at The Longyard was principally that of MC, although I always wanted to do a few songs myself, as that is the best way to promote product. Tutored by Herbie Marks, I think I've shown most of the Tamworth artists how to sell merchandise. It won't sell itself—you have to apply certain techniques and tactics.

I always wear a trademark hat, so I am obvious at the merchandise table after I sing. On stage, I always identify point of sale—'Wave to me, Nerys!'—and I have samples on stage to refer to. And deals! 'Special price for you, madam . . . CDs, books, $25 for one, $40 for two, $50 for three. Of course I can sign them!'

To this day, one of the highlights of every Tamworth Festival at The Longyard is *The Chardonnay Show*, run by the Bushwackers. On the last Sunday, the Bushies and their many mates get into a memorable concert, inspired, from its inception, by Dobe Newton's capacity to down chardonnay. At the first concert, back in about 1988, Dobe enhanced every other artist's performance with accompaniment on his famous lagerphone; at the end of each act, he asked if there was anybody out there prepared to buy a drink of 'chardy' for a thirsty virtuoso. At the end of the day, Dobe's son, Dan, looked at his dad despondently and said to me: 'The bastard's off his face.' Such is life!

June and Don Smyth had two mighty sons, Angus and Liam. We have grown to be like family to them, over many wonderful years. Sadly, June and Donny are no longer with us, but they will never be forgotten: we reckon they are out there in The Longyard, so do not rush them. Dear mates, in the truest sense of the term.

It is a cliché, but country music is one big, happy family. It is rare to meet prima donnas. Over the years, Nerys and I have enjoyed the talents of all artists, from the most to the least famous and we have loved the friendships established with our mates Sandra and Frank, Annette and Gordon, Jody and Rock. Tamworth, by and large, is a hugely successful festival. I always pay tribute to the originators, Max Ellis, John Minson and Nick

Erby, supported in later years by stalwarts such as June Smyth and Lorraine Pfitzner, and by the development of the Country Music Association of Australia. The residents of the very fine city of Tamworth are also loyal and relaxed about the invasion each January.

The essential difference between Tamworth and all other festivals I go to is that performers don't have to be invited. You front up, you find a venue and you go for it. Break a leg!

30

THE FILM INDUSTRY

I wrote 'The Drover's Boy' song in 1981, and it was well received from day one. I did get one complaint, from a white bloke, the partner of a strident Aboriginal activist. He accused me of 'sanitising Australian history'. I wrote him a polite reply, asking how he came to the conclusion that an exposé like mine could be interpreted thus, unfavourably. He did not respond, but my reply obviously did not appease him, for he ventured on a course of vitriol in various quarters for the next ten years. Crucially, in this era of photocopying, he had my letterhead and my signature.

In 1985, I had a phone call from Melbourne, from a man named Peter Oysten. A mutual friend, Debbie Sonenberg, had played 'The Drover's Boy' for him. The song 'rang bells', he said and asked if I would mind if he initiated a film treatment.

'Go for your life,' was my response.

About three months later, Peter rang to say he was coming to Alice Springs on another project, but asked to see me about 'The Drover's Boy'. All okay. It seems that he had been given funding to allow him to have five professionals write 'some draft film scenes' around my song. Would I have a look at these? Sure.

I had never read such nonsense. None of them had the faintest idea where I was coming from. Some had quite distorted views of frontier history. I gave Peter my opinion and he was very disappointed. So I said to him: 'How much time do you have up here?'

'Why do you ask?' he replied.

'I'd like to take you to Wave Hill Station to meet some of the women on whom the song is based.'

I drove him, over three days, to Wave Hill. We found five old women who had been 'born in the cattle' and they opened up to Peter beautifully. His response was emphatic: 'There's only one person to write a "Drover's Boy" screenplay and that's you.'

We agreed that I would try my hand—he was aware of my play, *No Need for Two Blankets*, which had been successfully staged in Sydney in 1969, with Galarrwuy Yunupingu and Albert Barunga starring.

Peter returned to Melbourne. I began to write a few scenes and he edited these, but then he announced that he had accepted a theatrical posting in London, and off he went. I thought that would be the end of things and I heard no more from Peter for many years. So I concentrated on other projects.

In 1990, Nerys and I received an invitation to travel to the United States, to participate in the Cowboy Poetry Gathering at Elko, Nevada. The other Australians invited were Bruce Simpson, Marion Fitzgerald and Ranald Chandler, vice-president of the Australian Stockman's Hall of Fame. All expenses were to be paid by George Gund, who had attended our house-warming party in 1989 with the legendary singer/songwriter Hal Cannon.

It was a marvellous experience, meeting all those fine people from the American West, who were so proud of their heritage, which is similar to ours. We were thrilled when Bill Gunn joined our group. Bill, the son of Sir William Gunn, was in the United States doing some impressive money things; I wasn't sure of the details.

I will never forget the opening of the Poetry Gathering. The Elko Town Hall was packed with 2000 American 'cowboys'—even the women referred to themselves as 'cowboy poets'—plus five fascinated Australians. Out onto the stage came 'Waddy' Mitchell, the legendary American poet. He had a droopy moustache and looked highly impressive in his high boots, big hat and colourful clothing.

'Ladies and gentlemen, stand please for the national anthem.'

Everybody stood. The Americans all placed their hands on their hearts, and 2000 voices went straight into 'Home on the Range'.

Then they sang 'The Star-Spangled Banner'.

On Australia Day, the local Elko school band played 'Advance Australia Fair', standing out in the snow and applauded by several hundred Americans and five proud Aussies. It was different, to say the least. Australia Day is usually so hot in Oz. We Aussies were much impressed.

We had a magical time. The Yanks loved my songs and Bruce's and Marion's poems. Boss drover Bruce Simpson was at ease, swapping yarns with real, tough old counterparts, the actual American cowboys; although Bruce is notorious for correcting Australians whenever they use American terms such as *cowboy* for *stockman* and *corral* for *stockyard*, he was among people who were genuine users of those American terms, and he loved the experience. They loved Bruce, too. Bill Gunn knocked the Yanks sideways with his spirited rendition of 'The Man from Snowy River'; we established at that point that most Americans at the festival had watched the great Aussie film four or five times. They were also impressed by Bill's whip-cracking ability, especially his 'Sydney Flash'.

Ranald Chandler gave the Americans a few laughs when he upbraided them for not taking their hats off inside buildings. Honestly, we thought they must have slept in those hats!

Nerys did some lovely readings of Henry Lawson stories, and she recited my poem 'Bush Woman' beautifully. The Montana women in particular said: 'Hey, she's talking about us.' The Montanans had a lovely affinity with Nerys and Marion.

The American poets were impressive, as much for their sincerity as for the content of their poems. Most of them were either ranchers or lovers of ranch life. A ranch, of course, could in our terms be a 50-acre farm, but the traditions were as old as the West itself.

At the end of the week at Elko, we flew to Oklahoma City and appeared at the Cowboy Hall of Fame to appreciative audiences. Then to Los Angeles, to the Gene Autry Museum, where we met the famous African-American cowboy movie star 'Woody' Strode—an affable, impressive man if ever I met one.

I sang 'The Drover's Boy' at Gene Autry and again received a very strong ovation. At the end of my set, I was approached by a woman named Claudia Salot-Engel, whom we had met briefly at Elko. Claudia had been assigned to look after us in LA.

She was wide-eyed. 'Ted,' she said breathlessly, 'that "Drover's Boy" song of yours—wow! We haven't begun to write songs like that in respect of our history. I'm in the film game here in LA, and that song is the basis for a red-hot movie.' She went on to say that she and her friend—Steve McQueen's widow, Barbara McQueen—had heard me sing 'The Drover's Boy' at Elko and they both felt the story had film prospects.

I didn't say anything about Peter Oysten, but let Claudia keep talking. She, Nerys and I drank into the early hours of the next morning, and Claudia made me promise that first thing on return to Australia I would write what I thought would make a good film treatment for my song and send it to her.

I did more than that. When I got back to Alice Springs, I quickly—and I'm talking about a week—wrote what I thought was a screenplay, and posted it to Claudia. There's confidence for you!

Our phone rang at 3 a.m. Claudia had no knowledge of the time difference; Americans think that everything in the world runs to US time and conditions.

'Hello,' I mumbled into the phone.

'Hey, Ted, it's Claudia. I received your post, but a screenplay is nothing like that.'

'Oh?' was all I could muster as a response.

'I'll post you a sample of a real screenplay.'

Which she did. I could immediately see just how tight was the play she sent me, compared to my wordy 150-page effort.

I thought about films and screenplays quite a lot, but I had other things on the go. Around Christmas 1990, there was a knock on our Alice Springs door. A tall stranger had driven to us in a hire car.

'My name's Bert Deling,' he said. 'I'm a film writer and I'm off to Broome to do some research. I've heard some of your songs and I'd like to get your permission to perhaps use some of them in some filming.'

He was a pleasant chap and we invited him in. He had only vague ideas of what might eventuate on his journey, but apparently he liked the songs on *The Overlanders* album, especially the principal song, 'Further Out'.

> Further out, we're the Overlanders,
> Riding further out
> We're undeterred by fire, flood and drought
> As we take up each selection
> We've a constant predilection
> To head in the right direction
> Further out!

'Further Out' (1981)

We got talking about films generally; Bert and Nerys were very compatible, with vast shared knowledge of films, actors and directors. He said that he was 'mainly a writer and a teacher of writers'. He was just what we needed.

I queried that there seemed to be 'something of a formula' surrounding screenplays?

'Certainly is. Do you have a big table and some butcher's paper?'

'Certainly do.' We spread a roll of butcher's paper onto our big table and gave him a felt pen.

He began to run up and down the length of the table. Act One, Act Two, Act Three. Lines were drawn. Then he inserted various 'turnarounds'. 'That's the formula. You need 110 pages. A scene a minute. Anything bigger than that goes straight into the wastepaper basket. If you haven't introduced the main characters by page twelve, ditto. At the final turnaround, you rush to the finish.'

I protested: 'Surely *Gone With the Wind* is nothing like *Mutiny on the Bounty*?'

'Act One, Act Two, Act Three, turnarounds—they are twins at the screenplay level.'

He produced a work in progress of his own, a beautiful coverage of the romance between Henry Lawson and Mary Gilmore and the involvement of Jack Lang—about which I had nil knowledge—and we could see where he was coming from.

Particularly Nerys. She and Bert began quickly discussing various great films, and I could see that I was totally out of my depth. The thought began to develop that Nerys was the best person to tackle a 'Drover's Boy' screenplay.

Away went Bert to Broome, but two weeks later I rang him, back in Sydney. How would he like to spend a fortnight with us in Alice, tutoring Nerys? Love to. We struck a deal.

He joined us in Alice. It was very beneficial. Nerys got the hang of the formula, to the point where she and Bert would analytically watch a film on the TV.

'End of Act One . . . turnaround.' Their voices would sync.

During the fortnight, Bert mentioned the name Joan Sauers a few times. He said she was a tough American screen-play editor, formerly employed by Francis Ford Coppola, now working in Sydney. He said that Joan enjoyed her nickname: 'the Butcher'!

Nerys and I took the decision that we would try to put a feature film together, based on 'The Drover's Boy'.

We had no spare money, but I had a huge mail-order clientele, accumulated over many years. So we put together a compilation album of my songs, titled *The Drover's Boy: A Celebration of Australian Women*—a nice contradiction in terms. We sent out a letter of intent, asking people to buy this album for $30, with all funds to go to 'The Friends of the Drover's Boy'. Each buyer would get an album, plus a badge with our Black Cockatoo emblem. We formed a company called Yirandi Productions—*yirandi* being the Warlpiri name for the red-tailed black cockatoo, my totem from Yuendumu days.

Artwork for the album cover was done by our mate Robert Ingpen. Bob based his illustration on an old photo I found of a beautiful young First Australian woman. Her hair is adorned with red-tailed black cockatoo feathers. Bob's original painting still hangs in our dining room. Bob has bequeathed to me all of the artwork for a popular book, *The Drover's Boy*, that he and I subsequently co-wrote.

We sold around 1000 albums!

Not quite sure how to tackle the future, we concentrated on Nerys getting her script together. When she was on about her fourth draft, getting better each time, we convened a meeting in Sydney, to get advice on how to stage our campaign. We invited John and Rhonda Mabey, plus Joan Sauers—'the Butcher'—the American lady Bert Deling had mentioned.

Joan Sauers is a vivacious, hugely intelligent woman. On Bert's advice, we had sent the fourth draft to her. The Butcher said, 'I am happy to go on record with this statement: "*The Drover's Boy* is the best and most commercial script I have seen in the last ten years. It could potentially be Australia's *Dances with Wolves*, but better."'

Nobody had anything clever to say about funding, but I was always confident of my many supporters. About all that came out of the meeting was that a 'name director' would be crucial; Joan Sauers mentioned Peter Weir, Bruce Beresford, Fred Schepisi and Phillip Noyce.

Cocky Ted Egan said: 'I'll give *each* of them a ring.'

That was my first lesson in the film game. I could not get within a mile of any of the four famous directors.

The next thing that happened was I got a phone call from the Australian Film Commission. 'What's this we hear about you making a film? Who are you? What do you know about film-making? You can't just collect money from people and make a film! There is a standard procedure.'

I was told in no uncertain terms that I must align with one of the 'licensed companies' authorised by the commission to raise public money for filmmaking. Taxation concessions were available if the proper conditions were fulfilled.

'Please make me legal,' I said to the bombastic bureaucrat.

I was sent a list of about twenty licensed companies. Further learning processes, Ted.

'The boss is out of the country/at Cannes/wherever'—anywhere but at her/his desk. Always lavishly spending somebody else's money. Their minders were determined that this upstart on the phone would be put in his place. 'We are too important and too busy spending other people's money to be bothered with a bloke in Alice Springs that we've never heard of. He obviously has no money, or we would have heard of him—and then we *would* be talking to him—so what's the point?'

Except for one company. Yes, we are licensed. Yes, we are successful filmmakers. Yes, we'd love you to fly us to Alice Springs to talk to you. We need to make one point: we will not be investing any of our own funds, but we are licensed to issue a prospectus on your behalf.

We met one of them and happily signed up, appointing their company as manager, as required.

It all seemed good at the outset. They were impressed that we had already raised around $30,000 through album sales. They were mightily impressed when I financed the printing of the prospectus and thrilled to bits when $1.5 million came in from my mail-order list, almost overnight, in $500 investment slices.

Unfortunately, I was not made aware—because from then on I had no access to the 'confidential film fund'—that the first cheque written by the new manager was to himself—a commission of $150,000 for raising the funds!

The second cheque covered the cost of fares to London—and Thailand, would you believe?—for him and 'an adviser', plus top accommodation, expenses and gifts of flowers on a couple of occasions. I did hear of that trip and was unimpressed, but was told it was a normal procedure to set up 'eventual distribution' of the film.

That started a very sad process of dwindling away our funds, with no sign of a film. I financed a second prospectus. All up, around $2.5 million came in from my punters, all of whom were thrilled by the newsletters I kept sending them, outlining how I intended to do what I had taught Alby Mangels to do with *Australian Safari*—showcase the film myself, as I had done with *A Drop of Rough Ted* in the late 1970s, especially in remote regions. And we would all get rich from VHS and DVD sales, wouldn't we? Little did I know.

It would take me an entire book to list all the shortcomings of this 'licensed company', but eventually I took the decision to get rid of them.

31

THE INDEPENDENT FILMMAKER

It was Russell Crowe who prompted me to take the bold step of seeking to regain control of our project. Russell met Nerys and me one day in Sydney. He said his agent had introduced him to 'The Drover's Boy'; that prompted him to ride a bicycle across Sydney to declare to a well-known lawyer that 'This is the best bloody song I have ever heard'. The lawyer convened a meeting.

Russell told us that he was interested in directing the film and acting in the leading male role, but he wanted also to be involved in the production itself. He said he knew our production company, but was not prepared to work with them.

To everybody's amazement, I was successful in getting rid of our management company. I asked the manager for a list of investors, but was told that that information was confidential. I had a fair idea where 95 per cent of the investment had originated, so I sent out a circular to my mail-order database, asking those who had invested in *The Drover's Boy* film to sign a form supporting me. I had to get the backing of 80 per cent of the investors, covering 75 per cent of the total amount invested, in order to get control. I achieved better than that, on both scores.

I engaged a top solicitor who identified fraudulent activity, after inspecting our books. I presented that paper to the Australian Film Commission and the Australian Securities Commission (now ASIC), asking their opinion of their licensed agent, but was told: 'It's an internal matter—you sort it out!'

I took control, under the name Yirandi Productions, and we really got organised. First up, though, I was sued for defamation by the previous company. I won the case, on the basis that what I had said was true, but it cost me $180,000 of my own funds to get the positive outcome. I was awarded costs, but my solicitor told me not to waste my time or money seeking reimbursement. He said it would cost $15,000 just to initiate proceedings, and there was nil prospect of getting any money from the plaintiff. As it was, it took years for me to cover my own legal expenses.

To work. We built sets at Ooraminna Station, south of Alice Springs. It was my decision to do that on private property, to avoid vandalism, so we built a little town called The Junction, featuring a pub, several houses, a windmill and tank, stockyards. My son Mark built a stone police station and cell block and a terrific team led by Ian 'Kincaid' Doig built the very effective shells of buildings. They were built to last only three months, but they are still in constant use at Ooraminna twenty years later. Many films have been shot there; Jan and Billy Hayes, the owners of Ooraminna, were enthusiastic about having the film set erected on their property, and they used it to great effect for outdoor functions over many years. Jan and Bill built additional structures, compatible with the 1920s setting we had created.

Sadly for us, Russell Crowe was by now well on his way to fame in Hollywood and committed for the next several years, so we lost touch.

We appointed a director and engaged Ningali Lawford to play the role of The Drover's Boy, plus William McInnes to play Dan Williams, the drover. Chris Haywood wrote to say that he had read the script and demanded to be cast as the villainous Sergeant Ryan. My old mate Buddy Tyson was perfect for the role of the venomous police tracker, Croc.

Bob Marchant, a Sulman Prize winner, produced a magnificent set of twelve huge paintings, *The Drover's Boy Series*, all based on my song. Bob then combined with Nerys and me to produce a full-colour book, which featured his paintings, some excellent old photographs and a discerning commentary by Nerys.

We did some preliminary filming, to enable a trailer reel to be sent to potential investors. Through the Australian Securities Commission and the Australian Taxation Office, I outlaid $50,000 and issued a new prospectus. The money was coming in fast.

Then I received the letter. The Australian Securities Commission announced that they had discontinued all prospectuses and instituted a new system of fundraising called Managed

Investment. I was instructed to return all investments received after the date of implementation of the new system. I was instructed that if I sent a substantial personal deposit as a security guarantee and also indicated that I had $2 million worth of 'private assets', Yirandi would be registered as a Managed Investment Company.

I must acknowledge I was quite angry by this stage. I contacted ASC to say: (1) I did not have sizeable cash amounts available; (2) I certainly did not have $2 million worth of certifiable assets; but (3) I was working to a recently issued legal document that the ASC authorised, a prospectus that had cost me $50,000.

I was told in no uncertain terms that they had the power to 'close me down' if I did not comply. The word 'prison' was used.

Our certified aim at all times had been to secure $11 million as our budget. We knew, from dealings with all parties, that the first question asked in the film game is: 'Do you have *all* the money in hand? If so, let's talk; if not, let's talk when *all* the money is in hand.' A portion of the budget, however impressive, was not enough.

One way out of our predicament was to secure the total budget quickly and make the film. There was no chance of getting major funding in Australia—I tried every known prospect and I had at all times been given bad advice and nil money by the various government funding agencies. It was suggested to me that there were overseas companies that might put up big money; I tried one of these in London, but they were crooks.

Next I tried a chap in Spain. He, too, was an English crook, living on what the Brits call 'the Costa del Crime'. I thought he might be a crook with money, so we skirted around one another for a few months, and finally I went to Spain for a meeting. The first time I saw him, he met me at Gibraltar in a Rolls-Royce! It was interesting to see how he operated. Smoothness itself. He used to go to North Africa a lot. At this first meeting he was normal, a tall, handsome bloke. The next time I saw him, he was driving a battered little Hillman. He was pale, drawn and his entire right arm was gone! He said a cement truck had collided with his Roller, but I suspect he may have run foul of some drug-dealing investors.

So, sadly, we were closed down. But not before the final blow was delivered by the ASC. Over the phone I was advised that the audit of our books had been conducted satisfactorily. Then the official said to me: 'Egan, I need to know the completion date for the film.'

Egan. Not *Mr Egan*.

'How do you mean?'

'The film you promised in the prospectus.'

'But you have cancelled prospectuses, so I was unable to raise the budget.'

'You must still finalise your commitment. The prospectus is still a legal document.' He gave me a date three months ahead. 'Egan, you are to submit the film *The Drover's Boy* to us by that date.' He hung up.

Wow! There was still about $80,000 left in the bank. I asked two filmmakers I knew, Craig Mathewson and Jean-Pierre Mignon, for their advice. They came back to tell me that for $150,000 they could hire some actors and create a documentary-type film; it would tell of a young First Australian woman hearing of her grandmother's story and it would outline how she would go about making a film called *The Drover's Boy* one day when she had the funds to do so. They said they could use some of the excellent footage we had done for the investment trailer.

I mortgaged our home for an additional $70,000, and Craig and Jean-Pierre did what they had promised. They made a commendable film under the circumstances, but it was nothing like the $11-million feature film I had aimed for.

The 'substitute' film was submitted to the ASC and the ATO. Both bodies indicated that I had, thereby, honoured my obligation to investors, who could now claim their investment as a taxation deduction.

Marketing experts viewed the 'substitute' film and agreed that it had no commercial value. THE END.

We had used all the remaining, but sadly depleted, invested money on sets, costumes and preliminary filming. Yirandi is still a legal company, but there won't be a *Drover's Boy* film on my watch. It will happen one day, as the story is still a vital part of the real Australian heritage.

Oh, I forgot! The man who accused me of 'sanitising Australian history'.

I was a member of the first Council for Aboriginal Reconciliation. One day I chaired a meeting at Newcastle. I gave a long talk on reconciliation issues, and I noticed that a particular Aboriginal man in the audience was watching me intently. He came to me after the meeting and introduced himself.

'You don't sound anything like the bloke in the petition,' he said amiably.

'Oh, what petition is that?'

'The petition initiated by—' and here he named my adversary—'and sent to all Aboriginal groups, urging them to pressure the Film Finance Corporation and all other government film-funding bodies, to ensure that no funds were issued to Ted Egan for his *Drover's Boy* film.'

32

COUNCIL FOR ABORIGINAL RECONCILIATION

Although I was always busy, I was nonetheless honoured to receive an invitation in December 1991 to become a member of the first Council for Aboriginal Reconciliation. The federal Minister for Aboriginal Affairs, the admirable Robert Tickner, had fought hard to promote the idea of coming to terms with our past treatment of First Australians, principally by instituting positive programs that would be of national benefit. It was all a bit pie in the sky, but worthy in my opinion: I was reminded of my experience establishing St Mary's Football Club as a means of creating equality in all matters, based on respect accumulated through sport. *Give it a go*, I thought.

Robert Tickner had obviously submitted a list of names to all governments, federal, state and territory, for consideration.

It was equally obvious that he had sought to propose a 'level-headed' council. There were no strident activists among the proponents—fourteen First Australians and eleven other Australians. Each state and territory was represented; the Labor, Liberal and Democrat parties had members, plus the Australian Council of Trade Unions. Torres Strait Islanders were among the First Australians. The chair was Pat Dodson; the vice-chair, Sir Ronald Wilson.

Obviously, the proposed council members had to be given unanimous approval before they could be confirmed. I was one of three NT representatives, with Galarrwuy Yunupingu and Wenten Rubuntja. I probably passed muster with the NT Legislature as being 'apolitical' but known to have fairly extensive experience among First Australians. Some people assume, because of my connections and experience, that I must be a left-winger, and I have heard certain rednecks describe me as a 'coon lover'. I am, in fact, very conservative on many issues, and I invariably vote for the person or party I see as the best parliamentary representative.

The Council for Aboriginal Reconciliation first met in early 1992 in Canberra. It was all very formal and 'how do you do' until Pat Dodson suggested that we might each provide a 'portrait' of ourselves. Pat gave a brief rundown of his own impressive life. He next asked Archie Barton to address us. The time was around 4 p.m.

Archie put his elbows on the table, tucked both thumbs under his chin and began, ruminatively: 'Archie Barton, who in the hell are you?'

He looked straight ahead; the air was electric.

'They named you Barton—same name as the Prime Minister—after the railway siding on the Nullarbor Plain, not far from where your mother gave birth to you . . .'

I looked at the other faces in the room. I had never seen concentration to match it.

'Your father was a white man, so it wasn't long before the government took you away to Port Augusta to give you a new identity, to teach you to be a stockman when you were old enough to be put to work . . .'

Archie spoke, dispassionately but reflectively, for the next hour. The light in the room was fading, but nobody thought to switch on lights. He told us of so many experiences, some tough, some brutal, some joyful. I loved this passage:

'. . . and so I was sent to work on this station. We'd been lamb marking all day and it was time for tea. I went to follow the other workers into the dining room, but the boss stopped me: "You get your food out on the woodheap with the other niggers." I looked at him and said: "I just lost my appetite," and I walked off, ten miles to the nearest road, and thumbed a lift to town.'

Devastating stuff. We had heard a short history of Australia. The rest of us gave biogs of ourselves that, I am sure, were more thoughtful than usual; at 7 p.m. somebody suggested that we might have our evening meal, scheduled for an hour earlier.

Those present all felt that we had established a link for life, thanks to Archie Barton.

I was on the council for its first term of three years. I have mixed feelings about the experience. Certainly I have an ongoing admiration for all the members, but I felt we were preaching to the converted. I am something of a head-kicker in social issues. I remember once proposing that instead of holding our next meeting at a five-star hotel in a capital city, we should convene on the riverbank at Wilcannia.

I am a good friend of Dick Smith, and I had heard Dick suggest that if Aboriginals were the owners of things such as motels and service stations in 'problem' towns such as Moree, Wilcannia and Brewarrina, there would be better incentives for their kids to get educated and learn to run such commercial operations.

I suggested that the Reconciliation Council meet with the citizens of Wilcannia, identify commercially viable businesses that were currently run by people who did not like Aboriginals and suggest change. Not actually writing cheques, as the council was not empowered to make grants or distribute money, but to help set the wheels in motion to place the businesses under sound management, answerable to Aboriginal ownership. My suggestion went down like a fart in a lift. The next meeting was in Hobart, and I don't recall meeting a single Aboriginal person there, other than council members.

I became less enthusiastic about the Reconciliation Council when the High Court delivered the *Mabo* judgment, in which it was held that native title may survive the declaration of sovereignty by a colonial power. I expected a forthright stance, but our council did not think it wise to enthuse publicly over this decision. I wondered: *What in the hell* does *excite us?* I stood down from the council on those grounds, but acceded to a request by Pat Dodson and Wenten Rubuntja—they came to my

Nerys and I on the day we first met, at the Toodyay Music Festival in 1981.

Building our dream house, Sinkatinny Downs, Alice Springs, 1987.

Nerys and I in 2015, the year I turned 83.

Me with author Dame Mary Durack, who did the voiceover for *The Overlanders* album in 1982.

The one and only Erik Kowarski, musical director on many of my albums.

Erik Kowarski and Nerys (far right) oversee the string group performing 'Song for Grace' for my album *The Anzacs*.

Above: Louisa Myers Wise playing the violin for *The Overlanders*.

Left: Me in full song recording *The Overlanders* at Soundwest Studios in Perth. 1982.

Below left: Dave Upson (left), owner of Soundwest Studios, Nerys and me, at the sound desk.

Below right: Mucky Duck bush band member Roger Montgomery (right) with his no. 1 fan Phil Beck (left).

The artwork for the cover of my album *The Drover's Boy* was painted by Robert Ingpen.

Ningali Lawford was cast for lead role in my film *The Drover's Boy*.

A group of 'drovers' boys', photographed working on Alexandria Station, NT, in 1915.

Edna Zigenbine regularly drove cattle from NT to Queensland, a journey of around 2000 km. She and the other women on this page are truly outstanding pioneers.

The incomparable Atte Racconello was the inspiration for my song 'Sotto la Croce del Sud', 2015.

Granny Lum Loy was a well-known figure about Darwin in the early twentieth century, and subject of my song 'Granny' (1990).

Alyandabu (Lucy McGinness), matriarch of the McGinness family of Darwin and of the Khungarakung people.

The frame and the first rammed earth wall of Sinkatinny Downs, the home Nerys and I started building outside Alice Springs in 1983.

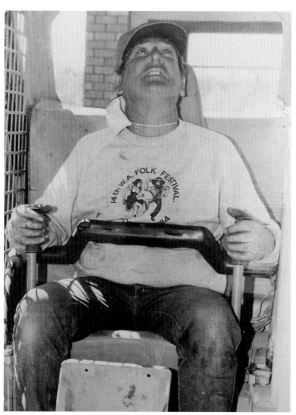

Working the bobcat to build the house was one of my tasks as 'all-round labourer'. I was the fittest I'd ever been.

The finished house was the product of six years of labour.

The interior of our house, constructed of rammed earth, stone and stained glass.

Our Aussie-shaped swimming pool, with spa in the shape of Tasmania.

Guests at our house-warming party
Cedar Prest (left) and Robin Turner
(right).

Also at the party, Geoff and
Tabby Mack.

Carmel Bogle, Geraldine Doyle,
Eric Bogle, and Sandra Dallen
(left to right).

Bessie Dingo (left) and Sallie Evans
cut the ribbon that kickstarted
the party.

Slim Dusty, Bill Hauritz, Mona
Byrnes, me, Geraldine Doyle and
Joy McKean (left to right).

Justine Saunders, Sallie Evans,
Lydia Miller (left to right).

Friends and family gathered on the first day of our house-warming party on 10 October 1989. The photo was taken from Dick Smith's helicopter.

The house-warming party was unforgettable: 400 guests, 10 days, 48 kegs of beer. Many guests camped on our property for the duration.

Delivering my 'Salute the Heroes' multimedia presentation at the National Library in Canberra, 2016.

WWI veteran Jack Nicholson, who landed at Gallipoli on 25 April 1915, lent the voice of authenticity as narrator for my album *The Anzacs*.

Above: Dhakiyarr Wirrpanda (Tuckiar) was involved in a series of murders and court cases in the 1930s. I researched these events for my book *Justice All Their Own*.

Right: I graduated with a Master's degree from The University of Adelaide in 1996, with my thesis (and book) 'Justice All Their Own'.

With Kris Kristoffersen, in Darwin, 2006.

Folk singer/songwriter Eric Bogle and I met on the festival circuit.

With Australian country music legend Smoky Dawson, in Tamworth, 1982.

John Williamson giving me his Golden Guitar award after covering my song 'The Drover's Boy' in 1990.

Me with 'special mate' Wayne Kraft ('Krafty') in 2017. He ran the Overlander Steakhouse for more than 30 years.

Margret RoadKnight performing on
my *Convicts* album as 'Molly Brown',
one of the 'Bunch of Damned Whores'.

Margot Moir, talented vocalist,
was 'Morag McDonald', another
'damned whore'.

Comedian and singer Geraldine
Doyle sang the role of 'damned
whore' Brigid O'Rourke.

Nerys Evans sang the part of
Megan Rhys on my album
The Convicts.

Above: Caroline Williams painted the artwork for my *Convicts* album, 'The Flash Mob' (1989).

Left: Dobe Newton, chair of the Country Music Association of Australia.

Judy Small, prolific folk singer, songwriter, and guitarist.

With June Smyth of the Country Music Association of Australia, in Tamworth, 2012.

Sheila and Peter Forrest, who shared their vast knowledge of Australian history with me.

Artist Narritjin Maymuru (left) and H.C. 'Nugget' Coombs. Coombs was the first head of the Council for Aboriginal Affairs, established as a result of the 1967 referendum.

Michael Harris (left) and Lou 'Decker' McManus, of the Bushwackers, playing for The Shearers album.

Me playing a variation of the Fosterphone, at the Top Half Folk Festival, Darwin.

Senator Pat Dodson, first Chair of the Reconciliation Council.

Ceremony to launch the *turtini* (Tiwi memorial poles) at Government House in Darwin, 2007 to mark its Indigenous connections.

Meeting with Prince Charles, on his visit to Alice Springs in 2006. A contingent from Hermannsburg (right) came to greet him.

Introducing the King and Queen of Sweden to the head ranger of Uluru National Park, 2006.

Nerys and I in
Government House,
our home for four years
from 2003–7 while I
was Administrator of
the Northern Territory.

My departure from Government House at the end of my term in October 2007
was marked with a parade.

house—to rejoin. I agreed, on the condition that we could meet Prime Minister Paul Keating to discuss 'Australia after *Mabo*'.

We subsequently had a quite cordial meeting with the PM. He said he understood that it was 'a very sensitive issue, not yet understood by most Australians'. He expressed his personal support for quick, symbolic recognition of traditional ownership, but indicated that there was bitter opposition to *Mabo* within his own caucus, not to mention 'across the floor' of the House. He said: 'I could go down over this issue.'

Probably the most interesting thing that happened during the Reconciliation Council was the dramatic change that occurred in Rick Farley. Australia had known him till then as a very articulate, obviously intelligent executive director of the National Farmers' Federation. He was connected to Ian McLachlan, known to be strongly opposed to the very notion of native title.

I recall that, at the first Reconciliation Council meeting, most of the other members were looking hard at Rick. I wondered: *What are you doing here?* I knew Rick's sister, Patti, from Darwin, so our meeting was cordial enough, but a few other councillors were not impressed at first.

Yet Rick turned out to be the most effective member of the council. He understood how government worked, he was adept at causing cynical people to 'give it a go', and he was extremely competent at drafting official submissions. He told us how he had helped Ian McLachlan improve his public image by becoming less forceful. I subsequently took notice of Ian's statements. Instead of saying: 'I am totally opposed to so and so . . .'

Ian would say: 'It saddens me to see such and such occurring', thereby getting his point across, but more amicably.

Further, we were all impressed at how popular Rick became among the First Australian councillors. He generously helped many of them with their local issues and personal matters.

Rick's accidental death at age 53 was most untimely. He had so much more to give to Australia. Fortunately, his beloved partner, the current federal Labor Member for Barton, Linda Burney, has set up the Rick Farley Scholarship for the educational benefit of bright young First Australians. May they also treasure his memory.

Under Minister Tickner, three major steps were taken to seek to correct the injustice to First Australians. The *Native Title Act* of 1993 introduced procedures for formal, legal recognition of traditional ownership. The Indigenous Land Corporation was set up to purchase land, if necessary, to enable traditional ownership to be restored; and the Aboriginal and Torres Strait Islander Commission (ATSIC) was set up as an elected body to cater to the specific needs of First Australians on a regional basis, in matters such as housing and employment.

The Howard government put paid to ATSIC in 2004, although it must be acknowledged that the task of the dismantlers was made easy by the thuggish behaviour of a couple of elected ATSIC members. By and large, though, on a national level, ATSIC did a commendable job during its existence.

I elected to stand down at the end of my three-year term, when it was necessary for half of the Council for Aboriginal Reconciliation to be replaced. I am not sure whether such bodies are effective. I guess the rednecks in Australia have been quietened down, in that they know they will be challenged if they go public, but the bastards are still out there, thinking their dark thoughts. Let's not kid ourselves: attitudes are nowhere near as positive as we are told by government.

Only the federal government has the power to create a better, more deserving status for First Australians, but it is hard to get politicians in Australia to see the big picture. They are too busy concentrating on winning the next election.

33

THE LAND DOWN UNDER

There were two reasons for winding up the *Faces of Australia* series after six of the projected ten titles. One, I had run out of spare money, and two, we had started to launch *The Drover's Boy* film project, which would absorb every available dollar for the next ten years.

Additionally, Greenhouse had been taken over by Penguin Books, so my connections to Marg Bowman and the team changed dramatically. I had lost a great supporter. It had been a good connection. Greenhouse did a great job putting the books together, but sales had been thwarted when they tried to have the series picked up by government education departments. A typical response had riled all of us. The Victorian Department of Education had knocked back *The Overlanders* because the album had 'that song' in it. They felt that 'Australian children should not be taught about white men associating with black women'.

However, the transfer to Penguin provided one stroke of luck for me. A week or so later, I had a phone call from one of the Penguin managers. 'Ted, I've checked our sales of your songbooks,' he said. 'They move surely, but very slowly, and we need space in our warehouse for quicker sellers. Are you interested in taking the stock from us?'

'Why not?' I replied. 'As long as you pay the freight costs to Alice. How many do you have in stock?'

'We've got 500 of each of the four titles. That's a total of 2000 books.'

The books retailed at $15.

'How about if I buy the lot from you at $1 each, and you pay the freight to Alice Springs?'

'You're a tough customer, Ted, but let's do it. We need the space. For $2000, we'll pay the freight.'

I posted the cheque.

A week later, I had a call from one of the big Melbourne bookshops. 'Ted, we're after your *Faces of Australia* books. We rang Penguin to get them, but they say you control them now. We like the series and I wonder if I can get 50 of each of the four books from you?'

My stock of books had not yet been freighted to me, although I had paid for them.

'Well, I have them in store in Melbourne. I can get 50 of each to you. As you know, they retail for $15 each, but I can let you have them for $10 each. I'll get them delivered to you.'

'Done! Many thanks.'

I rang Penguin and asked their warehouse to deliver 200 books to the bookshop. And I asked them to get the remainder forwarded to me as quickly as possible. Ho hum!

I still have stock on hand. They still retail for $15. As the man said, they move slowly but surely.

I have been able to rationalise somewhat my failure to complete the *Faces of Australia*, through a commendable project initiated by Colin and Susan Chapman. If ever there is an Aussiephile, it is Colin Chapman. He loves Australia to almost an embarrassing degree.

Colin and Sue suggested in 2002 that I write a book, a type of short history of Australia, using appropriate songs of mine as background to the various chapters. It followed the same approach as the *Faces*. I tried to model the book on Russel Ward's *The Australian Legend*.

The Chapmans were living in England at the time, but had made plans to migrate to Sydney. The idea was to publish the book and album both in the United Kingdom and Australia. They undertook to bear the costs involved, for which I was grateful. All I had to do was write the book and have the songs (all of which had already been recorded) placed in the proper sequence on two CDs. We combined our resources to get a set of photographs together. We were a good team.

The production came up well, especially the UK version. We titled it *The Land Down Under*. It gave me the opportunity to include chapters about explorers, immigrants and bushrangers, so I did eventually cover some of the ground that had been

missed in the original *Faces of Australia* series. My mate Bob
Marchant did the magnificent cover art.

We gave *TLDU* a good run, both in the United Kingdom
and at home. Nerys and I toured the United Kingdom fairly
extensively in 2003; we had a launch at Australia House, and
were interviewed at the various BBC Radio centres, such as
Cardiff, Newcastle and Northampton. The interviewers were
invariably ignorant of life in Australia, apart from asking fairly
gauche questions about the original penal colony. There was
no easy way out. Even at Northampton, where we located the
(neglected) grave of Caroline Chisholm, the great emancipist,
the creator of 'God's Police' in Australia—via her immigrant
girls—there was an abysmal ignorance of who she was, where
she had been and what she had done. I tried to get the locals
enthused about 'Caroline, your hero'—but no thanks. Minimal
UK sales reflected what we interpreted as a profound lack
of interest in Australia, apart from those Poms who were
angling to get to Oz to live. Those people posed a question
a minute.

Not that sales of *TLDU* in Australia were much better. I guess
it was the same buyer reluctance that applied to the original
Faces series. I set out to package and sell a book and a companion album of songs in each case. It seems that the problem is
that bookshops don't sell CDs and music shops don't sell history
books. Even shrink-wrapping them together has not helped.

34

LAND OF HER FATHERS

From around 1996, Nerys and I saved $500 per month in order to attend the Rugby World Cup in October–November 1999, for the main games and the final were to be played at the new Millennium Stadium, formerly known as Cardiff Arms Park, in Wales.

I was reared on Aussie Rules, but had come to love Rugby Union while at teachers' college in Brisbane in 1963. I never played a game, but I trained with the union boys and quickly realised that union is *the* great social game: thuggery itself on the field, but beer and singing after the match.

I am still critical of it as a game, for like many old things, it is done to a mindset. If you suggest changes, the eyes of the ardent union supporters glaze over. But when properly played, with what is called 'running rugby' as the principal aim, it is just so exciting. And unlike Aussie Rules, there is an international competition—and we were off to see it.

In 1993, I had recorded a highly acclaimed song called 'The Wonderful Wallabies', covering the unexpected triumph of Australia at the World Cup in 1991:

> He's tall, Rod McCall and the ball
> In the maul's his objective
> As you'll quickly find out.
> Towering John Eales
> Shows a clean pair of heels
> As he steals every catch
> In the lineout.
> Three cheers for Lynagh
> We've never seen finer
> World's highest scorer, you know.
> And it would be quite silly
> To overlook Willy
> Who was there, often 'having a go'.

'The Wonderful Wallabies' (1993)

'Willy' of course was Viliami Ofahengaue, born in Tonga, but a Wallaby star, whose name had been brutalised by 'Buddha'—Chris Handy, a tough ex-Wallaby prop and a genial commentator during our subsequent 1999 tour.

Nerys, being Welsh, was reared on rugby; the sport is the major religion of her native land. So we joined a wonderful group of Aussie supporters, in a tour led by Peter Norton, a rugby tragic, a fine poet and humorist to boot.

We met in London, had a few days there, then travelled by coach to Wales. Nerys and I were getting to know our fellow travellers: we could tell that they were a fine bunch, most of whom knew one another from rugby experiences. But we hadn't met any of them before.

As we crossed the magnificent Severn Bridge into Wales, Nerys involuntarily began singing the Welsh national anthem. Very quietly, but oh, the emotion! There was not another sound in the coach, not a dry eye, and the life of every person was dramatically affected by the experience on that day. From that point on, Nerys and I enjoyed a terrific camaraderie with our travelling companions.

Our first match was Australia vs Wales! It was a great treat walking the streets of Cardiff that morning. Everybody was in a festive mood, the pubs were jammed and drinkers spilled onto the streets, singing and carrying on. Faces were getting painted and we were all bedecked in green and gold.

Nerys was in a dilemma: she had two scarves around her neck, just to be sure! 'Schizophrenic, are yer?' called a Welsh drinker.

She laughed and gave a shrug, but at half time, when the score was 9–9, she found herself taking the Welsh scarf off. A big moment. Australia went on to win comfortably, but in the pubs afterwards—in typical Rugby Union-style—you wouldn't have known who had won. There is nothing to compare with being among Welsh people when they sing. It is such an essential part of them, and four-part harmonies seem to be intrinsic. Aussies just don't get it, no matter how hard we try.

I guess that's the essential difference: it is a component of being Welsh that you sing. They don't have to try, or even necessarily be good singers individually. It happens spontaneously. Among Nerys's rellies in North Wales, you get introduced to Gareth—'He's a baritone'—and his wife, Myfanwy—'She's a soprano'. You know who to sit with in the pub!

Next we travelled to France to see South Africa eliminate England from the competition. Paris and France were, of course, beautiful at that time of year. But I must admit that, while our Australian party loved the experience, we were unanimous in agreeing that Australian food and wines were at least as good as anything we sampled in France.

Back to London for the semi-finals, both played at Twickenham, where I had two unforgettable experiences. On the Saturday Australia played South Africa. I bet £100 at Ladbrokes—Australia to win. We won 27–21, after extra time, so I went to collect, but I was told that the payout was for a draw, as the scores had been level at full time! A sobering outcome and a lesson for a mug punter, but at least Australia was in the final the next week.

On the Sunday, France put on the most amazing display of Rugby Union I have ever seen. Down at half time, they ran the legs off the seemingly invincible All Blacks. The French were throwing 40-metre passes across the field, and the New Zealanders had no counter for the unorthodoxy. Even with Jonah Lomu in his prime, the All Blacks were done.

That was worth a celebration, for the All Blacks were favourites for the cup. We had backed France to beat them, though, so we collected our winnings and adjourned to the packed bar at the ground. There were no queues: the drinkers were five deep, trying to buy beers. Thousands of boisterous boozers.

All around the walls were signs reading 'BEWARE OF PICKPOCKETS'. I was in the middle of the throng, with a handful of notes clutched firmly in my hand, waiting for my turn to get served. I was wearing a suit and an overcoat. In my left-hand trouser pocket I had £500 in notes—my winnings from the match. In my right-hand hip pocket was my passport, in a wallet, together with assorted international banknotes, including an Aussie $100—all up, probably worth £100 or so.

I was conscious of the signs, but brashly thought: *No pick-pocket would dare take on a tough Aussie bloke like me.* I was crammed in the sardine tin of drinkers pushing towards the bar. Then I felt the slightest tickle around my right buttock. I looked immediately at the bloke alongside me; he looked straight ahead. What do you do? *Excuse me, old chap, did you just pick my pocket?*

I eventually got served at the bar, then I pushed through the crowd to our party, with four pints of beer spilling in all directions. I placed them on the table for our group and checked my hip pocket. The passport was gone. Fortunately, the roll of notes in the other pocket was okay. I looked around, but of course in the thousands of people I could not spot the pickpocket.

'Who would think that a pickpocket would go for a smart Australian?' I said in disbelief.

The general consensus was that I was the perfect target—overconfident, the prototypical sucker!

And try getting a new passport in London—what an ordeal!

Next it was off to Cardiff for the World Cup Final, Australia vs France. We backed the Aussies to win, and it was never really in doubt, the final score 35–12. We had seats close to the fence, right behind one set of goalposts—not the best in the house, but good enough, and we were able to see the face of Owen Finegan as he realised that he was going to score a try. I am sure that both he and I will never forget the moment. I'd love to meet him.

We drank all through the night. At 5 a.m., Geoffrey George and I were still looking at one another, raising our glasses and saying, 'Here's to the champions of the world!' A celebratory lunch the next day, and the tour was over: one of the best experiences of my life.

We're already saving for the next Rugby World Cup!

35

QUEENSLAND OPERA

I t has been great over the years meeting famous artists, watching careers develop, deriving enjoyment from it all.

Of the original country-music artists in this country, I never met Bob Dyer or Tex Morton, although I spoke to Tex on the phone one day. I admired both of them, because to me they represented 'hillbilly' music, deriving from the United States via people like Bob, but 'Australianised' by Kiwi Tex. Listening to the various hillbilly shows on Australian radio in the late 1930s and early 1940s was a daily breakfast routine for most families, as we munched our cornflakes and crunched our toast (plastered with Vegemite, of course). My father loved those programs, except for Tex Morton's 'Sister Dorrie': he referred to her as 'that squarking bloody female', which was quite out of character for Gentle Joe.

Bob Dyer never tried to present himself as anything other than the Yank he was. I know all the words of his terrific songs, such as 'The Big Rock Candy Mountain' and 'The Martins and the Coys'.

Tex, of course, was famous for his songs about his own travelling show, songs such as 'Mandrake', 'Aristocrat', 'Chain Lightning' and 'Rocky Ned', and I remember attending these events a couple of times, in the big tents, during my childhood.

It seems that only people as old as me (86 as I write) are aware that, during World War II, Australian country music came to be called 'Queensland opera', to distinguish it from the American hillbilly music presented by people like Bob Dyer and applauded by the hundreds of thousands of US servicemen based in Australia post-Pearl Harbor. Australians were quick to remind the Yanks that we had our own distinctive country music, based in Queensland, which was three times the size of Texas, so there!

I subsequently wrote a song titled 'Queensland Opera' and sang it at Tamworth. In the audience was my number-one fan, photographer Sandra Dallen. She said: 'Ted, I think I have photos of nearly every person or group that you mention in the song.' We did a count. We needed 101 photos, and Sandra had around 95. We were able to source the others, and then Sandra and I published a book, *Queensland Opera*, with a terrific poster beautifully designed by Elliat Rich.

* * *

Over the years, Nerys and I shared many lovely experiences with Slim Dusty and his wife, Joy McKean. They attended our second big house party, in 1994. Slim opened our cellar bar at Sinka-tinny Downs. I organised a few concerts for Slim and Joy in Alice Springs and Tennant Creek, at the instigation of Kevin Ritchie, a delightful man who often acted as tour manager for big overseas names such as Rod Stewart and Elton John and was also a lifelong friend of Joy and Slim.

Slim enjoyed Kevin's company; he also often travelled with 'GP', Gordon Parsons, the writer of 'A Pub with No Beer'. Gordon was such an easy, relaxed performer; he was good for the shy, nervous Slim.

It was fascinating travelling with Slim. If he did not want to be recognised—for that inevitably led to long periods of auto-graph signing—all he had to do was take his distinctive hat off! At that point, he was just another face in the crowd.

To their great credit, Joy and Slim have set the bar high for country-music performers and the rest of us have followed their example. Respect for the audience and value for money have been the catchwords since the early days of their tent shows, when they toured Australia from end to end and presented such worthwhile entertainment from so many star performers.

Performers such as Barry Thornton and Geoff Mack. Barry was one of those rare guitarists who could accompany anybody after hearing just the first note of their song. He taught so many people to play guitar, and was such delightful company in all circumstances. Geoff 'Tangletongue' Mack, of course, wrote 'I've Been Everywhere', which has been covered, around the world, by hundreds of other artists. Nerys and I are extremely pleased: Geoff reckoned our version—'I've Been Everywhere, Ma'am'—was his favourite! He probably said that to all the cover artists . . .

Nerys: 'So you've been to Llanfairpwllgwyngyllgogerychwyrndr-
   obwillllantysiliogogogoch?'
Ted: 'No, but I once drove slowly through Warawarapirililiyela
   malakupulanimalkanandrakurakurataraninna.'
[That's the Aboriginal name for Lake Howitt, on the Birdsville
   Track.]
Nerys: 'Oh, yes, on the Birdsville Track . . . Well, you'll have
   no trouble getting a lift! (*Slams door.*) Hoo-roo!'
Ted: 'Hey, come back! My swag . . . Come back!'
(*Car noise fades . . .*)

Geoff and his wife, Tabby, were the most romantic of couples. Tab was a gorgeous London showgirl who fell in love with the dashing Australian airman turned showman. They travelled from England to Australia on a motorbike, and lived for one another for every second of their wonderful married life.

I always thought that Geoff's star act was singing 'Old McDonald Had a Farm'—in Japanese. He learned to speak Japanese as a member of the British Commonwealth Occupational Force after the Japanese surrender in 1945. He turned the old song into the greatest tongue twister: hence his nickname.

I met Buddy Williams on many occasions, and had great reason to admire him. And in a similar capacity, it was great to see Brian Young in later years. These two pioneers gave great comfort and joy to the people in the *really* remote regions of Australia, particularly in the tribal lands of Central and Northern Australia. Aboriginal people loved Bud and Youngy, who were never motivated totally by the commercial outcome; they would put the show on the road regardless.

Another in this category was Larry Dulhunty, who used to take small band groups to outback festivals and race meetings. He would always get one of his minions to take around the hat and he would guarantee the crowd a show of whatever kind. He would offer himself as a boxing opponent, either bare-knuckle or with boxing gloves, or he would strap a surcingle on one of his (human) performers and invite local ringers to 'ride the feature horse'. I will never forget Larry at the Birdsville Races one year. His Aboriginal bass player, at the end of each second or third song, said, 'Larry, when am I going to get my pay?' Larry copped this for a bit and then said to the barmaid, 'Miss, give the bass player a double rum and a pastie—and charge it to my account!'

Larry possessed two unbelievable skills. He would get some-one from the audience to hold out a double-page newspaper spread. Using a stockwhip, he would then proceed to cut the paper down to the size of a postage stamp, without ever touching the holder's hands. Similarly, with a stockwhip he could 'flog' a person without actually touching their body with the whip, but it was so convincing. I volunteered for him a couple of times, so confident was I in his skills.

Another of Larry's stunts was to invite somebody from the audience to hold a cigarette in their mouth. First, he would crack that cigarette in half with a stockwhip. He would then shoot another cigarette in half—they weren't so expensive in those days—using a slug gun! Sometimes he would shoot backwards, looking intently into a mirror to get better aim, over his shoulder! All the time he would be ruing the fact that 'the old eyesight's not as good as she used to be'. The amazing thing is that he was never short of volunteers! How would he get on with today's health and safety regulations?

Mind you, 'Smoky' Dawson was adept at throwing eight to ten tomahawks at people from five metres away, creating an outline of their bodies on the board behind them; rarely did the tomahawk land more than a foot away from the volunteer's body.

In 1974, I was chosen by RCA to be the 'Australian presence' for the national tour of Charley Pride. There was a union insistence that any overseas tour had to have a local as a warm-up artist, so it did not bring any great kudos. I was under instructions to do 'exactly twenty minutes', and then Charley's American support artists would come on to complete the first half of the show. Then Charley would perform for about 90 minutes with his band. Audiences loved his laid-back style, his velvet voice and his impressive demeanour. He never failed to ask for a round of applause for 'my good buddy, Ted Egan'.

The shows, in every capital city, plus Burnie in Tasmania and Alice Springs, were all sell-outs. Alice Springs attracted 13,000 people to Traeger Park; rather nicely, the applause for me matched that for Charley on the night.

He was a lovely, sensitive man, Charley; he and his wife, Rozene, were very gracious to everybody they met. He was particularly interesting on racial issues. He was quite nonplussed by the many 'tribal' First Australians who attended the Alice concert, but he did not want to interact with them. The grandson of a slave, he said: 'I'm always pressured to align. Sometimes I'm told I'm "coloured"; well, I guess everyone is some sort of colour. Sometimes I'm called a Negro, occasionally a "nigger". Or a "black", an African American. But I'm simply me, Charley Pride.'

His band members, all white, were a bit different. They were very uneasy about the predominantly Aboriginal audience at Alice Springs. When we arrived for the next concert at Adelaide, one band member said, 'It's good to be back among real people.'

Charley was very relaxing company, and after the show each night he'd have either 'a double Drambooee' or a glass of Mateus. Asked one night if he'd like to taste the wine before it was poured, he said, 'Why, hell no. I'm a good pal of Mr Matoose and he don't make no mistakes.'

On the tour I had to appear with a 'local band', all of which was very expensive—and tedious for me, in that I rarely sing with a band, for all sorts of reasons, including that I can't 'talk the talk' about keys and bars. But it was another of the Musicians' Union of Australia's decrees. Herbie Marks did some charts for me and, at each venue, I would meet the band on the day of the performance, distribute the charts, have one rehearsal and appear with them that night.

It was interesting that the bigger the reputation of the band, the worse would be their performance. The so-called big names would have a brief look at the charts, say, 'We'll be okay,' and leave it at that. The lesser-known musos wanted to 'get it right', and often rehearsed for hours. In Sydney, before an audience of 10,000, I stopped the band early into my first song and said to them: 'Now, I can deliver this song better without you blokes, but I'll start again, and if you want to accompany me, have a look at the charts and follow me.' I got a big round of applause and the band sullenly played minimal accompaniment for the rest of my bracket.

It was interesting to meet Kris Kristofferson. In 1975, when I recorded his song 'Me and Bobby McGee', but in the Pitjant-jatjara language, RCA sent a copy to him. In 2006, when Kris toured Australia, the story was recalled and a very cordial meeting ensued. Nerys and I enjoyed his very straightforward concert in Darwin, where he just went from one song to the next, announcing the title and presenting the song. It was stag-gering to discover on that night just how many chartbusters Kris had written. We sat down afterwards, had a beer and I sang 'Bobbynya Ngali' for him. He loved it and demanded that I translate the entire song for him:

Kuka wiya, mai wiya
Mapitjangili
Pukulwiya
Bobbynya Ngali.

'Me and Bobby McGee', Kris Kristofferson (1969)

He roared with laughter when I explained that *mapitjangili* translated, roughly, as 'just about fucked'. He retorted, 'I should change the words to '*Mapitjangili* in Baton Rouge!'

I have followed with great interest the career of my mate John Williamson—or JW, as we call him. My particular favourites

277

among his songs are 'Galleries of Pink Galahs', 'Cootamundra Wattle' and 'A Bushman Can't Survive'. John did a cover of my song 'The Drover's Boy'; I covered his 'Cootamundra Wattle'. We both did well, I think.

I compare Eric Bogle to Nerys in many respects. They were both born in the United Kingdom, Eric in Scotland, Nerys in Wales. They both came to Australia as assisted migrants, and they have both developed a unique love of this country. They are not starry-eyed, but they see things in this land that native-born people often take for granted.

As Nerys and I drive around Australia, particularly in the more remote regions, she will say to me: 'Just have a look at that!' I look and say: 'Mmm . . .' Then she will tell me to *look* at the light, or the shadows, or the colour of those hills, or the afterglow of the sunset. Dopey me eventually concedes that, yeah, it *is* impressive.

Similarly, Eric, who can be a tough, somewhat cynical bloke, writes songs such as 'Shelter', which I think is the best song ever written by an Australian about Australia.

> I'm drowning in the sunshine
> As it falls down from the sky
> There's something stirring in my heart
> Bright colours fill my eyes
> From here to the horizon
> Your beauty does unfold
> And oh, you look so lovely
> Dressed in green and gold.

'Shelter', Eric Bogle (1995)

Eric is particularly renowned for his song 'And the Band Played Waltzing Matilda'. It is known throughout the world and is generally presented as an anti-war song; in its first few years of airplay, however, it was barred from many radio stations on the grounds that it was 'unpatriotic'. Sanity prevailed.

Nerys and I were with Bruce Woodley and Dobe Newton at John Dixon's house in 1987, on the day they started to develop 'I Am Australian'; it was the same day I began to write 'This Land Australia'. In fact, there was a competitive vibe as we exchanged notes on that day for the eventual content of the two embryonic songs.

John Dixon had written, in partnership with John Clarke, the very successful TV series *Anzacs*, starring Paul Hogan. As a result, he was commissioned by the Australian Stockman's Hall of Fame to put together some music suitable for their theatrical representation of 'Australian heritage'. John elected to use two of my songs, 'Captain Starlight' and 'Matt Savage: Boss Drover', for Longreach, but he wanted a third one, too—'a patriotic song'.

At a very boozy lunch at John's house that day, we threw ideas around. Bruce had been developing ideas for the song that eventually became 'I Am Australian' since 1984; he and Dobe then, over the following few weeks, took the song to a recordable stage. Nerys, with Bruce Woodley's daughter, Claire, and a lovely choir, sang on the first recorded version of that now immortal song.

Around the same time, I wrote my song 'This Land Australia', to be used as the theme song for my TV series.

Try to understand, this land Australia
Take her as she is, her moods, her mysteries

Mother of us all, beneath the Southern Cross
In her frame of peaceful seas.

'This Land Australia' (1987)

It's great to be a witness to the emergence and development of unique talent. Nerys and I have on several occasions been engaged to monitor emerging artists, musicians and songwriters. All the many young stars of country music have been encouraged by the 'family' of supporters and elders.

36

IT'S WHAT THEY DESERVE

I've mentioned that I have recorded 30 albums of songs, and that most of the songs are about, or inspired by, 'real' people—by which I mean those responsible for the proper ethos of Australia. I have not written, nor do I anticipate writing, a song about a politician, for I think that even the best politicians are invariably and necessarily compromised by their chosen calling.

Similarly, I don't write songs to put people down. I sometimes embellish facts, mostly as a means of delivering a punchline. Although it is totally farcical, I think my song 'The Man from Humpty Doo' presents a certain type of person, very common in outback Australia.

Humpty Doo, near Darwin, was the location for experimental rice-growing in the 1950s. Beautiful rice, but the problem was that thousands of magpie geese ate the rice as fast as it grew. Tall stories eventuated.

My song 'The Man from Humpty Doo' is actually based on two people, whose names don't really matter. They were both outrageous exaggerators, but they did it with such flair in the face of the reality that most of what they said was recognised as bullshit. The 'facts' as presented were always impressively accurate. I remember one of the pair telling a group of us about his boxing career. We had already established that I knew quite a bit about boxing in the era he was relating to, but in the pub 'the Man' said: 'I'll never forget the night I fought Jack Hassen for the lightweight title . . .'

I mentally ticked the boxes. Yes, Jack Hassen was a famous Aboriginal boxer in the late 1940s . . . lightweight, yes.

'. . . at Rushcutters Bay Stadium. Joe Wallis was the referee.'

That tallies, I thought.

'Jack got me in the corner of the ring and whispered in my ear, "You're the fastest backward runner I ever met." Now, chaps, whose shout is it?'

That was typical. To my recollection he never bought a beer, but he invariably had a story to 'pay his way'.

One night we were anticipating 'the Man's' arrival at the pub and somebody said: 'There must be something that he hasn't done!' So I was given the task of introducing the topic of jitterbugging.

He duly arrived and, after he'd accepted his schooner of beer, I said to him: 'We were talking, just before you arrived, about jitterbugging. Did you ever do any of that?'

He gave me the most pained look imaginable. 'Oh, mate—national champion for eight years!'

I watched him breaking in a goose
But he couldn't ride for nuts
He was useless as a rouseabout
And as a cook he'd rot your guts
But he said he'd rode with Skuthorpe
Shorn sheep with Jackie Howe
Been a chef at Menzies
And he'd milked the Sacred Cow
It's like he said: I've been around a bit
And I'll show you a trick or two
'Take a gander at my gaggle of geese'
Said the Man from Humpty Doo.

'The Man from Humpty Doo' (1970)

A dear friend who inspired another song, but on a totally different level, was Jim 'Yami' Lester. As a tribal boy, Yami lost his sight after the Maralinga atomic-bomb exercise in his homeland. The loss of sight was gradual, but Yami said to me one day: 'In the knowledge that I would eventually be totally without sight, I consciously concentrated on my other senses, particularly hearing. So I can discern just so much from a person's voice: old, young, male, female, Aboriginal, European, Asian—try me.' Indeed, his many friends will testify that you might go years between having contact with Yami, but as soon as he heard your voice, he delighted in identifying you.

Yet he insisted often: 'I can work people out when they talk, but when they laugh, they sound pretty much the same.'

So, Yami, my song 'The Laughing Game' is a tribute to you, old mate.

> It doesn't matter who you are
> Doesn't matter where you come from
> When we laugh, we all sound just the same
> Doesn't matter if you're rich or poor
> In a crowd or on your lonesome
> Everyone can play 'The Laughing Game'.

'The Laughing Game' (2000)

I was inspired to write my song 'John Flynn' not so much from the details of the life of the Reverend John Flynn, founder of the Australian Inland Mission and the Royal Flying Doctor Service, but after hearing about the event that prompted his actions.

In 1917, near Halls Creek, Western Australia, a horse fell and rolled on a stockman named Jimmy Darcy. He suffered extreme internal injuries. He was taken to the Halls Creek Post Office. There was no hospital, no doctor, but the postmaster, Fred Tuckett, had training in first aid. More importantly, he had access to the Morse code key, which enabled him to have an SOS message relayed down the line to Perth, where a doctor was summoned. By Morse code messages, the doctor established that Darcy must be operated on, and gave explicit instructions.

Using a pocket knife, Tuckett carried out these instructions and Jimmy Darcy's life was saved. Tuckett stitched the wounds with hair from a horse's tail. John Flynn heard of all this and said—many times—that this gave him the inspiration to establish the 'mantle of safety' that the RFDS provides for people in the remote regions of Australia.

> So rest easy in your grave now, Jimmy Darcy
> In the knowledge that your death was not in vain
> The Flying Doctor Service is 'a goer'
> To handle all the suffering and the pain
> The people in the bush now have a better life
> The furthest boundary rider, a lonely drover's wife
> Surely are protected, kept in touch, given a go
> And it took a man like Flynn to make it so.
>
> 'John Flynn' (1990)

* * *

In the awareness inculcated in me by the old Aboriginal 'drovers' boys'—that most songwriters are men who write songs about men—I am always on the lookout for great women as subjects for my songs. Although I never perform any of my songs that need to be sung by a woman and in the first person—say, 'A Song for Grace', 'Mary Broad', 'My Man's a Shearer'—I often take delight in presenting an entire concert where every one of my songs is about women.

I mentioned the compilation album (*The Drover's Boy: A Celebration of Australian Women*) that we issued to raise funds for the film. Every track on the album relates to Australian women: you simply have to recognise that *The Drover's Boy* is, in fact, a girl.

Some of the tracks were longstanding songs of mine; some of the new songs had come to me in thematic terms in recent months. One, 'Survivors', came to me after I saw a young First Australian woman sent to prison for life for killing her brutal husband: I felt she should have been given an award for bravery. What she had endured at the hands of that monster was truly appalling.

> Let's not forget the courage of sisters who've suffered
> They've been traded, degraded,
> Bashed, deserted and raped.
> Whenever we meet them all damaged and bruised
> Black eyes, busted noses and bloody confused,
> Spirits near-broken and bodies misused
> We must help them escape from it all.
>
> 'Survivors' (1990)

A must for the album was my poem 'Bush Woman'.

When we were filming *This Land Australia*, we travelled on the quaint little railmotor that runs from Normanton to Croydon, in North Queensland. During the journey, the train staggered to a halt and the driver announced: 'Ladies and gentlemen, I'm pleased to announce that we have arrived safely at Black Bull.'

'Black Bull,' enthused Gary Maunder, our cameraman. 'We must film Black Bull!'

Off the train we hopped, but it was a bit of a disappointment. There was a water tank, a little stockyard and the skull of a bull, perched on a star picket. We stretched our legs and decided that this was about the only benefit forthcoming at Black Bull. *But what's that noise?*

Chug, chug, chug. A tractor roared into the clearing, driven by a young woman, who stopped, switched off the ignition, grabbed two baskets and ran towards us. I can see her now. Good-looking, big hat, shorts, shirt, sandals. She reached us. Paused for breath.

'Sorry I'm late, folks. Would anybody like some cake and cool drink?' She placed her baskets on a little bench. 'Today, it's chocolate sponge cake and homemade ginger beer.'

The passengers and our crew gathered around. Looks good.

'Now, it's not free,' said the woman. 'It's $2 each. Every cent I raise goes to the Flying Doctor Service.'

I took my hat off and began to collect the money from the enthusiastic passengers as they lined up. She began to slice the cake and serve the ginger beer.

'So, who are you?' I asked.

'Oh, me,' she laughed. 'I'm not very important. I live on a cattle station a few miles away. Every week I come to meet the train. Out here we know how much we depend on the Flying Doctor Service and we do our best to raise funds to keep them in the air.'

'Good on you. Do you have a family?'

'Yes, there's my hubby and me, plus our six kids.'

'Six kids—wow! What are they up to?'

'I've left them doing their schoolwork. That'll keep them busy until I get back home. They're on correspondence lessons, and guess who's their teacher?' She smiled proudly. 'But when I get home, we leave the schoolwork for today. We have to muster the top paddock, and we'll all be in the saddle until late afternoon. So . . .'

She pocketed the money and repacked her baskets.

'. . . I'd better get going.'

And she was gone, in a cloud of red dust.

When we arrived at Croydon, I didn't head straight to the bar, as I normally do. I went upstairs to my room and began furiously writing a poem, which flowed onto the page. I realised, as I wrote, that it was not just the single admirable woman I was writing about, but the hundreds of stars that light up our lives—the wonderful women who think they are 'not very important'. I've got news for them.

> She's the backbone of this country
> She's alive and well today
> The mainstay of Australia
> That's all there is to say.
>
> 'Bush Woman' (1988)

Another song, 'She's Australian', was topical, for periodically there is debate about immigration, especially 'boat people'. While I am quite conservative on that issue, I'm also very aware of the positive impact of migrant women, especially the thousands of Vietnamese who came to Darwin: they transformed Australia's horticultural reputation. Over the years, I have been so impressed by the calibre of so many migrant women.

> She's not an alien, she's Australian
> And she's a pioneer.
>
> 'She's Australian' (1988)

In those productive months, I also achieved a long-held ambition to write a song about the legendary Granny Lum Loy of Darwin, grandmother of Ah Hoong Ah—Ron Chin, 'the Flying Chinaman'.

In her heyday, Granny was the best-known person in Darwin. She lived with her extended family at Stuart Park, and each day she walked into town, over the Daly Street Bridge, swinging her basket on a long pole. The basket was heavily laden with fruit, vegetables and eggs for sale to the general public, plus salty plums for the kids she met at each of the schools in Cavenagh Street. All Darwin kids love salty plums. She went to the temple (in those days called the Joss House) to pray on a daily basis. During the 1941–45 Pacific War, she refused to leave Darwin when all other civilian women were evacuated. Her self-appointed duty was to guard the temple.

> Watch her walking down Cavenagh Street
> Silk pyjamas, slippered feet
> Selling mangoes, vegies, eggs
> And she'll run you off your legs
> That's the way it is with Granny.

'Granny' (1990)

When Granny died, she was buried at the old Gardens Road cemetery. But for about an hour prior to the burial, we followed the hearse as she was taken to all her old garden sites, in various parts of Darwin, where she had demonstrated just what could and could not be grown in the Top End. I was in one of the family's mourning cars, with Ron and his brothers, Sydney and Cedric, plus the Minister for Education, Tom Harris Jr, son of the famous Tomaris (Tiwi spelling), proprietor of the Star

Cinema. We had a memorable wake for Granny. At the wake was her son-in-law, Dick Griffiths, who married the beautiful Rosemary Chin, Ron's sister. To this day, any time I see Dick he will find some way to get me to sing 'Granny's song'.

When I wrote the song, I wanted to have a chorus in Cantonese, so I sat with Albert Chan and a few old Chinese men and women at the Chung Wah Hall as they translated. I transcribed the words carefully and thought I had passed their scrutiny, but they said, 'Oh, no, not ready yet. You have to sing for Dr Lo.'

It was like being on *Young Talent Time*. Dr Lo was a holy man, and he sat solemnly in front of me. 'Ready!' He tapped his pencil on the table.

I nervously sang the unfamiliar words.

'One more time,' he said, about four times. Finally he was satisfied: 'Very good!' He gave me a polite clap.

Noice—as Kath and Kim would say.

* * *

So I can base a good concert on 'The Drover's Boy', 'Granny', 'Bush Woman', 'Jeannie Gunn', 'She's Australian', 'God's Police', 'Survivors', 'The Girls of Meekatharra' and 'Kitty Buchanan'. They all go down well. As does 'Edna'.

Edna Zigenbine became a 'boss drover' when she was just a teenager. She was working for her father, Harry, taking cattle from Victoria River Downs, Northern Territory, to Dajarra, in western Queensland, a journey of around 1200 miles (almost

2000 kilometres), at ten miles per day on average, riding horses and camping in swags for the entire journey.

At the famous Newcastle Waters Pub, Harry got into a fight and finished up in Tennant Creek hospital. Edna had to take over the mob—1200 head of cattle and the team of four drovers, cook and horsetailer. All men.

She successfully delivered the cattle to Dajarra. Consequently, for the next 30 years, she took droving contracts on the same footing as other boss drovers, except that she was a small, tough—and quite beautiful—woman.

I only knew her in later years, when she had retired and settled in Mount Isa; she was the ranger for the local town council, looking after any stray stock around the town. Edna became a great friend of Nerys and me and we had a sort of mutual admiration society. Edna liked my songs and liked to hear Nerys sing them; we loved to hear about her exploits over the years, either from her own lips or from others.

Military officers carry swagger sticks up their sleeves and constantly reaffirm their status with a tug of the wrist to display that little symbol of authority. Even when not carrying the swagger stick, the flick of the wrist is an automatic assertion of who is in charge. Old drovers are the same with stockwhips. If they are, in fact, holding a whip, the Turk's head handle is loosely held in the hand and the plaited leather strand of the whip is over the shoulder, ready to be used, adroitly, to show a beast that the whip holder is in control of things. If not holding a whip, the old-timers still twist the wrist, pretending to have a hold on the weapon—again, a demonstration of authority. Good whip wielders are always subtle; they never flog cattle but can flick the whip around the ears of a beast, as a gentle reminder to follow instructions. Control is the watchword. But mind you, in the wrong hands, a stockwhip can be a lethal weapon.

I was talking to Edna about her droving career one day. We sat quietly. I said to her: 'Edna, you were a boss drover all those years, which means you employed hundreds of men, on the road for months on end, in the most remote regions. A lot of them must have been difficult, to say the least. Did you ever have any major problems?'

She thought for a moment; I noticed her right hand clenching slowly but firmly into a fist, clutching an imaginary stockwhip.

'Not really,' was her laconic reply.

A member of the tough old school
Doesn't talk much as a rule
Quickly spots if you're a fool
But she probably won't despise you
Oh the droving days are over
It's time to take a look
At little old Edna Zigenbine
She's a walk-up history book.

'Edna' (2001)

I mentioned earlier that I planned to do an album titled *The Bushrangers* for my *Faces of Australia* series. The album never eventuated, but I subsequently wrote three songs that would have been included had it gone ahead.

'Such Is Life' is, of course, about Ned Kelly. Like most Australians, I have mixed feelings about Ned. The killing of three policemen at Stringybark Creek cannot be applauded. Further, I think Ned's 'Jerilderie Letter' indicates a very disturbed mind. But I come out on his side in my song.

I am definitely on the side of Tjandamara, the renowned Kimberley outlaw. Formerly a famous tracker for the police, he changed sides and led officialdom on a hefty chase for three years, until he was shot dead at Tunnel Creek in April 1897.

What do you say about Tjandamara?
What did you think about Che Guevara?
Were they justified?
Have they really died?
What's your opinion of Robin Hood?
Could you really call Ned Kelly 'good'?
Are you satisfied?
When you speak with pride?
Were they freedom fighters or agitators?
Bloody killers or liberators?
Jokes aside . . .
It's the people who make the legends
So let it be cut and dried
What's your verdict on Tjandamara?
The people will decide.

'Tjandamara' (1987)

Matthew Brady is one of the great Australian romantic heroes, in my opinion. Transported to Tasmania for forgery, he was eventually sent to Sarah Island, where escape was deemed impossible. But Brady escaped, becoming known as 'Brady the Bolter'. After an exciting Robin Hood-type career, he was eventually hanged, notwithstanding many petitions asking that he be pardoned.

> You certainly were a bolter, Matthew Brady
> You certainly were a wild colonial lad
> Admired by all the chaps and loved by every lady
> You very nearly drove old Governor Arthur mad.
>
> 'Brady the Bolter' (1986)

I also planned an album titled *The Immigrants* for the *Faces* series; that, too, did not eventuate. But I nonetheless wrote many songs that would have been suitable. I was particularly interested in migrant groups who settled in specific regions of Australia, especially where English was not the first language of the new arrivals.

Mind you, I have written songs about migrants more secure, in language terms, in their decision to come to Australia, particularly Kiwis and Poms. The vast majority of them have become wonderful settlers here, and I am always slightly mystified when they take up Australian citizenship, for they don't really need to. I admire the decision, though.

So I have to acknowledge that I wrote and sang two seemingly pejorative but, in fact, 'double-edged' songs—'Kiwis I Hev Mit', mentioning fush and chups, jandals, judder bars and chully buns, plus 'Willie the Whinging Pom', with due references to sandals and socks, jellied eel, Savile Row and

Marks & Spencer jocks! Thanks for coming, though, most of you!

The Germans in the Barossa; the Italians in the Riverina and North Queensland; the Greeks in Melbourne, Darwin and, indeed, throughout Australia; the Chinese in Darwin; the Japanese in Broome. They came in groups, they suffered hardship and privation, they stayed—often in the face of downright persecution. They thrived, they retained meaningful components of their 'old country' heritage, yet in many cases—for example, Eddy Quong—they became the most ocker of Australians. They need to have songs written about them! Get into it, Ted!

I was doing my show in Alice one night when there was a commotion in the foyer of the Stuart Arms. In burst 40 men, singing: *'Ein Prosit, ein Prosit, der Gemütlichkeit . . .'*

I can't speak German, but I am a good parrot, able to sing quite a few German songs accurately, so I joined in. They were members of the Nuriootpa Brass Band—South Australians—led in drinking terms by the inimitable D.R. Schulz; they were on tour in Alice Springs. I led them in singing *'In München steht ein Hofbräuhaus'* and *'O du Lieber Augustin'*, and they settled in to enjoy the rest of my show.

They were great blokes and we had a big drink afterwards. They introduced me to a Barossa Valley combination: a *Schluck*— a sip of wine—and a *Schnitte*—a snack (sandwich, cheese and biscuit, whatever). They endorsed something I had long since established as part of my life's patterns: never have alcohol without food. Alcohol must promote conviviality—otherwise, give it a miss!

D.R. Schulz commented on the very obvious fact that, while every second person in the Barossa has the same surname as his, there are a few different spellings. He said: 'I am Schulz without a T: we were so poor, we drank the tea.'

I wrote a poem about D.R.'s mother, Clara Schrapel Schulz, who was widowed with two young children in her late twenties; she worked the farm with D.R. for the next 50 years, harnessing horses, shearing sheep, tending the crops and growing the vines that nowadays produce the internationally famous Schulz wines. There is a delightful, crisp semillon named after Clara.

> It's history without tears
> For she never had time to cry
> And she wouldn't want it thought
> She couldn't cope . . .
> Clara Schrapel Schulz
> Daughter of the Pioneers
> In the latterday Heimatland
> The Valley of Hope.
>
> 'History Without Tears' (2017)

The Prussian/German/Silesian settlers in the Barossa had to endure mindless, hurtful persecution during the two world wars. Yet the 'Lest We Forget' tableaux in the Barossa are filled with Teutonic names of fourth- and fifth-generation Australian boys and men who died for this country. The Barossa Deutsch are my type of people. So it wasn't long before I wrote:

> Come and have a little *Schluck* and a *Schnitte* with me
> I'll tell you the story of the German families

They left their old homeland so they could be free
And they came out to Australia.
Komm und hab einen kleinen Schluck und Schnitte mit mir
Ich erzähle die Geschichte von Deutschen Familien
Sie verliessen ihr Heimatland, nun sind Sie frei
Und leben in Australien.

'A *Schluck* and a *Schnitte*' (1988)

To this day, I have minimal knowledge of the history of the Italians in North Queensland, but I am aware of their contribution to sugarcane farming and their esteemed status in the artistic and cultural life of the region. I had a magnificent introduction to one of Far North Queensland's leading figures when I met a woman named Atte Racconello at my show in Alice Springs.

There was an absolute aura to her. Tall and strikingly beautiful, she obviously had some knowledge of my music. She came, with her young daughter, from town to Chateau Hornsby (15 kilometres away), where I was doing my show. She introduced herself, and I noted that she, like Tom Burrows, had hands of steel. We spoke for no more than five minutes. She enjoyed my show and afterwards suggested that Nerys and I should visit Innisfail, her home town. Of course we said yes.

It was several years later that we fitted in a drive to Innisfail. I had ideas for a song. It's a long drive: we were a week on the road, getting there. I had no specific point of contact, but in Innisfail I asked a lady if she knew Atte Racconello. She gave me the strangest of looks and said: 'The whole town is in mourning. Atte died two days ago.'

I knew nobody in the impressive town, and saw no alternative other than to return to Alice Springs, which we did.

Quite a few years later, I received a letter from an Innisfail theatre group seeking permission to use some of my songs from *The Anzacs* in a production they had developed. The signature on the letter was Gina Racconello.

I rang, we had a very cordial chat and, yes, it was Gina who had accompanied her mother to my show many years earlier. Gina gave me wonderful material covering her mother's revered life. She drove tractors, was a mechanical wizard, did the most intricate needlework, ran the cane farm and cared for her husband, Mario, after he received permanent injuries. Later in life, Atte ran a pub renowned for its hospitality, became the mayoress, made wedding dresses and baked wedding cakes for all and sundry. What a woman!

> *Sotto la Croce del Sud*
> There she stood, looking good
> Under the Southern Cross
> Yes life was good
> *Sotto la Croce del Sud.*

'*Sotto la Croce del Sud*' (2015)

To cover Greek settlers, while I know the immense contribution they have made in building, fishing and pearling, I felt there was one other factor that made them unique in our heritage: the cafes they established throughout Australia, not serving Greek food, but establishing the basic Australian menu for diners: mixed grills, steak, eggs and onions, corned beef and mashed potatoes. And sweets to die for! Banana splits, fruit salad and ice-cream—yes, please! Nerys and I always, to this day, deviate into Goulburn, New South Wales, to have a meal at the Paragon Cafe.

The subject of this song is not a real person, nor did his cafe eventuate to my knowledge, but he is the prototype for so many wonderful individuals who have made this indelible mark. And Wagga Wagga deserves a Paragon!

> Konstantinos Pavrolatis, born in Kythera
> Journeyed to Australia in 1927
> He opened up the Paragon Cafe in Wagga Wagga
> And he never ever travelled back to Kythera again
> But every evening he would sit on his verandah
> Embrace his old bouzouki
> And sing the songs of Kythera . . .
> Boyhood songs, mantinades, tales of Aphrodite
> The Crying Stone of Potamos, memories of home.
>
> 'The Paragon Cafe' (2018)

Another song of mine is 'based on historical fact'. Yet I feel that 'Sayonara Nakamura' covers, poignantly, the presence of the hundreds of brave Japanese divers who died in Broome, Cossack, Darwin and Thursday Island in the early twentieth century. They were usually quite young, totally fatalistic and the majority of deaths were brought on by the bends—the paralysis they suffered when not 'staged' efficiently from the great depths to which they were prepared to dive.

> The agony's in his eyes, an old Malayman cries
> He knows that the bends have got young Nakamura

Helplessly they cursed, as the diver's lungs near burst
And he died on the deck, the boy from Okinawa.

'Sayonara Nakamura' (1981)

Robert Juniper, the famous Western Australian painter, was also an enthusiastic choral singer, and he sang 'Sayonara' beautifully with us when we recorded the song in Perth. On his next visit to Alice Springs, Bob gave Nerys and me a stunning painting. The Japanese characters read: 'In memory of Nakamura'. One of several Nakamura graves in Broome cemetery is number 442.

Along with 'Granny'—Granny Lum Loy—I love my poem 'Bill Wong', a tribute to the wonderful presence of Chinese in Darwin since the 1870s. Bill and I used to meet every morning on our runs/walks around the old Darwin streets. We shared many nostalgic memories:

He'd think about his ancestors, he could smell the joss
As he passed the Chung Wah Temple every morning on his
　　walk
Smell salty plums galore, as he walks past Yam Yan's store
Wing Cheong Sing's are open, so he pauses for a talk.
He thinks of Arthur Calwell, the Canberra politician
Reckoned it was smart to say: 'Two Wongs don't make a
　　white.'
But Bill Wong was quite content, his life had been well-spent
And we know Arthur Calwell just wasn't all that bright.

'Billy Wong' (2007)

37

DIFFERENT AUDIENCES, DIFFERENT SHOWS

My annual program from 1975 to 2003 was to present *The Ted Egan Outback Show* at Alice Springs during the tourist season—April to October. I started at the Stuart Arms Hotel, then I moved to Melanka Hostel, then to the Alice Springs Youth Centre and to Chateau Hornsby Winery, and I finished up doing ten years at The Settlers, owned by caterer Pam Holland.

As I've said, I earned huge money at the Stuart Arms in the days of the coaches. The historic old pub was in the middle of town, but sadly it was pulled down to make room for a shopping centre. Melanka and the youth centre were most unsatisfactory as venues, but I had no other options at the time.

I always wanted to have the opportunity to offer dinner and a show. That was easy with Pam Holland at The Settlers, but difficult at all the other places. Chateau Hornsby was a great venue for me, as I live nearby, but with the long distance from town (15 kilometres) and the introduction of the breathalyser, it became very hard to attract audiences there. Cab fares were prohibitive. It was a pleasant outdoor setting, but in the extremely cold Alice Springs winter—down to zero degrees Celsius most nights—I had to light huge fires. It was charming for the audience, but hard work for Tom Burrows and me, as we had to cut the wood and set five fires each night at 6 p.m.

Over the summer I'd head south—for cricket, gigs, family reunions and recording sessions, and to attend the delightful festivals held in different states. From 1982, Nerys joined me in my Toyota Land Cruiser.

For all sorts of nostalgic reasons, Nerys and I always wanted to attend the Toodyay Folk Festival, where we'd met; so, for as long as it existed, we did the five-day drive through the desert, from Alice to Perth, taking in the spiritual centres Uluru and Kata Tjuta, the splendid Petermann Ranges and Docker River, then onto the Giles Weather Station—set in GAFA country (Great Amounts of Fuck All)—Warburton, Leonora, Kalgoorlie and Coolgardie. We invariably had others with us, so sometimes we took two cars—Matilda, the old Peugeot, and the four-wheel-drive Toyota. It was rare to see another car on the dirt road.

As that trip was always in late September, if there had been rain in late summer or during the winter, the desert flats would be covered with miles of exotic wildflowers: Sturt's desert pea, parakeelya and the like. One night, camped under the stars, Nerys said: 'Here I am, a Welsh daffodil, travelling through the centre of Australia with a buffalo shooter [Bill Easton], a male stripper [Rob Schard] and the world champion beer-carton player [Ted Egan], camped, in our swags, on a bed of wildflowers.' She came to no harm.

Toodyay was special, as it created so many new, lifelong friends for me; usually former UK residents who, like Nerys, had come to 'Enhance Australia Fair'. But nowadays the big WA festival is at Fairbridge. It is equally good, but we don't get there so often. Must be getting old . . .

Each of the major festivals around Australia has its own flavour; I have attended and enjoyed many, over the 50 years of my career. I am usually accepted if I apply to be a performer, as I try to set a reasonable artist's fee. I am always supremely confident that I will make more from merchandise sales than from performance fees, but I need to get there and perform, so negotiation is necessary. I am a solo performer, and Nerys and I usually drive to the various venues, as we need to carry so much merchandise. We always request motel accommodation: a twin unit on, as we get older and slower, the ground floor. So our travel and accommodation costs are minimal, compared to those of bands and international performers, who usually have managers and various roadies with them.

I am rarely listed among the top-line artists, but I'm relaxed about that, for I get easy gigs, usually two or three concerts of an hour each, plus perhaps a workshop. And the earlier in the day I perform, the better I like it. That gives Nerys and me maximum opportunity to meet our many mates, share a drink or several, and do unprogrammed things not available to the stars. We have had such mighty adventures over the years—all you need is a rock-solid constitution.

The National Folk Festival always runs over Easter. In former years it moved from state to state, in sequence. We had two in Alice Springs, in 1980 and 1987, which were brilliant. In other states, the organisation was often not up to scratch, so the decision was taken in 1992 to hold all Nationals in Canberra. I was invited to perform at the first in the Australian Capital Territory.

I opposed that idea originally, but after some wondrous festivals in the national capital, I am now totally in favour. The prime attribute of the Canberra Nationals is that not only do the folkies support it, but multicultural Canberra kicks in, via the various embassies and consulates. It's a superb way to spend Easter. Great food as well as top artists. Good coffee, and they never run out of toilet paper—that's the test of a good festival.

The Port Fairy Folk Festival was the inspiration of the Geelong Folk Club members, led by Dr Jamie McKew, who recognised the cultural importance of this charming seaside town, Port Fairy, which in its early decades was called Belfast. The first festival, which locals call 'The Folkie', was in 1977. Nerys and I were invited to attend in 1984, when the tiny shows were held in various buildings in the town itself. So popular had it become by 1992 that the festival was relocated to the present site, South-combe Park, where, each year, on the Labour Day weekend in March, huge Hokka tents are erected and thousands of eager patrons head for heaven. Local and international artists conduct breathtaking concerts.

At the outset the townsfolk were somewhat apathetic, but nowadays half the audiences at concerts are locals. They were won over, in the mid-1980s, by the presence of Roger Montgomery, who went around the local schools, where he charmed students and parents alike with his musical talent and enthusiasm. Now the town itself runs the festival, still supported by the Geelong Folk Club.

The Woodford Festival is the brainchild of the one and only Bill Hauritz, the most fearless person I know. Bill is a dedicated folkie himself and kicked off with a small festival at Maleny, in south-eastern Queensland. Maleny wasn't big enough, so Bill and the committee now own a magnificent festival ground called Woodfordia, just a few miles from the town of Woodford, near Caboolture. Bill Hauritz is never satisfied. Next year will always be better and bigger—and, yes, Bill will be in charge. You have never seen a more subtle manipulator of the hundreds of volunteers he engages to run Woodford in the week between Christmas and New Year. They invariably fulfil his every wish, and it is the only place to be at that time of year. I am the chairman of their 500 Year Plan Committee; we are serious!

Wondrously, I have heard many parents say that Woodford is the safest place for their teenage children on New Year's Eve; sometimes you can't move, so dense is the happy throng attending the various concerts, but there are no security or other issues. The variety of the international cultural exchanges is most impressive and financially audacious: the festival has welcomed twenty Gyuto monks creating a huge mandala, dancers from Kiribasi and large contingents of First Australian dancers and singers. Woodford is also world-renowned for the spectacular 'Fire Event'—always to a theme, started by First Australians developing fire from friction, and culminating in enthralling choral singing as the huge principal edifice is burned.

I have been connected to the Illawarra Folk Festival since its second year, 1987, when I met a politically admirable young chap named Russell Hannah and he asked for my thoughts on festivals generally. We agreed that it made good sense to 'be courageous', so they booked a huge circus tent the following year, and Eric Bogle and I were the 'big-name artists' who charmed the local folk enthusiasts. Illawarra has never looked back!

The festival was originally held in the charming little town of Jamberoo, but it became so big it was necessary to switch to Bulli, where, each January, anything can happen and usually does. Alongside fantastic concerts and workshops, they have a 'very revolting' (a direct quote from Nerys) Tripe Appreciation Night, where Neanderthal offal-munchers assemble to congratulate one another on their epicurean perspicacity. I have sung for this particular crowd on occasion, but they are not in my top 100 audiences, because they are too busy with their noses in the trough to appreciate real culture. Fortunately, they are a minuscule minority of the attendees at Bulli; most of the others are superb in every respect.

Young Russell Hannah is very selective about the artists engaged for Illawarra. He likes performers who 'make me want to fight'; Cooper's beer does that for you. Elevates your thought processes. Makes you discerning. Seriously, though, the Illawarra region is *the* folk-music centre of Australia. It revolves around an old-fashioned bush band, Wongawilli, which has combined, over many years now, with the two greatest-ever Australian folk stalwarts—Peter Ellis and Shirley Andrews—to revive colonial dancing and the proper presentation of traditional songs.

Illawarra and Russell Hannah brought about the recognition of chronicler Col Wilson, aka 'Blue the Shearer'. Blue—named thus by Russell—was an accountant who had never shorn a sheep in his life, but his presentation of the 'weekly news' on the ABC, in poetry form, became legend. My WA mates Bernard Carney and Roger Montgomery do the same in Perth. It's a difficult task, presenting a song or poem to a topic, on demand. My dad was also good at it.

* * *

It's interesting for me to look back at the different types of audiences I have had over the years when presenting *The Ted Egan Outback Show*. In one respect, I have been consistent: I relate to outback Australia and the various people who are the subjects of my songs and stories. But the shows I presented for coach tours to Alice Springs bore little resemblance to the one I presented for Amnesty International in Melbourne.

For the coach groups I could get away with chorus-type songs, especially the 'relevant' ones such as 'Our Coach Captain', 'The Hosties and the Cooks', 'Have You Been to the Rock Named Uluru?', plus 50 verses of 'The Drinkers of the Territory'. The stories I told were inevitably related to intrepid outback travellers like them. They particularly liked the ones about

Greasy Biggins, the cook: 'He was so greasy, dogs used to lick his shadow.'

For Amnesty and comparable audiences, I would sing 'Poor Fella My Country', 'Vincent', 'Gurindji Blues', 'Survivors', 'She's Australian', 'Granny', 'Sayonara Nakamura' and 'The Drover's Boy'. To lighten things a bit, I would sing 'Me and Bobby McGee' in Pitjantjatjara, or 'The Canoe Song' in Tiwi. I wouldn't try any bush humour on them—too risky.

The most challenging groups were Sunday afternoon pub drinkers. I like to brag that I was always well received at the famous Humpty Doo Pub, up near Darwin, when the audience of around 200 drinkers was mainly bikies. I would get them going with 'The Characters' and 'The Drinkers', particularly as they liked to identify with the people who were the subjects of the various verses. But every now and again, I would insert a provocative or sensitive song; it was interesting how protective of me they became, shooshing any peasant who was making the slightest sound. The publican could never believe the hushed silence I invariably received as I sang 'The Drover's Boy'. It was always requested, so it became a great encore number when I deliberately finished my set without it. I was taught that trick by Willy Nelson: 'Folks, do you have time for "Stardust"?'

The nature of tourism to Alice Springs changed dramatically after the 1989 pilots' strike, and I had to rethink things quickly. The coaches stopped coming in large groups. Where I used to attract five or six coachloads of patrons a night in the earlier days, by around 2000 I would be lucky if I scored five coaches in the entire year.

Travellers were fewer, older, more experienced, more affluent and more demanding, and a vast proportion came from the United States or Canada. So I had a language problem as well as a heritage problem. I worked to the principle: 'Hang on a minute.'

At 8 p.m. I would come onto the little stage, throw just one switch for the sound system, sit on a barstool and say (hopefully) engagingly: 'Good evening. May I introduce myself? I am Ted Egan, the world champion beer-carton player.' I knew I had about one minute.

The looks people exchanged were inevitably apprehensive. 'Doris, what in the hell are we doing here? We've just paid $15 to hear this Ted Whatsisname! He's local, supposed to be famous, but what's this? A boozy-looking old fellow with an empty beer carton? There's no band, no strobe lighting, no anything . . .'

I'd continue: 'I travel around the outback and I meet people like you. I write my songs. This one is called "The Characters of the Outback".'

Quickly I'd go into a couple of verses of 'The Characters'— simple, not crude, with a (hopefully) funny line at the end. I'd be 'working the eyes' furiously: *Please love me!*

If they got the joke, I'd breathe easier. If they didn't, I'd try a different tack. Hang on a minute. Slowly, I'd alternate. A funny one, a serious one. A provocative one. A nice simple story. A clean, but funny joke. The song 'Granny' usually worked. So did 'Sayonara Nakamura'. They loved the story that introduces 'Bush Woman'. Then I'd try another funny song, a more obscure story. 'The Drover's Boy' usually got them relaxed and wanting more 'real Australian' songs.

Quite often people would line up to buy merchandise at the end of the show, and I'd hear comments like this: 'Ted, I was just saying to Doris that they won't believe us when we get back to Philadelphia—that we sat and listened to an old Australian singing for two and a half hours, and his only accompaniment was an empty beer carton. What do you call it?'

'A Fosterphone,' I'd say. 'I'm the world champion. A photo? Yes, of course—and I'll sign your book. How would you like me to personalise it? Nerys will do the finance. A special price for you . . .'

Beats working!

38

HANG ON A MINUTE

And so life progressed, until 2003. Nerys and I were in Adelaide, preparing to go to the United Kingdom to work on the launch of *The Land Down Under*.

My four children—Greg (then 49), Margaret (46), Mark (44) and Jacki (40)—were all well, happy and always in touch. Greg and his wife, Rosie, lived in Adelaide, Marg was in Darwin, while Mark lived in Alice Springs, as did Jacki. I had seven grandchildren, all of them 'inheritors of good genes'.

Nerys and I were content also. Short of funds as usual, but better than married because we were CFLs—Companions For Life—and about to embark on yet another 'adventure', as we described each new stage of our relationship.

We were staying at Scotty's Motel in North Adelaide. The phone rang.

'Hello, Ted Egan,' I said.

'Mr Egan, I'm ringing from Parliament House in Darwin. I have Ms Martin, Chief Minister, on the line. May I put you through?'

I mouthed, '*Clare Martin*,' to Nerys. Impressed!

'Of course. Hello, Clare . . . Ted Egan.'

'Ted, you're a hard bloke to track. Where are you?'

'Adelaide . . . [*sings*] "On the road again . . ."'

'And Nerys? Both well?'

'Couldn't be better. What can I do for you?'

'Well . . . I'm ringing to ask you if you'd like to be appointed the next Administrator of the Northern Territory.'

A pause.

'Clare, are you talking to the right bloke?'

'I think so.'

'Do you know how old I am?'

'No idea, but it doesn't matter. So, what do you think?'

I noted that Nerys, sitting in an easy chair, was tuned in to the conversation. She was furiously signalling that I had to get control of the situation.

'Well, I'm inclined to say no, because it would change my lifestyle pretty savagely . . .'

Nerys is giving me an intense look. Eyes wide. Head nodding. She had put two and two together.

'Clare, can you give me a couple of days to think about it?'

'Okay, Ted, understood. Let's talk on Friday.'

39

A GERIATRIC FAIRYTALE

I had just been offered the position of Administrator of the Northern Territory—I guess the highest appointment available to any NT citizen. My initial response had been to say 'no' on the grounds that it would change my lifestyle so drastically.

I knew a lot about NT Administrators. I had read of the earlier appointees, especially the renowned John Anderson Gilruth (in office 1912–19), who had been 'run out of town by the unions'—or so the story went. I knew of his successor, Frederic Urquhart, former head of the Queensland Native Police, who was responsible for the massacre of the Kalkadoons at Cloncurry.

I had researched Colonel Weddell, who had supported the proposal to 'teach the blacks a lesson' at Caledon Bay, Arnhem Land, following the killing—by the Yolngu of that region—of five Japanese, two derelict white men and Mounted Constable McColl, in 1932–3.

Because of my many bush postings to remote regions with the Native Affairs Branch, I had met every post–World War II Administrator, from Mick Driver to John Anictomatis. The Administrator (equivalent to the Governor in the various states) traditionally visited bush stations, and the local 'government man' was required to feed him, accommodate him and cater to his every wish. By and large they had been a pleasant bunch of old men. But they had all been *old* men, in my judgement.

So here I was, being offered the job. It was April 2003 and I was almost 71 years of age—older than any occupant of the position for a hundred years. Not that I considered myself an *old* man! I was just hitting my straps.

The conversation with Clare Martin, Chief Minister of the Northern Territory, could have ended quickly and peremptorily, but for Nerys. As soon as I put the phone down, Nerys said, 'Get on the phone to Joan Johnston.'

Joan is the widow of a man who is perhaps the most revered of all the NT Administrators, Commodore Eric Johnston. Eric was Naval Officer in Charge (NOIC) in Darwin in 1974, when he weathered Cyclone Tracy in his office, the lovely old stone building on The Esplanade (formerly the Supreme Court building, but acquired by the RAN in 1942 and kept as naval headquarters).

In the absolute devastation of 'post-Tracy' Darwin, Eric was a supreme figure. He and his naval ratings were magnificent in the immediate aftermath of the disaster, so much so that in 1978 he was asked to become Administrator. He served for eight years and gave the position a total facelift. He was everywhere, always bright, cheerful, innovative. Nerys and I were good friends of Eric and Joan; whenever they visited Alice Springs, we met up with them.

I rang Joan in Perth, and told her of the offer. She said: 'Go for it. You two are perfect for the role.'

So, two days later, Clare Martin and I agreed that, subject to the necessary clearances, I would succeed John Anictomatis in October 2003 and become the eighteenth Administrator of the Northern Territory.

My background was extensively investigated under the anticipated headings—business, health, taxation, personal— and I must have passed the test comfortably, for there was no impediment to my appointment. I guess that the appointee must also be considered to be apolitical, despite the fact that the appointment is made by the government of the day—in this case, a Labor government—because, if there was to be a change of government, the Administrator is still the head of state. Over the years, despite being offered safe seats by both sides of politics, I had kept aloof from party membership.

When the announcement of my forthcoming appointment was made, there was an enthusiastic response, especially from Central Australia, because 'Jock' Nelson had been the only previous Administrator with connections to Alice and the Centre. There was one dissenter: in a letter to the editor, the question was asked: 'Must we have a left-wing demagogue as Administrator?' I had to look up the meaning of the word *demagogue*. I checked out the name of the letter writer, but could not find her/him on any electoral roll, so I was not too upset. I'm happy to be recognised as a demagogue. But I certainly don't think I am left-wing; I'm a hard-headed right-winger in a few social areas.

October raced into existence. Nerys and Drury Piper were a formidable team as our effects were packed and dispatched. We had decided to rent out our Alice Springs house, furnished, but there was a hefty truckload of personal effects to transport to Government House, Darwin.

There, our predecessors, John and Jeanette Anictomatis, welcomed us and graciously introduced us to the staff of nineteen who would be in support at Government House. Without exception, we were so very fortunate that, for the next four years, we were cared for by such fine staff members. An ongoing delight is that most of them remain in contact as lifelong friends.

On 31 October 2003, I was sworn in by His Excellency the Governor-General, Major-General Michael Jeffery, at Parliament House, and it was a great day in my life. Memorable speeches were made by the GG, the Chief Minister, Clare Martin, and the Leader of the Opposition, Terry Mills.

For my response, I wanted to be a bit different and asked three prominent First Australian men to 'endorse' my acceptance. Koolpinyah Barnes represented the local Larakia people and presented me with a woomera, the Larakia symbol of authority. Former Member of the Legislative Assembly Hyacinth Tungutalum and I sang 'Kupunyi Dandu' together, and Hyacinth welcomed my appointment on behalf of the Tiwi. Galarr-wuy Yunupingu asked me to sing with him the Gumatj song

'*Bardikan*', which his father, Munggurrawuy Yunupingu, had taught me many years previously. He then said how pleased were his Yolngu people, most of whom I knew so well.

In the presence of many dignitaries and a large group of my own relatives and friends, I promised to do my utmost to preserve the honour and dignity of the role of Administrator and concluded my speech with the sentence: 'And wouldn't my dear parents be proud of me today?'

Nerys and I hosted our first of many wonderful lunches at Government House that day and we agreed with the Governor-General that we should share 'a few bush experiences' in the future. Later, in 2006, we organised a tour at the Governor-General's request, where we escorted Michael and Marlena Jeffery on a journey that began at Government House, Adelaide. There, we were treated royally by the wonderful 'Lithgow Flash', Her Excellency Marjorie Jackson-Nelson, Governor of South Australia. Marj is a long-term friend whose company Nerys and I have loved for many years. Dear Marj, of course, is one of Australia's great group of 'golden girls'—champions in their various sports.

We went up the Birdsville Track, with three days' camping en route. Memorable stops at bush pubs, station homesteads and Aboriginal centres saw the vice-regals at their best, always polite, courteous, interested. The bushies loved them. What a delight-ful trip it was. The Birdsville leg was organised to the last detail by the irrepressible Ian Doyle and Keith Rasheed.

After Birdsville, it was arranged that the RAAF would fly us out. We went first to a goldmine in remote Western Australia,

where the Governor-General opened proceedings and participated in a smoking ceremony with local Aboriginal people, who
were to enjoy substantial royalty proceeds. Then, at our suggestion, the plane diverted to Wiluna, Michael Jeffery's birthplace.
At the time of his birth, in 1937, Michael's father was a stockman
and Wiluna had 10,000 residents and huge gold diggings, but
the ruins of many old buildings are there today to remind us
of the history of the place.

On our visit to his birthplace, the Governor-General was
appalled that the school at Wiluna was located next to the sewage
ponds. He furiously rang the premier of Western Australia and
was able to get immediate approval for funds to create a new
school in a better location. The local population was immensely
impressed with their home-town boy. And so were we.

Nerys quickly called our term at Government House,
Darwin, 'a geriatric fairytale'. Yes, it was a demanding appointment, seven days and nights a week, but there was not a negative
second in the next four years. As head of state, the Administrator has to approve all Northern Territory legislation, opens
each new session of parliament and appoints and swears in all
ministers, judges and other senior officials. There is a minimal
requirement to sit at a desk, but the major expectation is that
Her/His Honour gets out among the people. We were thrilled
to be offered such a challenge.

Government House in Darwin was built by Chinese labour in
the 1860s, as South Australia took control of its 'northern territory'. There was promise of big things to come. Explorer John
McDouall Stuart had completed his epic south–north–south

journey across Australia, and thereby established the route for the Overland Telegraph Line, which was completed in 1872—one of the great engineering feats of its time.

The cable link with Asia and thereby the rest of the world removed the issue of isolation for the emerging Australian nation. But South Australia was ill-equipped to take advantage of the new maritime and communications links, and in 1911 sold off its 'territorial rights' to the new federal government. The first Commonwealth Administrator, John Anderson Gilruth, was appointed in 1912.

Stoutly built from the porcellanite stone quarried from the cliffs nearby, the 'House of Seven Gables' has survived three major cyclones and dozens of lesser ones, plus over 60 Japanese bombing raids in its vicinity during World War II. It was often badly damaged, but was faithfully restored each time. There are just four principal spaces, today known as the Queen's Room, the Prince of Wales' Room, the Drawing Room and the Dining Room. Lovely louvred verandahs are on three sides and give the building, which sits on a superb block of real estate overlooking Darwin Harbour, a unique atmosphere.

The Administrator—and her/his partner, if relevant—immediately assumes patronage of many worthy organisations and causes. Nerys and I particularly enjoyed our connection to the Scouts and Guides, horseracing, all codes of football, cricket, the Duke of Edinburgh Awards and St John Ambulance. I was an Honorary Colonel in Norforce. Nerys loved her workshops with the Country Women's Association and the Quilters; she was stimulating in her role as chair of the Government House Foundation, charged with the responsibility for producing 'luxuries' such as artworks, renovations and furnishings. She implemented several exciting undertakings, especially the purchase of traditional paintings and historic quilts. The big fundraising event each year was the Government House Ball, organised by Nerys and her committee.

Organisations expect the patronage to be much more than just a name on their letterhead. They all want a close, involved and detailed affiliation. It was refreshing to learn just how many good things were happening, and how many real achievers there are in life. Pinning on medals for bravery, long service and the many forms of endeavour was an absolute delight. But it was demanding.

Nerys and I lived in a comfortable flat at the rear of the official building, where we had privacy, together with a pool and barbecue area. On a few occasions we entertained our private guests or relatives, but so much happened on an official level that any spare time or free nights were cherished as an opportunity for the two of us just to be together. Phew!

Official highlights? Well, we met Her Majesty the Queen and Prince Philip twice, once at a lunch in Canberra at Government House, and then at the Commonwealth Games in Melbourne in 2006. We entertained the King and Queen of Sweden at Uluru. We escorted Prince Charles on a brief visit to Alice Springs. We met and entertained His Royal Highness, the Crown Prince of the Netherlands. We met every Ambassador and High Commissioner as they paid their routine visits to the Northern Territory.

The King of Sweden is a very reserved man—I felt he was quite shy—and it was hard work making conversation. I had decided to present him with a special little gift, although that sort of thing was frowned upon. I gave him a woomera and explained what an ingenious invention it is, for the 'extra arm' it creates enables a skilful spear-thrower to easily beat the world javelin record. His Majesty was interested and impressed. He had been an Olympic sportsman himself.

I had also done a bit of homework and announced that I would like to sing a song for Their Majesties. There was a gathering of about 80 people at the 'Dinner Under the Stars' that Nerys and I hosted at Uluru, among them Senator Amanda Vanstone, who was the federal Minister for Aboriginal Affairs at the time. When I mentioned 'a song', I noticed Amanda's eyes roll, plus a certain level of disdain. I nonetheless sang my song 'Have You Been to the Rock?', with a chorus first in English, then in Pitjantjatjara, then in Swedish. Their Majesties and staff applauded rapturously and the ice was broken.

Magistrate Hugh Bradley was at the dinner, as he is the Swedish consul in the Northern Territory; Hugh and I sat on either side of the King and plied him with a few good Barossa reds. The Queen, sitting on my left, is a most vivacious woman: she offered to sing in Swedish, then in German; she was an interpreter at the Olympics, where she met her husband. Eventually, everybody was singing. At the end of the evening, one of the Swedish staff said to me: 'Most of us have never seen our King smile, let alone sing!'

When we entertained the Crown Prince of the Netherlands, once more at Uluru, I again did some homework. I rang my mate Feiko Bouman—the famous Dutch–Australian architect who designed the Australian Stockman's Hall of Fame at Longreach. I asked Feiko to translate the Uluru song into Dutch, and then sought his advice. He said: 'Whatever you do, Ted, don't say "Holland". It's "the Netherlands".'

When I shook hands with the Prince, his first question was: 'Have you ever been to Holland?'

I replied: 'I was told not to say Holland.'

He laughed and said, 'Well, I'm the Crown Prince of the Netherlands, born in the region known as Holland, so I'm allowed.' The Prince is now King Willem-Alexander of the Netherlands. He and Queen Máxima are an admirable couple.

Our day with Prince Charles at Alice Springs was unforgettable. It was 45 degrees Celsius when he flew in, and I was staggered to discover, at Alice Springs airport, that a group of traditional First Australian women were there and wanted to greet His Highness. They were barefoot, bare-breasted, painted in ochre and wearing traditional headdresses. As I knew all of them well, I was sure that nothing offensive or provocative was on their minds, so I was quite relaxed when the women joined our official party.

In came the plane, and Prince Charles and his party descended. He did the official handshakes and then I said, 'Your Royal Highness, a group of women has come from Hermannsburg to greet you.' He went straight to them. They had been standing, barefoot, on the hot asphalt tarmac—it was showing signs of melting—for about twenty minutes, but they were serene.

The elderly women had apparently left important ceremonies to welcome the Prince. They had asked my good friend

Alison Nararula Anderson to accompany them as interpreter, as she speaks excellent English as well as six First Australian languages.

The women did a short but impressive dance and song for Prince Charles, and he listened intently as Nararula explained that the women wanted to show their loyalty to 'the sovereign'; they felt that a continuing connection would ensure that 'the killing times' would never occur again.

Prince Charles is a most impressive man and he received the delegation with due dignity. He has that remarkable skill, even in the briefest of exchanges, to give you his absolute attention and make you think that you are the most important person he has ever met. As I sat with him in the back seat of the official car that day, he revealed that he had been given a detailed brief on me and my background among First Australians, so we had exchanges that will impress me forever.

Everywhere he went in Alice Springs, he gave people his undivided attention. In sharing a drink with Nerys at the social gathering late in the afternoon, he said: 'Do I detect a Welsh accent?' When she informed him that she was born in Barry, near Cardiff, the Prince of Wales laughed and reminisced. 'Barry, what a harbour! When I was in the Royal Navy, I had to bring a minesweeper into Barry Harbour, and it was like a dog chasing its tail.' It is not widely known—particularly in Australia—that South Wales has the second-biggest tidal changes in the world. The Bay of Fundy (Canada) registers sixteen metres, and Barry (Wales, United Kindom) fifteen metres. King George Sound (in Derby, Western Australia) comes third with twelve metres.

Because I knew so much about the position of Administrator—and because I was mindful of Sir John Kerr—I did not want to do anything contentious or groundbreaking during my term. I dodged a few tricky engagements and was determined to set no dangerous precedents. But I was also determined, given my vast experience, to make a stand concerning First Australian issues, so I was never backward in giving an opinion. As a consequence, I got on the wrong side of one ABC journalist.

She was interviewing me about Galarrwuy Yunupingu, whom I have known since his youth. She obviously did not like Galarrwuy and asked me: 'So why is he so disgruntled?'

'Well, with justification, he gets annoyed when white people sound off on traditional Aboriginal issues, where they have no real knowledge,' I said.

The question of 'promised marriages' had been in the news at that time. I said to the interviewer: 'I was talking to the Chief Justice about that matter the other day, as a means of supporting Galarrwuy.'

She concluded the interview abruptly.

The next day, I had a phone call from a friend at the ABC. 'Ted, I just rang to warn you that *Stateline* [the regional 7.30 p.m. TV report] is going to take you to task tonight, on the issue of the separation of powers.'

'You're joking,' I said, but I asked our private secretary, Frank Leverett, to check.

Frank rang the producer, then reported back. 'It's true, Ted. They're going to have a go at you for seeking to influence the Chief Justice in the performance of his duty.'

I rang the ABC TV producer and asked if they intended to interview me on the program. He replied, smugly, 'No, we've got all we want, thanks.'

Chief Justice Brian Martin and I are very good personal friends. We both played Aussie Rules football at a good level as young blokes. On a regular basis we would go to the Darwin footy matches together, and discuss all sorts of issues over a few beers as we watched the game. I rang Brian—His Honour—who in turn rang the ABC and insisted that, short of an interview, he had the right to make a public statement.

They agreed to read Brian's statement and, fortunately for me, they interviewed Chief Minister Clare Martin, who said she was sure that both the Chief Justice and I were well aware of our respective roles in terms of the separation of powers. She went on to say that she felt it was 'an unnecessary beat-up'. That was the end of the matter. I have been a bit warier around journalists as a consequence.

* * *

One thing I was determined to implement was recognition of my mate Steve Abala. Steve was a First Australian of Khungarakung descent—he was a grandson of the wonderful matriarch Alyandabu (Lucy McGinness). Steve was born in Darwin and joined the AIF in 1941. He served in New Guinea, and immediately after the war went to Japan as a member of the British and Commonwealth Occupation Force.

On his return to Darwin, he married his childhood sweetheart, Lorna Cooper. That was the point where he realised that, despite his service in defence of his country, he was still subject to the Aboriginals Ordinance: in all aspects of his life, he was under the control of the Director of Aboriginal Affairs. With good humour all round, Steve applied for and was given permission to marry Lorna. Displaying amazing tolerance, Steve laughingly announced, often, that he refused to apply for the 'dog collar'— the local way of referring to the exemption certificate—but by law he was not allowed to drink alcohol. He nonetheless drank on an admirable social level at sports gatherings.

Steve Abala was one of the first people I met in Darwin, and he and I were best mates. Many a night I spent with Steve, Lorna and other friends at the former Army 118 Camp, at Parap, where most First Australians of mixed descent were accommodated after the war. We loved to sing the old songs as we lowered many convivial beers.

Steve was a wonderful athlete and played Aussie Rules, basketball and soccer at top level. He was captain of Buffaloes in the Aussie Rules competition, and won the Nichols Medal for the league's best and fairest player in 1951, as well as taking Buffs to four premierships. When Rugby League was introduced as a new game in Darwin in 1950, Steve tried out with the Navy team.

Tragically, in February 1956 he was killed when he tackled an opponent in a Rugby League match at Gardens Oval. Darwin was in mourning for weeks, and many thousands of pounds were collected in order to provide a new house for Lorna and the kids.

Now, as Administrator, I wanted formally to commemorate Steve, so I recruited research officer Barbara Vos to join me. In 2004, we established a committee of Steve's old friends and announced the creation of the Steve Abala Role Model Administrator's Medal. Henceforth, on an annual basis, a Top End athlete would be selected for this award—females and males, in alternate years. The criteria for selection: 'an illustrious sporting career combined with an impeccable lifestyle'. We collected hundreds of old photographs, recorded reminiscences and published a fine book.

We had a magnificent function at Government House on 14 February 2006, the 50th anniversary of Steve's death. We had gone back 60 years and selected retrospectively, year by year up to the present time, 60 previous and appropriate winners of the Steve Abala Role Model Administrator's Medal. Steve himself was selected as winner for 1951, and his children attended to receive his award. What an event it was, for only a few awardees were dead; almost every winner was there! Some had travelled from interstate. It was especially rewarding for me, as I had been connected to sport in Darwin from 1950 and knew every winner personally.

I have always believed that cities achieve real maturity only at the point where appropriate statuary is commissioned. Using my own money, I brought a renowned bronze sculptor named Peter Latona to Darwin and initiated a campaign to raise $150,000 to create a life-size Steve Abala statue to be erected at Abala Road, at the entrance to the Darwin Sports Facility at Marrara. We selected Xavier Clark, a local footballer then playing in the AFL for St Kilda, as the physical model for Steve; Xavier was similar to Steve in size. I paid Peter $10,000 to create a maquette, a small bronze statue that we mounted on a revolving wooden platform, with the embossed names of all the Role Model Medal winners.

Sadly, the big statue never eventuated. I thought it might be misconstrued—the Administrator collecting money for a private cause—so Darwin City Council agreed to take over the campaign. I transferred the $80,000 I had raised and gave the council a thousand books that we had printed as a means of raising additional money. Council then became strangely obtuse on this project—I guess none of their elected members had any knowledge of the wonderful man whose memory I was seeking to revive—and they refused to carry on the fundraising campaign. They returned the money to donors; to my knowledge, there are still many boxes of books somewhere in the premises of Darwin City Council. What a pity!

Vale, Steve. *Nimbangi mandani. Nginta arnungka padjuwani.*

* * *

Just as Eric and Joan Johnston had done, Nerys and I were determined to establish close and constant relationships with as many town schools as possible, and also visit as many regions and remote events as we could. Bush-race meetings, bush schools, Aboriginal communities—all were exciting visits. As Norforce Colonel, I attended quite a few Army exercises, but I have to admit that they did not do much for me, although at all times I was impressed by the quality of those in charge of our essential defence forces.

From my youth, I have always had a strong affiliation for Aussie Rules in Darwin, Alice Springs and at my many bush postings.

In each of the four years of our appointment at Government House, Nerys and I were invited to the MCG to attend the Grand Final as official representatives of the Territory, and I was thrilled when given a Merit Award by the AFL to honour my lifelong connection with the sport.

Another great event we sponsored was the reunion of all persons connected previously with Government House. I was talking to Philip 'Doc' Baban one day, and he said, casually, 'My grandpa was head gardener at Government House for many years—but do you know, Ted, I've never been inside the grounds.' That prompted me to send out invitations; our staff established as many connections as possible, in any capacity, going back as far as we had records.

We knew that in the 1930s a local band named Rondalla, mainly comprising Filipino/Aboriginal members, had played regularly at Government House. We contacted these families; yes, the music traditions were alive and well, and there were many who 'knew all the old songs'.

The outcome was a tremendous afternoon when around 200 people gathered on The Terrace for the happiest event imaginable. There were no longer class barriers. Joan Johnston, widow of Eric, came from Perth. Scott Wise, son of F.J.S. Wise, Administrator from 1953 to 1957, came from Margaret River. Scott's daughter, Rowena, had been named after Rowena Abala (Steve's sister), who had cared for Scott at Government House as a little boy. She came too and it was great to see her and Scott together again. People of every race, colour and background attended, mostly grandchildren of cooks, kitchenhands, housemaids, gardeners, stewards, you name it. The Rondalla music was superb, and I was able to lead the singing of most of the old Darwin songs.

That, in turn, prompted us to do something to commemorate the Aboriginal connection to Government House. With the permission of the Larakia, the traditional Aboriginal people of Darwin, it was agreed that a set of *turtini*—Tiwi memorial poles—be commissioned. There has been almost an equal number of Larakia and Tiwi staff members over the years at Government House.

Bede Tungutalum accepted the commission and the poles were duly made, painted and delivered to Government House. They were erected and, in the presence of around a hundred Aboriginal people, we had an appropriate *yoi* (ceremony) to celebrate the history of that vital contribution. Freshly painted, the poles looked pristine, but they are not to be repainted. Tradition is that the poles must remain untouched as they disintegrate. As they are made of ironwood, they will probably survive for a hundred years. In my judgement, the older and more seasoned they are, the better they look.

Open days, when Government House was thrown open to the general public, were always good fun, as we engaged local folk musicians and singers to participate. Nerys and I knew them all and joined in many of the songs, to the delight of the hundreds of people who came to visit. A concert and afternoon tea, combined with the opportunity to inspect the famous house, proved to be a great way to conduct such days. On the same basis, we had children's days that catered especially for kids with disabilities. Clowns and various animals gave us all lots of laughs, and The Patriots (Vietnam veterans) treated kids to rides on their motorbikes. It was also a good opportunity for me to sing a song or two, rather than bore the kids with an incomprehensible speech.

It was a historic day for the Northern Territory when the railway link from Adelaide to Darwin was completed on 4 February 2004. The first agreement to provide that link had been in 1911, at federal takeover time! At the ceremony, I was sitting with members of the McGinness family—Alyandabu's descendants—who had a long history of employment on the old Darwin–Birdum railway. As three parachutists appeared above us, carrying the Australian, Northern Territory and Aboriginal flags, I said to Sadie McGinness Ludwig: 'Sadie, what would your father, Jack, think of this? The train eventually coming through is great stuff, but how about the inclusion of the Aboriginal flag as a vital component of this great day?' We shared a lovely memory of her dear old dad.

Gough Whitlam was there that day. I had not seen him since my appointment as Administrator, but was greeted by his booming voice: 'Your Honour!' It was great to see him again. Gough often visited Tamworth and always got along to my show to demand that I sing 'Gurindji Blues'.

When our four-year term expired, Nerys and I were able to welcome some old friends, Tom and Tessa Pauling, to Government House as our successors. Tom, a long-term legal eagle, was Solicitor-General prior to becoming the nineteenth Administrator.

One of the joys of having lived at Government House is that all the former incumbents who are still alive as I write—Neil and Lesley Conn, Austin and Val Asche, John and Jeanette Anictomatis, Nerys and me, Tom and Tessa Pauling—share with our successors great respect for the position, and retain a strong personal friendship. We have subsequently welcomed Sally Thomas (the first to be called *Her* Honour), John Hardy and Vicki O'Halloran as appointees. It is such an exciting role.

40

AFTERMATH: BRING IT ON!

In 2007, Nerys and I resumed life at Sinkatinny Downs, Alice Springs. We made the standard comments—'I had to relearn how to park a car' and 'Don't you wish Ben was here to drive us home?'—but in many respects it was good to get back to a normal routine.

In my eighties as I write, I have had a few health issues, some of them quite major, but as a result of the wonderful medical treatment we expect and receive in Australia, along with the skill of individual doctors, I have new knees—Ted Kneegan!—and a pacemaker. I've had heart surgery (a new aortic valve), and I am grateful that my medication has been prescribed with inimitable accuracy.

I look forward to quite a few more active years; I am slow physically, but have never been busier between the ears. My mate Sandra Cline says—perceptively, I think—'Ted, you're probably getting a better oxygen supply to the brain, after the heart surgery.'

I don't write songs at the old rate, but occasionally one emerges. I must acknowledge that the word *legacy* is on my mind; I am brash enough to think that nobody else can claim authorship of as many songs that relate to the history and ethos of Australia. So I am working on a couple of musicals and using exciting things such as iBooks, where the principal challenge is that I am not a child of the computer age!

I can use a word processor effectively—I am a hotshot typist, from earlier experiences with old typewriters—but the minute people start talking in acronyms or electronic terms, I struggle to stay abreast. Fortunately, my dear son Greg, a computer wizard from the first days of computers in schools, is aware of my short-comings and can usually fill in the gaps for me. Indeed, he and I are working on a few promising projects together, where he is often grateful for my experience in old procedures.

Nerys and I enjoy a limited amount of travel, particularly to music festivals, country and folk. I am not an adventur-ous traveller and have limited overseas ambitions. But I love driving in Australia, especially on the long trips—Alice to Darwin, Alice to Adelaide, the Nullarbor, the Gunbarrel. It is the ultimate escapism, and I reflect happily on the fact that most of the hundreds of songs I have composed originated on similar trips.

Nerys and I are creatures of habit, usually staying at the same motels, often in the same rooms. We have favourite coffee shops, bakeries, public toilets—Renmark, South Australia, has the best of all three, all in one spot—and we are constantly on the lookout for 'differences': seasons, crops, wildlife (sadly often judged by the roadkill), wildflowers, the whiteness of salt lakes, that sort of thing.

Nerys acknowledges my love of driving. She often does a crossword puzzle and we may go for hours without exchanging a word; then we'll talk animatedly for the next 100 kilometres, play some music and then lapse into private thought. It is a joy to be with such a beautiful companion.

We delight in living in the unique home we built, with the help of so many longstanding friends, most of whom still live in wonderful Alice Springs: Dave and Mary Evans, Marg Friedel and Dick Kimber, Annie and Chris Tangey, Scott Balfour, Mandy Webb. A special mate is 'Krafty' (Wayne Kraft), who ran the wonderful Overlander Steakhouse for over 30 years; he and I share many a pleasant afternoon together, as he invariably arrives with a top-class Barossa shiraz to decant. We have also done many tourism promotional tours together; I'm happy to go on record and say that no individual has done more to promote effective tourism to the Northern Territory than Krafty.

My family ties are strong. My first wife, Rae, still lives in Darwin, where she was born. Nerys and I get on well with Rae and we all share the love of four children, Greg, Margie, Mark and Jacki, with their children Bunji, Rory, Jack, Jess, Steve and Sandi Lee. Very sadly, Mark's elder son, Joe, died in 2017, aged only 34. He is much missed, especially when I make my standard call at beer time: 'Youngest shouts!' Joseph will always be young in our hearts. RIP.

Our great-grandchildren are just beautiful. At the time of writing, we have Charlotte Rae, Amani, Frank, Jacob, Jayden, Phoenix, Ethan, Tiahna, twins Maya and Emily, and young Eddie. Rory and Agata, parents of the twins, live in London, so we don't see much of them, but there are photos galore, plus Skype—although I must admit that I am edgy about Skype. The most exciting thing for me is what good parents each of those children has. I keep telling them it's caused by the inheritance of good genes, so they may all anticipate bunions!

Ad familiam felicem!

Acknowledgements

Thanks to:

- Allen & Unwin for agreeing to publish this book. It happened through the combined and valued expertise of Richard Walsh, Elizabeth Weiss and Samantha Kent, advised by John Kerr and Margot Hilton.
- my family members (the AFF Society), who have been benign influences on me during my 80-plus years: my parents, Grace and Joe; my siblings, Pat, Peg, Sal and Tim; my wonderful children, Greg, Marg, Mark and Jacki, and their mother, Rae; my many grandchildren and great-grandchildren. My nieces and nephews. But especially my beautiful CFL, Nerys Evans.
- those scholars whose writings, attitudes and opinions have helped shape mine: Tim and Ros Bowden, Sandra and

Colin Tatz, H.C. 'Nugget' Coombs, Jan and Bill Gammage, Michael Kirby, Father Frank Brennan S.J., Manning and Dymphna Clark, Mary and Elizabeth Durack, Dr Nancy Williams, boss drover Bruce Simpson.

- those discerning people who have paid good money to see my shows, support my projects and buy my merchandise over so many years. It beats working!

- those painters who, to me, capture the real Australian ethos: Russell Drysdale, Sidney Nolan, Elizabeth Durack, Bob Juniper, Robert Ingpen, Tom Roberts, Bob Marchant, Albert Namatjira and, especially, the 'X-ray painters' of western Arnhem Land.

- my First Australian mentors: Aloysius Puantulura ('bookim down my language'), Munggurrawuy Yunupingu, Narritjin Maymuru, Raphael Apuatimi, Burayuwa Mununggurr, Tim Jabangadi and Uni Nambijinba, Reg Saunders, Phillip Roberts, Dottie Daby, Alyandabu, Sadie McGinness Ludwig, Vai Stanton and, especially, Vincent Lingiari ('We gotta look after the whitefellers in this country'). Oh, yes!

- my old Native Affairs Branch mentors: Ted Evans, Bill Harney, Roger Jose, Fred Gray and Paul Hasluck, who stressed at all times the need to 'respect' our First Australians.

- the many Darwin Chinese families: the Chins, Wongs, Quongs, Lees and Wus, who are so uniquely Australian in their attitudes and achievements. Despite the deplorable discrimination their ancestors endured, they are role models for the world.

- the wonderfully talented musos whose skills have helped me in my many achievements: Herbie Marks, George Golla,

Terry Walker, Erik Kowarski, the Bushwackers, Bloodwood, Margret RoadKnight, Robyn Payne—and again, Nerys. Where would I be without them?

- the photographers who have been around me to help record and remember the heady days of showbiz, whose photos are in this book with their permission: Allan Howard, Sandra Dallen, Carmel Sears, Di Calder, Dianne Howard, Barry Skipsey, Chris Tangey, Mark Marcelis and Tim Palmer—proprietors of the magnificent *ResideNT Magazine*—and the staff of Government House, Darwin.

- the poets and songwriters I admire, to the extent that I have done 'covers' of their works or included excerpts in this book: Bruce Simpson, John Williamson, Norma O'Hara Murphy, Judy Small, Eric Bogle, Kris Kristoffersen and Kelly Dixon.

- the great Australians on whom I have based hundreds of songs: the Faces of Australia.

- the three geniuses in design and layout who have enabled me to undertake so many projects of consequence: my granddaughter, Bunji Elcoate; Marg Bowman; and Casey Heintzel. *Sine quae non.*

- two real historians, Sheila and Peter Forrest, who are available to social commentators like me at all times, to share their wisdom, overview and immense knowledge.

- my mates in sport, where discussions and my modest achievements have brought me such joy, over so many years: my dad, Joe; the St Mary's football and basketball teams of the 1950s; Steve Abala; Ron Smith; the Flying Chinaman;

Joe Sarib; Neil Davies; Coll Portley; Wayne Kraft; Frank 'Comenius' Brennan; Peter 'Peemite' Brennan; Karen Schneider; my brother, Tim; my nephews, Mike Toone and Shane Gleeson; and Artie and Carol Byrnes.

- my 'next generation' mentors, Greg Egan, Frank Brennan and Colin Plowman, to whom I regularly turn, seeking a 'younger perspective'.
- my many mates in country and folk music—hundreds of them—who are all so important. Let us continue to marvel at the accord established around music.
- my partners in convivial drinking. BYO! *Ein Prosit!* To the Regiment!
- those cherished friends who have written endorsements for this book: Bails and Sarah Myer, Dick and Pip Smith, Geraldine Doyle and Paddy Fitzpatrick, Margret RoadKnight, Jan and Bill Gammage, Russell Crowe and family.

Ted Egan
Alice Springs

Index